PENGUIN HANDBOOKS

THE PENGUIN WINE BOOK

Pamela Vandyke Price was born in Coventry and educated at Somerville College, Oxford, and The Central School of Speech Training and Dramatic Art. Having spent her working life in feature journalism, she began to specialize in the study of wines and spirits after the early death of her doctor husband. In this book she relates for the first time how it came about that she was taught wine by one of the trade's most respected authorities. She was the first person outside the wine trade to be permitted to take the examinations for the trade's students, in which, over five years, she gained four certificates of merit.

After editing *Wine & Food* for three years, she became the gastronomic correspondent of the *Spectator* and for articles in this and *Catering Times* she won the first Glenfiddich Trophy and gold medal in 1971 as wine and food writer of the year and the silver medal in 1973. For nearly twelve years she was wine correspondent of *The Times*. As well as writing and broadcasting, she lectures and teaches on wine, including contributing to both the introductory and the advanced courses organized by Christie's. She belongs to a number of wine orders, being made the first woman member of the Jurade of St Émilion, founded in 1199. In 1978 she received the special diplôme d'honneur from the Comité International du Vin de Champagne and in 1981 was made a Chevalier de l'Ordre du Mérite Agricole by the French Government. Her twenty-one books include *The Taste of Wine*, *A Dictionary of Wines & Spirits*, *Entertaining with Wine*, *Understanding Wines & Spirits*, *Enjoying Wine – a taster's companion*, *The Penguin Book of Spirits and Liqueurs* and *Alsace Wines and Spirits*. She edits the Century wine guides, to which she has contributed the volumes on Bordeaux and Champagne.

THE PENGUIN
WINE BOOK

PAMELA
VANDYKE PRICE

PENGUIN BOOKS

Penguin Books Ltd, Harmondsworth, Middlesex, England
Viking Penguin Inc, 40 West 23rd Street, New York, New York 10010, U.S.A.
Penguin Books Australia Ltd, Ringwood, Victoria, Australia
Penguin Books Canada Ltd, 2801 John Street, Markham, Ontario, Canada L3R 1B4
Penguin Books (N.Z.) Ltd, 182–190 Wairau Road, Auckland 10, New Zealand

First published by Allen Lane 1984
Published in Penguin Books 1984

Made and printed in Great Britain by
Richard Clay (The Chaucer Press) Ltd,
Bungay, Suffolk
Typeset in Monophoto Photina

Text illustrations by Sally Seymour

CONTENTS

For
Allan Sichel
(1900–1965)
from the last of his many pupils
with love

ACKNOWLEDGEMENTS

The wine trade throughout the world is traditionally generous – so I hope they will understand that in this short space it is not possible to name all of the many who have contributed to my being able to write this book. It has, after all, been the result of study during more than a quarter of a century. Many of those who helped me for years are no longer with us, although I do not forget them.

Because I have tried to write about wine as it is now, instead of concentrating, as many colleagues do, on the historic and traditional aspects, I am particularly indebted to the wine makers of today, notably those of the southern hemisphere.

Concerning South African wines, I owe many thanks to the Cape Wine Centre in London, where Michael Stokes-Rees and his colleagues have been stalwart friends; Nicholas Clark, M W, of Henry Collison, has been of invaluable assistance. In what are rightly termed the 'fairest vineyards', the K W V, Oude Meester and Stellenbosch Farmers Winery, together with the wine makers and owners of many of the great properties, have been my indulgent hosts on many occasions. If I single out the names of N. C. Krone of Twee Jongegezellen, Dr A. Schickerling, Dr C. Niehaus and Dr Van Zyl, I will not, I trust, seem discourteous to many others – the reputation of these friends is so high that I am proud to say I have learned much from them.

The Australian Wine and Brandy Board gave me unforgettable experiences on two visits to their impressive vineyards, and the many wine makers and estate owners were endlessly hospitable and instructive; their Australian colleagues in London and those with specialist knowledge of Australian wines have likewise been extremely helpful. Dr Bryce Rankine, of Roseworthy College in the Barossa Valley, has launched so many pupils into the world of wine that they will, I hope, understand my naming him alone in this mighty continent, as I have been privileged to know and learn from him also.

ACKNOWLEDGEMENTS

Cook's New Zealand Wine Company twice invited me to their glorious country and, in addition to providing superlative hospitality and kindness, enabled me to meet many other wine makers, all of whom contributed to my understanding of these exciting 'classics of the future'. In London, Donald Walker of the New Zealand High Commission has enabled many of us to continue our study of 'kiwi wines' in impeccable style. But it is to John Adams of Cook's that I particularly owe my thanks, for so patiently explaining to me many of the basics concerning the growing of vines and the effect of soils.

The appropriate departments of the Italian, Portuguese, Spanish, Austrian and German governments in London have been most helpful with information and hospitality and, as a member of the Paladini dei Vini de Sicilia, I have been able to visit that beautiful island several times. For many years Food and Wine from France has been a valued source of information and a kind friend – the entire organization in London has contributed to so much of my work that any thanks to them must remain wholly inadequate. H. Sichel & Sons, both in London and Mainz, have been both friends and much appreciated sources of advice, and their kindness enabled me to visit the vineyards of Franconia as well as many in the Rhine; W. I. Baverstock Brooks, now of Russell & McIver, most kindly arranged for me to visit the Palatinate in some detail, also the Achaia Clauss installations in Greece, and the house of Langenbach gave me a particularly valuable visit to Worms. O. W. Loeb, a host on a visit to the Mosel, have been endlessly patient in answering queries and for many years have been a valued source of information on many classic wines of both France and Germany.

In Spain there are a number of helpful friends, but perhaps Miguel Torres Jnr, whom I met through Andrew Henderson in London, himself an enthusiast for fine wine, is primarily responsible for teaching me about Spanish wines in general and the remarkable wines of Penedés in particular – the Torres family is only one of those to whom thanks are inadequate, but who have a special place in my heart. Others are many members of the port trade: I have been lucky enough to visit Portugal several times, but my hosts at several *quintas* during a port vintage provided an unforgettable experience – they and their families will always be very dear to me and they will excuse me for not naming all of them. I hope I learned something about this magnificent wine.

Other very dear friends include the wine makers of Cyprus – 'the perfect island' as it will always be to me and where, in spite of many troubles, good wines are made, carrying on the traditions of their proud history. To

KEO, SODAP and ETKO in particular I send my thanks – but there are so many to whom I owe much in that beautiful country. Other islands where I have enjoyed much kindness and whose wines have been freely explained to me include Corsica, Crete, Madeira – where Noel Cossart is only one of the great wine dynasties who so indulgently taught me.

The wines of Hungary have been shown to me by Colman's of Norwich and, thanks to the thoughtfulness of John Lipitch, now consultant to them, I have twice been able to visit this impressive country and try a wide range of their fascinating wines. The great vermouth establishments have always been free with information, so thanks to Martini & Rossi and Noilly Prat. In Champagne there are so many friends that I can only thank the CIVC and hope that individuals will understand the omission of their names, as in Alsace, where the CIVA have also been extremely helpful and there are also an infinite number of friends. This is so in the Loire and – although, alas, I haven't been there for many years – in Burgundy, with which my friend Christopher Fielden has kept me in touch, as have many friends in the UK wine trade with this region, the Rhône and the Beaujolais.

In Bordeaux, the list of thanks could be very long! Peter Sichel and his family and establishment, including those at Château Palmer; Ronald Barton of Châteaux Langoa and Léoville Barton; John Davies, MW, formerly of Château Lascombes; William and Trudy Bolter in Bordeaux; all these have helped me over many years. Peter Vinding Diers and his colleagues at Château Rahoul in the Graves gave me most valuable information about vinification and the work of yeasts. To Alain Querre and his family and, as I may now say, my colleagues in the Jurade of St Émilion, I owe many years of learning about and loving the wines of this region. It is also a source of pride that I have enjoyed not only the hospitality but the instruction of Château Lafite-Rothschild and also of Château Mouton-Rothschild. But perhaps the greatest debt here is owed to my very dear friend, the late Martin Bamford, MW, who, with his colleagues at Château Loudenne, enabled me to understand something of the way in which the wines of France are such a jewel in the setting of fine food – not, let it be understood, pretentious 'cuisine', but the most delicate and unforgettable type of hospitality. To be Martin's guest was a precious and rewarding experience.

The British wine trade might well line up in alphabetical order to be thanked! Their tastings, their individual kindness, their patience with answering questions, cannot ever be evaluated – only remembered with delight and gratitude. Among a very large number of friends, I can only name Graham Chidgey of Laytons (and all his colleagues), David Rutherford of Rutherford Osborne & Perkin, Robin Kernick of Corney & Barrow, Patrick Grubb, MW, Michael Broadbent, MW, and, at International Distillers & Vintners, James Long, Ben Howkins, Don Lovell, MW, and Alan Simpson, whose help with the technical aspects of this book have been invaluable and enlightening. To John Avery, MW, I owe a great deal: his father, my dear friend Ronald, was a most respected and appreciated tutor in wine to me and his son has continued teaching me, especially about the wines of the New World, the United States and other vineyards, where he is such an admired judge and authority.

The processing of this book owes much to the patience of Geraldine Cooke, of Penguin, also to her colleagues, Annie Lee, who did a masterly job on the text, and Jessica Smith, who was particularly efficient about the illustrations. My old friend, Margaret Bird, coped in her inimitable fashion with the typescript. Those who read how the text came into being will perhaps be able to associate themselves with the many who taught me – also with those to whom I have spoken, broadcast and lectured, who have also taught me much by their lively interest. The good things in this little book are due to the many of them; the deficiencies are my own. I hope that the good may prevail!

London, 1983   PAMELA VANDYKE PRICE

PREFACE

How this book came to be written is, I think, a charming story. Indeed, although it is not directly relevant to the contents of *The Penguin Wine Book*, I have insisted that I should be able to relate the background; it may be an encouragement to the reader – a tale that ends well.

Nearly sixty years ago I was an only child in a middle-class family in the English Midlands. My parents lived modestly, my father, a clock and watchmaker, being somewhat looked down on as not a 'professional man' by at least one of the small schools I attended. Wine never accompanied meals in our house although, for special celebrations, there might be an apéritif: gin and 'It' (sweet vermouth), sherry, sparkling Muscatel. Before my head reached the level of the dining-table I was offered a sip from a glass held down to me at the start of some birthday lunch; I drank – and drank, commenting, 'Good, more please.' It was my luck that my first wine was Champagne.

As a toddler I was taken to play in the big public gardens. Having a huge head covered with a mop of curls, I attracted some attention and, at Christmas time, there were often presents from elderly people who'd asked who I was. One year a book arrived, called *The Dreamland Express*, about a magic train; I loved it and, as I was then beginning to read, went through it again and again. But we never discovered the donor.

At the end of the Second World War, when I'd just completed a course at a dramatic school, a friend introduced a medical student keen on producing plays. Together with another potential actor, the four of us went to a dance and, after this second meeting, I went home and told my parents I'd met the man I was going to marry. It seemed impossible. He, as one of the bright stars of his year, not only had to qualify but it had been understood he must put his career first and not marry until he was over thirty; as one of the medical students who'd volunteered to go and 'help' when the concentration camp was liberated at Belsen, he had a particularly tough outlook on life and, as a member of a distinguished Jewish family, he was eventually supposed to pick a bride with money. Our backgrounds were totally different.

One evening we were talking outside the station before I went home and we discussed the books we'd loved as children. Alan Vandyke Price told me that he'd once had a wonderful book that had disappeared after a children's party and he had never been able to get another copy. It was about a magic train.

'Oh,' I said, 'that's *The Dreamland Express* – I've got it.' He went home and told his parents, 'I've met the only woman who's got *The Dreamland Express* – I shall have to marry her.'

Alan qualified and, after three years, our wedding was fixed. Then it had to be put off because he caught a form of hepatitis from a patient. As a result, he never drank anything alcoholic for the rest of his life. Eventually we were married, but we had no home although when he did part of his RAF national service in south Wales, we were able to get a furnished flat. On his discharge, we returned to London, moved into where I still live, and Alan went back to St Mary's Hospital, on the staff. We were considered thriftless because, when we could go abroad, we went to France, Italy and Switzerland, Alan, the grandson of a well-known hotelier, teaching me about food. Then the hepatitis, which had recurred while we were in Wales, returned; I was lucky when I virtually bluffed my way into becoming 'Household Editor' on a glossy magazine, for I had to keep us. This was when I began to come into contact with the wine trade. I knew absolutely nothing of the subject – once I telephoned the chairman of the Rhine & Moselle Shippers Association to ask the difference between Rheingau and Rheinhessen – but there was one personality of whom many tales were told and yet whom I never ventured to tackle.

In the autumn of 1955 the Jurade of St Émilion came to London to institute the first British chapter of this historic wine order (founded in 1199); because Alan and I had visited St Émilion, I took up the invitation to attend on business and, later, told my husband, 'I've seen the great Allan Sichel. Not at all what I thought he'd be like.'

We were, I must emphasize, happy in a way that one is supposed only to read about in fairy stories – yet about us, through nearly ten years, it was true. There are still many who remember that our delight in each other was so great that, as one friend wrote to me, 'We almost hesitated ever to interrupt you.' Not only was Alan a true physician, much loved by those he helped, but his wisdom and tenderness to me, his delight in many aspects of life and his insistence on 'doing things not merely as well as anyone else, but better' made him the most compassionate and interesting man I've ever known. To this day I am part of him.

A fortnight after the Jurade meeting Alan began to worry about me – 'You're not in a state to stand any sort of shock.' Yet the future seemed bright, he was set for one of the big hospital jobs and, if I had a child, part of a substantial inheritance from his grandfather would come to us. But one Sunday afternoon he died, in front of my eyes, from a brain haemorrhage, and the post mortem showed that at most he would have had only a few more months before a painful end. His chiefs said they must have been blind not to have noticed certain signs of imminent death, but he knew although he didn't tell me.

The wine trade sent me bottles – 'To help you sleep' – and asked me to many luncheons and dinners. I was like a block, without life. Yet around their hospitable tables the talk, all of wine, was something to hear and, in those days, there were not only many unusual characters in the trade, there were great wines at prices even I could afford. Sometimes I would go across Regent Street to buy a half bottle at the historic wine merchant, Hedges & Butler, the shop then looking as it had done half a century earlier; behind the counter was a man I'd begun to know slightly, who would occasionally invite me to have a drink and then one day asked if I would care to be shown how to taste. One day Hedges & Butler held a tasting and this friend asked if I'd care to meet Allan Sichel who was present. He said something that made me really laugh for the first time in perhaps three or four months.

Later that year, when I was going to France with two of my husband's colleagues who didn't speak French, the same friend asked if I'd like some introductions. No, I couldn't bear to go back where we had been – but within forty-eight hours I had five invitations, including some to stay, all from people I'd never previously known. The last call came from Allan Sichel's office and an elderly man told me, 'Mr Sichel is away, but said if you ever went to Bordeaux we were to give you any help you wanted. And what relation are you to Marjorie Vandyke?' 'She's my mother-in-law.' 'You will please to give her my kindest regards.'

In Bordeaux we went to lunch with Allan at Château Palmer, a wonderful experience for the youngish, shy threesome, a meal that began with the 1937 white Domaine de Chevalier, the first great white Bordeaux I'd ever had. I tried to thank the host, using the formal address that seemed correct. 'For heaven's sake don't call me Mr Sichel – unless you mind using my name.' That was typical of the good manners of the heart, in which, when he chose, he excelled. Back home, I told my in-laws about the trip and how when we went to Château Palmer, Allan Sichel said –

'Allan Sichel!' exclaimed Marjorie. 'Is he still as charming as ever?' and then told me how her hotelier father used to buy wine from his father's company and how, as a young married in Hampstead, they'd all known each other and she had said she would name her first son after him. I didn't know then, but Allan had wanted to be a doctor himself though, as the heir, he had been expected to follow his father into the family firm.

During the next few months I was advised by another dear friend to take up the study of wine seriously and was allowed to attend the courses and take the examinations of what was then the Wine Trade Club Education Committee; no one was willing to talk to me – many of the lecturers would begin, 'Gentlemen – and lady,' or 'How nice to see you here Pamela.' (And being the first 'outsider' it was inevitable that, although we did the exams under supposedly anonymous numbers, everyone knew the mistakes in my papers.)

14

In the spring of 1957 Allan asked if I would come on one of his regular buying trips, to Alsace and Burgundy. These were prized invitations. Some excellent customers were never asked but those who were recounted the experience with awe and delight. I was surprised, apprehensive.

'Why are you asking me?'

'Not, my dear child, for the reason you so obviously think. I'm getting old and I've been ill' – the first coronary had been in the previous year – 'so I don't want to travel alone and my wife doesn't care for the long drives.'

'But I'm still very sad – you might be bored.'

'With you I should never be bored.'

'Would I be your guest?'

We were having lunch, so he didn't put up his monocle, but he did look down his particularly straight nose. 'Certainly you would be my guest.' No one could be more *grand seigneur* than Allan when he wished.

'And are you a very rich man?' I supposed he must be – the big Bentley, the respected firm, the way in which he and his opinions seemed so important.

'Yes, very!' (In after years, I used to be told to repeat this again and again.)

'Good. I'll come.'

It was typical that the other man accompanying us was a member of the wine trade who'd just had a bad nervous breakdown after serious family trouble. But I didn't know this until years later.

On the journey, I tried to be useful by reading the maps, as my husband had taught me, doing any odd shopping for the men, making bookings – my French was quite good, but it had to get better, as anyone who's grappled with interdepartmental telephone calls in France will understand. Hour after hour I'd listen to Allan talking to his sources of supply, watch him and the other men tasting, in offices, in cellars, in tasting-rooms . . . It was a little like the times I had spent in the labs at St Mary's Hospital, watching my Alan and listening to the doctors talking, only now the subject was easier to understand.

After one tasting in Beaune I tried to explain to him how the wines all stood up and 'spoke' as individuals, like people. The next day he left the tasting-room for a few moments and returned, bearing a tastevin specially for me. When Allan put me on the airport bus at Lyon he said, 'Things won't bite so hard now.' When Jeanne, his adored wife, read my diary of the trip, she said, 'She's in love with you.' This was nothing new. One of his most appreciated secretaries found him 'very difficult' even though she, like many of those in his office, would have done almost anything for him; one of his 'young men' was always attracting wrath – Allan in a bad temper was terrifying and could inflict hurt, just as he could be so sensitively kind and comforting – and, frequently being dismissed, would stay away for a couple of days until the boss's temper subsided, when he'd return. To me, he was endlessly interesting and I suppose that, having been so perfectly happy and rewardingly loved, it was something of a challenge for me to love him. Sometimes he admitted that he did everything to stop me, to send me away; his was a happy marriage. I, as I naïvely thought, presented no complications, I'd had my happiness in that way. I simply wanted to be with him, to learn, if necessary to do the odd jobs which I, the doctor's widow, was able to manage when he wasn't well.

From then on, I went on all but one of his buying trips. He was a relentless master, often pushing himself to the point of near collapse. Tasting in the morning, vineyards and cellars after no lunch, business talk until around six in the evening, then 'Meet you downstairs at eight' (ladies did not, to his eighteenth-century notions, sit in bars), after which we'd have dinner, he opting invariably for simple food and early nights, to be ready for a day that might involve tasting 300 samples of young wines.

On the long drives and, if he was in a good mood, over dinner, we talked about everything. He was the only person I've ever known who showed complete understanding about my feelings for my husband; often I used to feel that the two men were talking to each other through me. Naturally he would speak about wine, the days when he started in the trade, tell me about the wines we were drinking, which he would discuss gently and tenderly when they

were the great ones, having a command of language that sometimes infuriated me, the journalist with the Oxford degree. 'Why
can't I do anything better than you?'

My stories, often told to divert his attention when he became
tired and on edge in travelling, were those of the child to whom
books are as essential as water. I could ask or tell him anything.
The notebook would come out, to record a quotation, a book he'd
liked, set down a little verse:

> I care not whence the bubbles came
> That sparkle gaily in Champagne,
> I only hate the one that goes
> So insolently up my nose.

Allan never taught his many pupils – he made us make up our
own minds. We might choose our moment and ask the odd ques-
tion. Always, any lack of precision in a descriptive term aroused
annoyance – 'You don't mean "dozens of times", you mean "a few
times" . . . you don't really think that, you only think you ought to
. . . listen to the wine talking – what does it have to say?' Sometimes
one felt strained to the limits by the inability to understand and
interpret. He expected that one should continue and, always, 'tell
the truth'. He cared about 'the vision of beauty that is part of the
revelation of absolute truth' more than, I think, almost anything
else.

For Allan's sixtieth birthday I, unable to think of anything I
might give him, wrote a 'profile' about him, including the dark
side of the character. But 'after the sixtieth, the years fly by', and
sometimes it seemed as if he needed much more devotion, unques-
tioning admiration. 'He needs so much love,' Marjorie Vandyke
used to say about her son and Allan Sichel certainly did, as if he
felt a chill round him.

Penguin asked him to write a book about wine. I was able to
help with the search for information, I went on the visits to parts
of France he'd never visited, to Germany, taking the notes, subsequently typing the drafts. (How did I manage to hold down various
jobs as well? One year I went to Bordeaux, taking the plane like a
bus, thirteen times.) To see Allan tackle unknown wines was to see
that, as he used to say, 'If you can taste claret, you can taste

anything.' He had drunk it for breakfast for three months when he first went to Bordeaux 'to see what it had to tell me'. And the most reserved French would admit his exceptional ability in tasting strange wines. Even when supposedly on holiday, he went on writing the book. The original manuscript is rather different from that published, more idiosyncratic, possibly less practical, but it must be stated that, contrary to what some supposed, I never dared alter more than the smallest punctuation mark in the final version.

The Sichels' Hampstead house had become almost a second home to me. It was where I rang when my father died and I had to have my mother certified, when I lost my job – all in the same week – and where both Jeanne and Allan were present with kindness as well as offers of practical help at bad times. There were wine dinners still talked about, parties in the garden, many happy occasions. I was 'the child', a source of amusement, sometimes, I suppose, useful. The children of the house had married and left home.

In 1965 the vintage was terrible, rained out, but Allan, ill 'with my usual Bordeaux cold', wrote asking me if I'd like to come out and travel a bit 'but it won't be much fun'. I finished a book I was doing against the clock and, once I was there, the weather changed to one of those golden autumns; we went over to Burgundy, then up to the coast where, on the last evening, I reminded him of a time when he'd refused to 'adjust' a wine for a very important buyer, even though his wine had come top in the tasting and he needed the sale. He spoke of 'when I'm burnt – and you're not to make a scene when that happens – and I shall be forgotten in eighteen months.'

'Not as long as I'm alive.'

A fortnight later, he telephoned to say the advance copies of the book had arrived and invited me to Hampstead on the Sunday. I'd made a list of trade friends to whom copies might be sent, but he suddenly decided to sign only those for the family and, at last, mine, on which he altered the original inscription to one that 'will make the wine trade talk!' To Jeanne and myself he said it was strange that he felt nothing about the book – nothing. I told him to wait until the reviews came in. It was a misty evening, one month away from the anniversary of my husband's death; Allan came out to the porch and said 'Goodbye my child,' instead of his usual 'Au revoir, petit.'

Tuesday morning Jeanne rang me to say that he'd died on the Monday night. Before the funeral, the family gave the minister – in the same chapel where I'd been almost ten years before – my profile, so as to prepare the address. I obeyed instructions – I didn't cry.

Later, Peter Sichel allowed me to help with such revisions as were possible for subsequent editions of his father's book. Later, I achieved some of the successes and even honours that I would have liked to lay at his feet. Yet, when Penguin asked me to write this book, they didn't know why it was such a moving and, I would like to think, beautiful end to a good story. Any reader will understand that it has been possibly the most intimidating commission of my career and the many pupils of Allan will share in the wish that I, the last one he taught, have been able to pass on his inspiring love of wine.

This is a totally different book from Allan's, it deals with wines he never knew, conditions in which he never worked. But . . . each time I tackle a difficult tasting, I tell myself 'Allan Sichel taught me' (and then, rightly, I forget about him and concentrate on the wines), just as, when I am faced with a problem about life, I tell myself, 'Alan Vandyke Price loved me.' Even though I long, as I will always long, to be with them again, I can only be grateful for what they made of me.

Allan Sichel once said, 'I leave you my love of wine.' If this book, a demanding assignment, gives any reader something of that love and delight in wine that he gave me, his time may not have been wasted and my account of how *The Penguin Wine Book* came into being will have been, as it should be, a true labour of love.

INTRODUCTION

A definition is helpful as a start. Unfortunately, there is no definition of 'wine' that is recognized throughout the world in regions where wine is produced. This means that there are inevitable qualifications and reminders when general statements have to be made and, even within the English-speaking countries, words do not always carry the same meaning or implications. Until there is some kind of international organization in charge of definitions and labelling – of spirits as well as wines – there seems no simple way of using terms without some explanations along the way. The Wine and Spirit Association of Great Britain has, however, formulated a possible definition of what wine is and, therefore, it seems helpful to state it: 'Wine is the alcoholic beverage obtained from the juice of freshly gathered grapes, the fermentation of which has been carried through in the district of its origin and according to local tradition and practice.'

Various drinks that may sometimes be loosely termed 'wine', therefore, can be considered as being outside this definition and the scope of this book. 'Wine' cannot be made from fruits other than freshly gathered grapes. There are many pleasant beverages of an alcoholic nature that are produced from berries, fruits, vegetables, flowers; these have certainly been made in Britain and elsewhere for many centuries. Today, they are categorized in the UK as 'country wines'. Although they were originally made in Britain as part of the countryman's domestic routine, just as ale was brewed, cider was made and – it should not be forgotten – wine was made from domestically grown grapes, these country wines have revived enormously in popularity in the UK, where they are made commercially as well as in the homes of many enthusiastic amateurs.

This is not simply a matter of making something as a saving – some of the equipment is not cheap and the commercial products in this category are by no means inexpensive. But people enjoy making their 'country wines' even if they have to buy the basic material instead of finding it in their own gardens. There is much satisfaction derived from making a good drink of this type and, assuredly, skill and experience are involved. In order to produce this sort of beverage some knowledge of the process of fermentation is necessary and, unless the maker of 'country wines' is obstinately blind to the possible qualities and intricacies of the wine made from freshly gathered grapes, he or she is likely to acquire much from the making of 'country wines' and will find that contact with true wine will be more enjoyable and interesting because of the previous experience of making alcoholic beverages from fruits or vegetables. I think that, at least in the past, farmers' wives and owners of large gardens in many parts of the world have utilized produce to make 'wine'. And pleasure has resulted.

There are, however, instances of intense snobbery. Claims are made that 'elderflower Champagne' or similar alcoholic fruit drinks are 'virtually the same as' wines made from grapes in one of the classic regions of production – but people who voice such opinions are clinging, for some reason, to the limitations of their own capacity for appreciation. They may *prefer* their own products – but they ought to be able to see that there *is* a difference between them and, for example, a real Champagne. This sort of snobbery is rather as if the home dressmaker says that something run up from a pattern is 'virtually the same' as the product of a great tailor, or couture house. The difference *is* there and it is apparent to the intelligent and sensitive, although there is no reflection on the achievement represented by either product.

Then, there must be an exclusion of alcoholic beverages made, as many are nowadays, from imported dried grapes, grape juice,

* Explanations of wine terms will be found in the Glossary on page 262.

imported musts* and similar things included in wine-making kits that can be bought at chemists as well as shops specializing in equipment for the 'home wine maker'. These drinks probably do represent a wish on the part of their makers to drink an agreeable alcoholic beverage fairly frequently without its costing more than a modest sum; for the most part, the 'wines' are ready to drink almost as soon as they are made, whereas many country wines definitely improve with some maturation (although not necessarily for more than a shorter time than would be regarded usual for an ordinary wine to develop adequately in bottle). Again, the makers of these reconstructed drinks must exercise a certain amount of intelligence – there is no 'mix up the powder and bottle' as far as I know; they have to observe, even momentarily, some of the procedures that are routine in conventional wine making: cleanliness of equipment and containers, the importance of stoppers and seals, know the rôle of yeasts and the action of certain bacteria, such as *acetobacter* which 'turns' wine to vinegar. If somebody is able to follow the instructions in the wine-making kit and produce a drink that gives enjoyment, then they may more easily be able to understand and appreciate wine.

This also, of course, applies to those who make or simply discriminatingly enjoy beer – all these things are, after all, fermented drinks. It astonished me when I, who don't drink beer or ale, was invited to visit a huge brewery and could actually understand the processes going on there – because I already knew a little about wine!

It might have been wise if my parents, moving to a flat with a garden in which there were several damson trees, which they finally decided to make into damson wine (having utilized every other damson recipe they could think of), had known something about fermentation. They made the wine but bottled it almost immediately, pushing in the corks and standing the bottles upright on a shelf in a corridor. The footfall of my four-year-old self passing by was, shortly, sufficient vibration to cause the angry liquid inside the bottles to blow out the corks. I can still remember the shrieks of horror that greeted my sticky entrance into the drawing-room – apparently drenched in blood.

A part of the definition that has to be borne in mind throughout any consideration of the world's wines is that referring to 'district of origin' of the grapes. To many people in non-wine-making regions, the concept of a 'vineyard' is probably that of a large estate, like a big farm, with all the vines involved in making the wine being grown within a fairly short distance of the house or winery, the boundaries between this estate and its neighbours being defined. This is understandable. Even those whose wine drinking is restricted to rather modest bottles will probably have heard more about certain world-famous wine estates, or know of their existence, than they will have been aware of the giant co-operatives and huge modern wineries or installations that make the production of these modest bottles feasible – causing wine to be big business today. It is the great wines, the costly bottles, the famous personalities among the growers, producers and merchants who get the publicity and it is fair that this should be so: the glamour that surrounds such wines may lure the novice drinker into trying something slightly more 'special' from time to time and, while reading about the record price fetched for a particular estate's wines, resolve that, maybe one day, he too will hope to try one of these precious wines. But the estate wines and the estates themselves represent only a minute fraction of the world's wine production. Indeed, as there is seldom enough fine wine to satisfy demand – hence the way prices soar – we should be thankful that this is so, for otherwise few of us would be able to find a drink for everyday occasions.

The wines that are made on a large scale may not be produced from grapes grown in one particular place. Indeed, in many countries, the grapes may come – in cooled container lorries – from plantations hundreds of miles away to the wineries. The grapes may be grown by farmers who contract to sell them to the wine makers; supervision is exercised, but this, it must be admitted, is not always quite at the same level as when the owner of an estate walks round his vineyard with his manager and cellarmaster.

Sometimes, farmers actually make the wine in their individual wineries. This is then bought in by the big establishments to be 'finished' in their own installations; this often occurs in that utterly traditional vineyard, the upper Douro, source of port. Sometimes the big establishments do own vineyards but combine the produce of these with other grapes or wines that they buy. Sometimes, for a branded wine required in vast quantities, the wine makers will buy their supplies from numerous different regions. They may change the source of supply or the principal source of supply from time to time. They may alter the components of a non-vintage everyday wine from year to year. They may find that the whole system of nomenclature is complex – one wine may be legally entitled to bear one name in its homeland but be prohibited from being labelled in the same way on a particular export market.

All this, therefore, makes it difficult to pin down 'district of origin'. It must be understood, however, that the controls regulating all the classic wines of Europe and many of those of the New World do define districts of origin, sometimes very strictly. There are some vineyards in France that wish to extend their boundaries, indeed, some have done so in the past, but, if the regulations specify that the area to which the name on their label is to apply is bounded by a line that goes straight through the vineyard, then that name cannot go on the produce of that particular section; the wines made from these grapes must bear another name. In practice this makes life extremely difficult and some exceptions obviously have to be made, but permission for them is very hard to obtain. Wine makers in expanding vineyards, such as those in many regions of the southern hemisphere, can often simply start cultivating a suitable adjacent plot when they feel inclined. One does not, of course, plant any vine at random, but there are many New World estates within wine regions where, in certain areas of a vineyard, it is simply not possible to plant vines – outcrops of rock, river banks and so on. There are also vineyards that have gone completely out of production – and been built on – in quite esteemed areas. One I know is in the suburbs of Bordeaux, another actually in the Médoc; one is under houses, the other at least partly under a huge warehouse; it depends on the local and proprietorial priorities of the time.

Then, 'local tradition and practice' are usually complex. A local tradition may be simply that – not necessarily detailing what is contemporary wine-making procedure. It surprises some people that grapes are seldom crushed by the foot these days. Indeed, from very early times various devices were being used so as to achieve more juice by crushing in a more effective way than simply by trampling on the fruit. A 'local tradition' may also be too expensive and too inefficient to continue in any commercial undertaking. There are contradictions: when I visited the port region at vintage time and saw a number of different *quintas* (a *quinta* is a farm), it at once was obvious that there is no one single way of making port. One port house, respected throughout the world, would make its wines with the traditional treaders, 'cutting' or trampling the grapes in the *lagar* day and night; its neighbour, equally famous and respected, would be completely mechanized, using the autovinificator. One great port authority would refuse to have a 'trodden wine' received in his winery, one equally eminent would be just as firm that no autovinificator contributed to any of his firm's ports!

Much the same occurs with wines that are 'wooded', i.e. matured in wooden casks, and those that are not. Before the invention of stainless steel, enamel, glass-lined and reinforced concrete tanks for maturation, of course wood was the only container. It isn't now – and for some wines, it may not be ideal.

The origin of the 'local tradition and practice' section of the definition was to avoid the distortion of any wines by the unscrupulous. Of course, local regulations today govern the methods of wine making that are allowed in different regions. In Italy, for example, the DOC regulations require that wines submitted for tasting and approval so as to gain this right to use the term on their labels must be made in the way that is generally accepted as traditional in their respective regions. But it must often be difficult to decide where tradition ends and somebody's personal routines begin. Nor, in these days of rapid changes in wine making and general wine farming, is it possible to resist progress: as soon as innovations are known they tend to be tried out if they seem to have achieved success – and may then be copied.

'Freshly gathered grapes' cannot be exactly defined – what, in these days of refrigeration, really is 'fresh'? Grapes may have travelled long distances in cooled containers, they may have been grown outside the region that will be on the label of the wine, they are not, overall, subject to controls other than those locally exercised, such as types of vines, cultivation methods, quantity of yield; but in many areas these controls do not apply – and if 'local traditions' involve grapes being semi-dried or reserved for late picking, the definition of 'fresh' is tricky.

This 'local tradition and practice' cannot be exactly defined unless it is agreed that these traditions and practices depend on where you are – and, additionally, are according to the detailed controls exercised so as to maintain the standard of wine farming and wine making, plus, as far as the origin of a wine is concerned, to define this origin for the benefit of the consumer.

There is another difficulty with a definition. Wines made in one place according to the methods whereby other wines are made are not and cannot be 'the same' as the wines that they are either imitating or emulating, although, in some instances, their makers put the same names on them. They are like pupils of a school – there will be some similarities, some dissimilarities and some rogues when all are surveyed. It is pleasant to see that certain great wines have inspired imitation and, subsequently, the early imitations have evolved their own individuality. There may remain a family resemblance – or not. It may be a compliment to the progenitor to acknowledge the inheritance, although *not* by presenting one wine under the name of another, not or only partly protected by law. It is permitted to refer to Australian or California 'Champagne', but illegal to do so anywhere in the EEC. Names such as 'Chablis', 'Sauternes', 'Burgundy' appear on many labels of New World wines and nothing can be done about this, as long as the wines are not offered for sale in countries where such names are legally protected and restricted. It has been thought, in the past, that the use of names that are possibly familiar to the beginner in wine may be a guide, especially when the regional or national name of the wine concerned is likely to pose problems as to pronunciation – Anglo-Saxons are supposedly shy of attempting to get their tongues round difficult foreign words. Today, however, the growing tendency, even when it is not enforced by law, is to use either the true local name for a wine and explain its style on the label or back label, or else, with cheap wines, simply to call them 'Dry white' or use a brand name that is explained in the advertising or some other way. The love of tradition and history does result in some New World wines continuing to be labelled with European names, but I must admit that I have never encountered a wine bearing any such name to have more than a very slight resemblance to its classic counterpart: a 'Chablis' might, say, be a dryish white wine, or a 'hock' a slightly soft one, but the kinship with the real thing is remote indeed. To say, as used to be common practice, that certain cheap Spanish wines were 'Burgundy' or 'Sauternes' could have been inversely confusing – someone accustomed to a wine bearing this classic name would certainly have received a surprise when tasting the real thing! But there are fashions in names, especially those that are easy to pronounce.

Today, it is becoming increasingly usual to put the name of the grape that makes the wine on its label: Sauvignon, Chardonnay, Pinot Noir, Cabernet Sauvignon and so on. I think that, especially in some countries, there is a belief that a wine made from a single grape variety is somehow 'better', although the misconception is obvious when one thinks of claret (red Bordeaux), which *must* be a blend of several grapes, as are most Champagnes, all port, sherry and most of the greater Spanish and Portuguese table wines. These are all usually made from several grapes.

More will be said later about the misuse of the word 'blend' and appraisal of quality, but, in the context of labelling, it should be remembered that the regulations applying to one region and one wine do not necessarily hold for another even adjacent region and another wine: the amount of the grape named on the label need not *always* be 100% and, as if there were not sufficient confusion, the grape's name need not be the *exact* name! 'Riesling' by itself can be one of several sorts of Riesling, each slightly or very different; 'Cabernet' is sometimes the Cabernet Sauvignon, but in many regions more often the Cabernet Franc – again, rather a different wine resulting; in Australia the 'Hunter River Riesling' is actually the Sémillon.

Labelling regulations will also be discussed later, but the fact that they vary should be stressed. The person who reads this book and has mostly been drinking wines produced from within Europe will have a very different viewpoint about what wine is and should be from the reader in a wine country that is 'new' by Old World notions, who will be untrammelled by near-archaic conventions and whose attitude to drinking wine has been conditioned by a different way of life. Even though ease of communications and improved living standards have made the social life of many people throughout the world at least somewhat similar, there are still differences resulting from climate, economic pressures, education and simply local preferences and personal or temperamental idiosyncrasies.

Therefore, in this book I am assuming that everybody accepts 'wine' to be the produce of grapes; these grapes will be crushed while they are still whole as they were first gathered. Then they will be made into an alcoholic beverage by procedures that have been proved satisfactory and that, according to local regulations, national restrictions and general scientific knowledge, are harmless to drinkers and intended by the makers to be enjoyable.

Many people think of wine in a rather too respectful way. But it is something made to be sold – and destined to be successfully sold because it pleases. Here there is immediately the dichotomy between the commercial and the aesthetic. It is misguided to be either too respectful or too casual. Earlier, I indicated how it is the finest wines that create the publicity – rarely do they make the profit, however astonishing this may seem to anyone reading of the prices attained in any sale of 'finest and rarest' bottles. Indeed, it is anyway difficult for any very fine wine to make a profit, because it costs so much to produce: Château Lafite-Rothschild, for example, never made any profit for eighty years after Baron James de Rothschild bought the estate – such money as came in went back to improve the vineyard, the *cuverie*, the details of the production. Any owner of a world-famous property will find it impossible to 'cost' the work that went into the making of the contents of even one bottle – fine wine is not something trundled off a production line! 'It takes two years to make a vintage,' say some growers, meaning that what happened one year may produce certain results in the next – but these are, still, unpredictable with any certainty.

It might seem absurd that anybody finds it worth while to try to make fine wine – and how 'fine', the inexperienced may say, can it be anyway? It is to be hoped that this book may explain something of the fascination of the great wines of the world, but it must be accepted that it is one thing to recognize and, if possible, appreciate quality; it is another to find it personally enjoyable. There is one world-famous, invariably costly wine that I admire, that I respect for its detailed quality, but I find it difficult to enjoy, simply because of its particular character – the very thing that appeals to many other people and sends its price to the top of many wine lists. There is nothing odd or 'wrong' about this. If we all liked the same wines, there would be three large vats labelled 'Red', 'White' and 'Rosé' and the taps of each could be turned on to meet requirements.

It is the 'bread and butter' wines that keep the wine trade going – from historic merchants to cut-price shops and cash-and-carry outlets. Sometimes a lot of publicity accrues to the destructive comments made in public by those not involved in the wine trade, except by writing or speaking about it. What, I wonder, do such people think they achieve? As one who drank a lot of very ordinary branded wines and then went on to the revelation of the fine wine world, I deprecate the destroying of confidence – those who taught me lured me on to the delights of fine wine. But it's the cheap and branded lines that start drinkers drinking and so, for those who have the inclination, can lead to the non-profitable but rewarding wines. The 'bread and butter' wines can be both revealing as to the house style of various concerns marketing them and en-couraging to the potential and future drinker.

It is, however, only the fine wines that give the ultimate experi-ence of both sensuous and cerebral satisfaction – which is what accounts for so much 'purple prose', inspired by sessions over great bottles. The reader must take my word for this, if so far the revelation has not come his or her way. It can happen – if you continue to love and learn about wine, it certainly will happen. And, when it does, you will see, as someone gratified me by saying once at my dinner-table (apropos the 1926 Château La Lagune), 'Now I see what all the fuss is about!' But love, in all its heightened forms, is not usually manifested as a peak of excitement every day of the week.

Then there are the wines that give enormous pleasure – the stimulation of discovery, of finding quality where the price of the bottle might not have assured it, of exploring a new wine that provides a slightly different but rewarding delight – as happened to me when I first tried some of the old Muscat wines of Australia. These are also the sort of wines that can offer great enjoyment among the more 'tried and trusted' lines: the small-scale bourgeois claret of a good year and an estate now impeccably organized, the Italian wine produced according to the most modern methods, the Spanish wine incorporating the old grapes and traditions of a region with the contemporary resources of technology, the California wine or one from Chile that seem to be at the beginning of a new tradition . . .

There are, also, the wines that can make an enormous difference, not merely to the social drinking patterns of an export market, but to the economy of the producing country. Over 14% of the adult French population has something to do with the wine trade, even if many of those concerned are in its bureaucracy. These, of course, are concerned with the mass market lines, intended as pleasant drinks rather than memorable experiences and, usually, made to be consumed within a short period of first being offered for sale. They are the wines with which most of us start our experiences of wine drinking. They are very important – not merely in the commercial sense, but because of their very existence. A century ago nothing quite like the 'house wines' and the 'big brands' of today existed.

True, customers ordered 'three dozen of Firm X's claret'. Wines were not even regionally or estate labelled until the twentieth century, except for the very greatest properties. What then was wanted were wines to drink – not wines to think about; the greatest wines then available sometimes made an impression of a lasting name; they did not often inspire recorded impressions of pleasure, only, usually, of excessive consumption.

What has changed the pattern of trading and the scope of merchants' lists has been the availability of so many more wines –

starting with the small-scale classics of the period after the Second World War; these have usually had to be extended to the wines of the world, both low and high in price.

The extension of knowledge about viticulture and viniculture even in the past fifty years has transformed and is transforming the wine scene to an extent that would have been considered impossible even a quarter of a century ago. The fathers of those who now make wine still find many current practices difficult to accept. The peasant proprietor inevitably feels that 'What was good enough for my grandfather ought to be good enough for me – and my son', but it has to be recognized that, whereas not all that is new is good, not all that is old is worthy of respect. Achievement in many fields has been so wonderful in recent years that it is disgraceful that humanity still suffers from so many problems. Human beings break athletic records almost weekly. craftsmen produce works of art that are sometimes not applauded as they should be because they are utilitarian – masterpieces of mechanics, such as medical appliances, kitchen equipment; costume jewellery may be more beautiful than the heirlooms worn by past monarchs: the flick of a switch can within seconds make a culinary creation that would previously have taken many pairs of hands hours to evolve.

So with wine. It is now made where, formerly, the vine could certainly not have been cultivated commercially. Wines and vines that are vulnerable to disasters and mishaps that would have made them total losses fifty years ago are now protected – as humans are against many killer diseases; if anything does go wrong there is generally a way of putting it right. The interchange of information between wine makers throughout the world is extraordinary: naturally, establishments have their secrets, but discoveries and adaptations of technology are freely shared, so that one wine maker may influence the world's wine trade, if he is able to break through in some discovery.

It should be stressed that a gigantic installation, equipped with every device known to oenologists, with white-coated technicians in the laboratories and mechanical harvesters in the vineyards, is wonderful – just as wonderful as the sight of an estate that has looked the same for a couple of centuries, where the personnel are all third or fourth generation and where many routine tasks still have to be performed by hand. Both strands in the cable of wine-making are wonderful – the cheap wine, well made, is to be as respected as the virtually handcrafted liquid that some of us only get to drink on a few occasions in a lifetime. And it is from the cheap wine that the impecunious enthusiast can learn a great deal, enjoying the experience too.

What the lover of wine may find it helpful to know is what I hope to explain in this book. It cannot be a directory of 'what is made where', because the scene changes too quickly. Nor can it be a series of judgements on a variety of wines – even the smaller supermarkets these days have too wide a range and the 'authority' who pronounces on these risks making generalizations that will be out of date within months. What does not change, however, is the things that basically influence wine – the climate, the vineyard, the grapes, and, these days, the way wine is made. To understand something of these is to be equipped to understand more about the wine – any wine – that you may be offered to drink. This additional knowledge is, in my opinion, a way of increasing enjoyment: if you know how, you know why, and when you know why you are likely to experience extra satisfaction as well as – I hope – pleasure.

[ONE]

WHERE WINE COMES FROM – THE VINEYARD AND THE VINES

A flat map of the world, indicating the main wine-growing regions, will show that there is a strip of propitious land in the northern and the southern hemispheres in which the wine vine can flourish. It will not grow in the extreme north and south, nor in the tropics, and, curiously, the very finest wines are produced at the extremities of the regions of production – where the vine has to fight to exist, aided by all the resources that man can provide.

There are frequent pronouncements these days by the enthusiasts proposing to create new vineyards in the New World, to the effect that good, even fine, wine can nowadays be made on sites that would previously not have been thought suitable, in areas where it would certainly not have been attempted fifty years ago and, even, without much regard for the soil of the vineyard itself. It is true that so much is known now about the potential capabilities of the various wine vines, and so much can be done to alleviate hazards and create some forms of assistance – irrigation, soil treatment, protection against pests – that enormous areas can now go under vines, providing the necessary capital is available to establish and maintain such vineyards.

But the vine is still a plant, growing outside, not in a greenhouse or laboratory; it is still to a certain extent dependent on the conditions of soil and climate in which it is planted, even before the grapes are picked and processed so as to make wine. Just as you cannot grow roses at the north or south poles, or cultivate gentians or certain conifers on the equator, so the wine vine cannot be grown just anywhere. Nor, indeed, can it yield more than one crop a year – something that surprises many people who, accustomed to hearing about double cropping of some agricultural products, ask naïvely if they cannot see a vintage in Europe in the spring, also one in the southern hemisphere in September, as well as at the more 'usual' times!

In this book only wine vines are dealt with. But there are huge amounts of vines producing grapes destined for consumption at the table, or for making grape juice, or preserving in various forms, of which the currant – so called because it was originally the dried raisins of Corinth in ancient Greece that were so much esteemed – is only one.

Vines have been cultivated since the earliest records and not simply because of their pleasant fruit. This fruit provided a valuable source of nourishment (which is why it is still traditional to take grapes to invalids because of the sugars in the fruit, mainly glucose and fructose). By careful planning, a vineyard owner then could count on enjoying fresh grapes during several months; the grape arbours – in many regions of classical times vines were trained up posts and across trellises – provided shade and freshness in hot countries. The vine will grow and yield in very poor soil, so that, in the Middle East, where the first vines were probably cultivated, whether or not one believes that it was Noah who planted the first vineyard, the vine, like the olive, could be allocated those sections of garden or plantation otherwise unsuitable for vegetables or other fruit. Ownership of a vineyard was significant – definitely a status symbol. As sweetening in the ancient world could only be done with honey, the value of grapes was considerable. But the odd row of vines could be most valuable to even a modest smallholder.

There are more than fifty species of the plant *Vitis*. Many of these are supposed to originate in various parts of north and south America, some in Asia and even Japan. These, according to the great US authority, Dr A. J. Winkler, consist of two types – *Euvitis*, or true grapes, and a species called *Muscadinia*, which is dissimilar in construction. The difficulty of working out where certain grapes originated or where they have flourished since being transplanted and how, in so doing, they have altered in character and attributes is something that still engages the oenologists, but the existence of so many vines explains perhaps at least partly why, from very early times, sculptors, painters and engravers have represented vines and grapes, sometimes, as in certain Scandinavian works of art, where it might be supposed real vines would have been quite unknown. The theory that 'Vinland', discovered by Leif Ericsson in AD 1000, was in fact 'Vineland' is sound, because Leif Ericsson found vines bearing grapes in abundance on what would probably have been the shores of Massachusetts. But this, in the history of the vine, is almost recent: the discovery of *Vitis sezannensis* in fossil form of a leaf was made at Sézanne in the south of the Champagne region and has been dated to the Tertiary period, millions of years ago. (It is now thought, however, that this particular type of vine would not have made wine.)

The first discovery of a wine vine, ancestor of all of today's wine-producing vines, seems to have been around 8000 BC, and this was traced in the south of France and in Italy. This is *Vitis vinifera*, which makes nearly all of the wines of the world through the various versions that have been evolved. Within the EEC alone there are at least 300 varieties of *Vitis vinifera*, although only about half of these are allowed to be used for wine and, in certain of the classic vineyard regions, the varieties permitted are even more restricted. But vines and wines had their origin in the Middle East and, with the examples of works of art, engineering and many highly civilized artifacts having been revealed by explorers and archaeologists, it is a reasonable thing to assume that, even if it was the wild plants that yielded the first grapes, the inhabitants of those regions soon acquired the ability to grow such vines for their own purposes and, in consequence, to make wine from their fruit.

Even in pre-Christian religious ceremonies and some early records of medicinal practices, wine, made from grapes, is frequently mentioned. In myths, legends and sagas from Homer onwards wine often plays an important part. The practical uses of wine were at least as important as the pleasures it gave: always regarded as a mysterious thing, according to accounts of the effect of alcohol on the drinker, it was at once sedative, digestive, disinfectant, tonic. Those who first listened to the parable of the Good Samaritan, who arranged for the man who fell among thieves to have his wounds washed with wine and dressed with oil, would have found this standard practice. Later on something will be said about these wines of ancient times and their descendants. Now it is only necessary to give the steps whereby the wine vine, *Vitis vinifera*, rather charmingly known by some as 'the Old World grape', came to be so important.

Any information of a general sort about vines must be prefaced by the warning that it is sometimes difficult, even for the greatest authorities, to determine whether a vine that has been cultivated somewhere outside the area where it is to a certain extent traditional and has recognizable characteristics is actually a relation of a classic vine – and, if it is, will the grapes it produces make the same kind of wine? The difference between some vine varieties and others is difficult even for ampelographers (those who study grapes) always to determine and sometimes, after years of everyone assuming that a vine is a strain of one particular variety, it is then found that in fact it belongs to another branch of the family. Even as recently as thirty years ago, it was usual for students of the wine trade to be told that the 'Steen' or 'Stein' grape, cultivated in South Africa, was a native vine, a 'sport' that had been civilized. Then it was stated that this was in fact a type of Sauvignon – but today it is known to be the Chenin Blanc. So it is essential always to be open-minded about what is what – and a study of the work already done about wine vines will reveal how much more has yet to be done.

The study of vines – ampelography – is a Greek word made up of *amphelos* (vine) and *graphía* (description) and, as Lucie C. Morton comments in her wonderful study of vines (*A Practical Ampelography* by Pierre Galet and Lucie C. Morton), this was something to which growers devoted scant attention until they were virtually forced to do so by the several serious plagues afflicting vines in the middle and latter part of the nineteenth century. Interestingly, the early ampelographers concentrated more on describing the fruit than on giving many details of the rest of the plant. Lucie Morton's work convinced her of the need to classify and relate vines to each

Leaves of some wine vines, showing the variations in leaf formation, especially indentations and serrations.

Cabernet Sauvignon

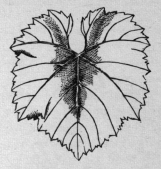

Chardonnay

Gamay Noir à Jus Blanc

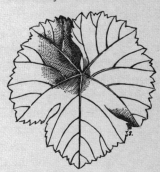

Gewurztraminer

Pinot Noir

Chenin Blanc

GRAPE CLUSTERS

Basic shapes of some grape bunches, showing how the overall formation and closeness or looseness of the individual berries can affect their exposure to the atmosphere and, in consequence, relate to the various methods of training and pruning.

Winged Cluster

Cylindrical Cluster

Conical Cluster

Shouldered Cluster

other, not only by giving an account of wine grapes, but by providing detailed accounts of canes (her term is 'dormant wood'), and, most important, of leaves and shoots. Indeed, she has worked out what she calls 'ampelographic geometry', whereby leaf structure may be measured and codified; her ability to identify vines that previously puzzled researchers is remarkable. There are, in her book, sixteen basic leaf shapes – looking somewhat like the diagrams that used to illustrate Victorian and Edwardian books on napkin-folding.

There are, according to Miss Morton, four basic shapes of bunches: the cylindrical cluster, which looks like a set of globular shapes strung along and pendent from a central stem; the conical cluster, which is triangular or vaguely so, ending in a very small cluster like the apex of the triangle; the shouldered cluster, which has a roughly triangular shape too, but with more width at the top near the stem; and the winged cluster, which has a little 'wing' or alongside bunch dependent from the main stem falling to about half-way down the main bunch from its own stem. There are also, in this detailed study, ten basic grape shapes, but some of these relate to table grapes or truly obscure varieties as far as the ordinary drinker is concerned. What I think is important to realize, however, is that these numerous variations do exist, because their existence stresses the complexity and wonder aroused by even a superficial study of the fruit of the vine and what it makes.

In studies of vines, the shape and style of the leaves and every detail of the plant is subjected to examination, but, as it is the fruit, the grape, that is the reason the wine vine is cultivated, some information about this seems more pertinent here.

The relevant part of the grape starts at the stalk, the point at which the individual berry or grape is attached to the main bunch. The overall shape of the bunch and whether it holds the grapes together tightly or loosely is another factor that anyone planting a vineyard must take into consideration. But the stalk, or, rather, the part of it that joins the grape to the main stem where other grapes are joined, tends to be less important in wine making than in the cultivation of table grapes, when, as is obvious, this must remain green and supple during the time that the bunch of grapes is in transit from vineyard to market and that it must hold on to the grape. With wine grapes, this tiny section of the stalk is not, these days, always included in the 'crush' or fruit put into the mechanism (whatever it is) whereby the grapes are crushed; the stalk's contribution can be to add more liquid, substance, tannin, but too much stalkiness can make a wine acquire a slightly bitter, flat and almost astringent flavour. Sometimes this can be remedied; sometimes, as with wines lacking in acidity and general intensity, it can be a useful element if not exaggerated; sometimes, with youngish vines, it can unbalance the wine if great care is not taken. In past times, when little was known about the effect of each part of the vine, stalks went into the press or vat in far greater quantity than they do today, and the *'goût de tige'* ('taste of stalk') is definitely a criticism, not just a comment.

The skin of the grape is of considerable importance. Some grapes have thin skins, easily broken, sometimes split open by heavy rain or hail, sometimes bursting in extreme heat or, even if they are picked in prime condition, requiring careful handling before they are ultimately crushed. Other grape varieties, however, have very tough skins and the presses or whatever mechanical device is used for making the wine must be adjusted so as to cope with them. This toughness is carried through to the wine; once in the Douro Valley at vintage time I asked why the filters I saw in the wineries were fitted with thick cloths, of the consistency of sailcloth, instead of the more usual filter paper – though this is quite robust. The port grapes are very tough-skinned and the wine coming off them would literally destroy the normal filter paper in a short time. (Now there is indeed a thicker type of 'paper' often in use.)

It is the thickness or thinness of the skin that makes certain grapes suitable for certain climates, because the grape, like the egg, is a perfect example of packaging, protecting and containing its contents during maturation. But the skins of grapes that are black (very few grape varieties are referred to as 'red' even though there are gradations of colour, including inky-blue, deep purple, violet, crimson, blue-black) contain the pigments that tint the 'must' or unfermented grape juice, and thereby make red wine. Most actual grape juice is yellowish-green, rather similar to grapefruit juice and, although there are some grape varieties that have a pinkish juice, which are known as *'teinturiers'* or 'tinters', these are seldom included in any of the grape combinations that make fine wine. The skins of 'white' grapes are, as everyone will know, also a variety of tones, from a definite green, like a green apple skin, a paler, lemony or lime green, a more yellow tone, a golden shade, a pale bronze-gold, to a straw colour and, even, a pinkish tinge added to the yellow. As grapes ripen, their colour may or may not change – some white grapes turn brownish yellow or even pale orange.

Within the skin of each grape are the flesh and the pips. Wine grapes do, as far as I know, all have pips. The flesh of the berry is slightly different in the main layers of which it is composed, from the section nearest the skin to that surrounding the pips. It is this flesh that is the main source of the juice, from which the eventual wine is made, but all the components of a grape on its stem contribute in various ways to what this juice will contain.

It is astonishing to realize that, in fresh grape juice, the principal element is water. This accounts for about 70–85% of the juice. Carbohydrates account for 15–25%. Here the glucose and fructose elements are significant, although they account for only 8–13% and 7–12% respectively, according to Dr Winkler. The tannins, derived from the stalks, skins and pips, account for a mere 0.01–0.05% and, of the other things listed, nitrogenous compounds are 0.03–0.17% and mineral compounds 0.3–0.5%. Yet from these apparently minute 'extras' in the make-up of the grape are derived the differences and complexities that can make one wine memorable, another highly successful commercially – and yet another totally insipid.

The world of wine receives contributions from other types of vine, as will be seen, but only a few of these make wine by themselves. *Vitis labrusca* is possibly the best known and one of the native wild vines of North America; others in use include *Vitis rupestris* and *Vitis riparia* and there are a number of others.

Hybrids, however, are crossings. They are of some importance these days: in many European countries their use for wine is forbidden by the various systems of controls, but the British reader may find it interesting to know that a number are in use in English vineyards, some by themselves, others in conjunction with classic vines. A high proportion of hybrids, however, more than one-third of those planted, appear to have some relationship to both the *vinifera* and *labrusca* vines, albeit a distant one. The wine made from many hybrids has not been found particularly agreeable, which is why their planting is so often controlled – to protect pure strains. There are, however, those who do like wines made from the *labrusca* vine but, it is probably fair to say, these tend to be people native to the regions where it not only grows but is cultivated for some kind of wine.

The rôle of most hybrids at the present time is for experimentation, especially in places that are being considered as possible sites for vineyards. In the past, however, the high yield of these vines resulted in their being far more widely grown, as obviously farmers wanted the big crops. It was difficult to persuade anyone enjoying short-term profits from the cultivation of prolific hybrids to uproot them and, as far as many peasant farmers were concerned, a vine that can make wine is – a vine that can make wine, nothing more. Indeed, the terrible disaster of the *phylloxera* plague in the nineteenth century (see pp. 47–8) was probably long-term beneficial, in that the destruction of so many vineyards by the aphis at that time made it possible for the authorities at least to try to encourage and even insist on the planting of *vinifera* vines when the vineyards were rehabilitated.

Today, however, with a greater knowledge of vines, work on hybrids is of increasing importance. Some of them – they are often named apparently rather strangely, commemorating those who evolved them – are especially hardy and resistant to vine diseases. Some of the wine made from hybrids in English vineyards has achieved more than basic acceptability. So it is possible that, in the future, careful and controlled use of certain hybrid strains may create a new 'family' of vines, possibly never able to achieve the highest quality of wine possible with vines from classic strains, but nevertheless pleasant and useful.

There are a vast number of hybrid vines being grown today –

but, in areas already established as important in making classic wines, the hybrids are very strictly controlled and producers must be registered with the authorities. Grapes used both for the table and for wine fall into three categories: recommended, authorized – again strictly controlled and sometimes restricted – and what EEC regulations term 'temporarily authorized'. These are the vines that will not usually be permitted to be replanted once the vineyard has been ploughed up, and they may not be used for wines. The hybrids do not come into the 'recommended' category, with the exception of one that is used in the making of Armagnac.

As a plant, the vine is somewhat like the iceberg – there is far more below than what is seen on the surface. When one reflects where the vine grows, it will be realized that this must be so, because few plants of the size of a full-grown vine could live in the shallow surface soil that covers some of the world's vineyards. Wild vines, of course, literally run wild. In their native state they are not trained and run along the ground, rather like brambles; sometimes they put out subterranean shoots from their own roots which extend sideways, sometimes they simply spread on the surface.

In the earliest days of vine growing, farmers would prop up the vine shoots, both because this enabled vines to serve as types of hedges or bushes, even arbours if trained really high, and because, by raising the fruiting branches away from the earth, the animals could not eat the grapes. The biblical reference to the 'little foxes' who damage the vineyards may seem odd to someone familiar only with the impeccably ranged vines of famous vineyards today, but the odd plot of vines would have been at risk from the smaller four-footed animals, also cattle – enjoying a juicy feed – and, of course, birds. As knowledge of plant cultivation in general increased it was found that, if a vine was supported upwards, either by being tied to a stake or post or even a tree, or if its branches were coiled in towards the main trunk, in a basket-like shape, not only was the plant itself healthier but the fruit it gave was much superior to that of the old wild vine.

The pruning of vines also started early. Any husbandman would have noticed the improvement in the yield of vines not indulged by allowing their shoots to grow and take too much away from the eventual fruit. It is remarkable how, in *De Re Rustica*, Lucius Junius Moderatus Columella, born in Cadiz and living mostly near Rome, where he owned and ran several farms, gives an account of how to lay down and care for vineyards, both for table and wine grapes, such as might be a handbook for the primitive vine cultivator even today; he gives considerable detailed instruction on pruning. He also mentions a number of specific vines, describing their characters, and therefore it is clear that by his time (the first century BC) a great deal was known about this aspect of farming.

Another advantage of training vines on poles and trellises was that, as well as acting as windbreaks or arbours, as the ancient Egyptians often portray in wall inscriptions, a second crop could be planted actually underneath the vines. This system may be seen in Madeira today, with a huge range of market garden produce being grown under the shade of the vine canopies; in very hot vineyards this type of shade made it possible to grow vegetables that would otherwise not have been able to withstand the direct sun. Plantations of this type would both hold such topsoil as did exist and, if turned in by ploughing, serve to revitalize it, long before it was realized that land requires regular resting and nourishing if it is to be profitably planted for useful crops.

Below ground, however, man does not – as yet – influence the roots of a vine to any great extent. The sort of soils in which these roots can exist so as to provide nourishment to the plant, in addition to that taken from the leaves, will be dealt with later, but the root system of the vine is yet one more of the astonishing things about this remarkable plant. The taproot or main root stem of a mature vine can plunge down twelve to fifteen feet below the surface of the vineyard and, from this taproot, several other fairly sturdy roots extend, both downwards and sideways, with many other stalk and tendril-like roots extending from them, occupying a considerable space within the ground. This huge root system is why, when vineyards are grubbed up and left to lie fallow before being replanted, it is so difficult to remove all of the roots, which are, as far as the thinner ones are concerned, usually left to rot in the ground.

The vine's roots work through all sorts of layers in the earth but it is the depth to which they penetrate that accounts for much of what was previously thought mysterious about the vine. It is a mysterious plant, but some of its mysteries have been explained and, at least to me, prove wonderful even when one understands some of the causes and effects. To see a tree heave up a paving stone or crack the lid of a tomb is no more amazing than to see a photograph of the various layers of soils through which a vine's root will penetrate and from which it draws various forms of nourishment.

In many vineyards today, however, the roots of the vines are not quite the same as in past times. Although it was as early as 1536 that the Spaniards who, under Cortez, had settled in Mexico were grafting vines brought over from Europe on to the vinestocks growing wild, so as to resist the attacks of an aphis that fed on the roots of the European vines, this practice appears to have been forgotten or at least ignored until the nineteenth century. Then this aphis, *phylloxera vastatrix*, was discovered in Hammersmith in London, having been brought from the United States, ironically enough in cuttings of vines which were coming in to provide scientists in Europe with the means to experiment with methods of counteracting downy mildew, a plague that had attacked the vines previously and that was eventually defeated by the use of sprays. But the invasion of the aphis was far more serious because its peculiar life cycle is such that there is no point at which it can be definitely destroyed and, unless a vineyard is flooded – when vines cannot be cultivated anyway – or is situated on sand, where the aphis cannot live, which only a few vineyards are, then any vine attacked by the *phylloxera* will be dead in about three years.

After an appalling crisis in all major European vineyards and the most desperate and sometimes far-fetched attempts to counteract the plague, it was found that the aphis does not attack the roots of American vinestocks, such as *labrusca*, and vineyards were replanted with these, on to which the classic vines, reared in a nursery, could be grafted.

This was a complete change in the history of the vine's cultivation. The *phylloxera*-resistant rootstocks are somewhat different in form from those of the 'national' or ungrafted vines, apparently being thinner. It also usually takes longer for a vine grafted on to another rootstock to bear satisfactorily for wine, so that the life of its productive period does not begin until later. Lengthy discussions, as will be supposed, have taken place about the difference in quality between the wine from grafted and ungrafted vines and, today, it is possible to make at least some kind of comparison, because there are some vineyards – such as Chile – where there are no grafted vines at all, *phylloxera* never having invaded the country; there are also many regions in Australia and New Zealand where ungrafted vines apparently flourish, thanks to regulations governing the import of vegetation that might carry all sorts of pests affecting many plants. Thus, although it is possible to say that virtually all European vines today are grafted (the exceptions are Colares in the sand dunes outside Lisbon, a section of the Great Plain of Hungary, certain Cyprus vineyards – *phylloxera* has never come to the island – and a few patches in Douro vineyards), it is not true, as was generally stated until quite recently, that all the vines in the world are grafted.

There is also the extremely important business of 'clonal selection'. This means that, from a single vine, all cuttings taken for study can be traced back to the original 'parent'; the way in which each cutting develops is recorded and its individual particularities observed. This enables ampelographers to evolve strains that are disease-resistant or have certain specially desirable attributes – such as ripening at a particular time – or are suited to certain conditions. It is no longer possible, therefore, to make too many complete generalizations about the type of wine produced from a specific vine – the individual clone, or result of several clones, and the contribution of the particular rootstock must all be taken into account. This revolution in the world of vines has been a quiet one, but it is probably true to say that never in one period of fifty years has so much changed in the vineyards of the world.

The wine vine is mostly hermaphrodite, that is, a single plant possesses both male and female organs. This means that the plant is able to fertilize itself – it is completely independent. There appear to be a few unisexual vines that have to be cross-pollinated. The vine has only tiny flowers, so does not attract large quantities of insects; indeed, it would seem that there is considerable divergence of opinion as to whether vines in general self-pollinate, or whether this is done by the wind. It is not, however, a matter that need concern the wine lover.

From the foregoing, it will be understood that the vine, although a remarkable and still somewhat mysterious plant, is, essentially, a plant; it is subject to the seasons in its development and, in cultivated form, requires constant care throughout the year, although it is mainly at the time of the vintage, when the grapes are picked, that the public are much aware of what it is doing.

The other highly important event in the vine's year is the flowering, in the spring: the flowers have an odd, slightly sweet but also slightly musky smell, which, for a brief time, is wafted over the vineyard, but there is nothing very picturesque about this. A quick flowering is desirable, because this means a good 'set' of the minute remnants of the flowers that, eventually, will form clusters and swell into grapes. If the set is poor or prolonged, the grapes do not mature in a regular way. Generally, the vintage is within two or three days of being a hundred days after the vine's flowering, although some New World vine growers have recently asserted that they do not see that this is inevitable, as certain treatments can, if necessary, push on the progress of the maturation of the grapes. I should not suppose, however, that this is likely to occur in most classic vineyards within the lifetime of this book – progress is a good thing but conflict with nature is seldom wholly satisfactory!

PRUNING

There are a fairly large number of basic methods of pruning and training vines, but the aims of all are the same: to produce grapes in prime condition and to protect and assist the development of the vine in a variety of vineyards. Thus, the part of the vine where leaves and fruit will grow must be raised above the ground, to escape damage by wild creatures – the new shoots as well as the actual grapes are delicious to these – and the branches must be supported so as to bear the weight of the grapes. At the same time, the maximum yield of grapes must not be so great that the vine is exhausted, quality having to be borne in mind as well as quantity and also the circumstance of the vine having to bear fruit year after year satisfactorily. Thus, it is important to cut down unnecessary foliage and shoots, even if they are likely to bear fruit. Also, too many leaves will take nourishment from the grapes. Topping and slicing away superfluous vegetation is routine, nowadays often being done by machine.

The leaves, however, must shield the vine from both hot sun and possibly battering rain. Against hail foliage is scant protection; even the stems of the vines can be split and scarred by a hailstorm lasting only a few minutes. If the vine is trained low in a vineyard that suffers several months of cold, wet weather and possibly night frosts with some frequency, then lifting the part of the plant that bears fruit away from the coldness and damp of the soil is a safeguard; air, held within a vineyard, is warm. But adequate circulation of air within the vine plants is also important, as a safeguard against rot and certain diseases likely to attack if the weather is damp and hot.

The method of pruning also caters for the fruiting of the vine over the years, so that shoots selected from the growing plant will develop and bear in succession, other shoots emerging in turn, with, if possible, some that can also be, as it were, reserves, to be allowed to bear if some disaster has destroyed the main branch or branches destined to fruit at one time.

So it is that you may see several different sorts of pruning practised within even a fairly small area, because different vines have different characteristics and may be more satisfactorily adapted to one method than another in different sites. Training the shoots along wires is a common method, either all to one side of the vine, or branching out on both sides; there are usually several strands of wire, secured at the ends of the rows by posts or stakes, and these can be used to pull up and tighten the rows and support the vines as they get heavier. In some vineyards, such as many making the fine wines on steep slopes in Germany, each vine will be trained up a single stake or post, often just higher than a human being's head. In the hot vineyards of the southern Rhône each vine is

VINE PRUNING AND TRAINING

The double Guyot method of pruning and training, developed in the mid nineteenth century by Dr J. Guyot and used for many of the classic wines of the world. Essentially, the Guyot method aims to prevent overcropping in any one year, but to enable shoots that will bear in the next year to replace those that have already yielded.

Top left, the *taille courte*; *top right*, the *taille longue*; *bottom*, the much-used *taille Guyot, mixte*. These methods are used in many vineyards, according to the terrain and the vine variety. Note that the branch that is to fruit this year is backed up by the branch that will fruit next year.

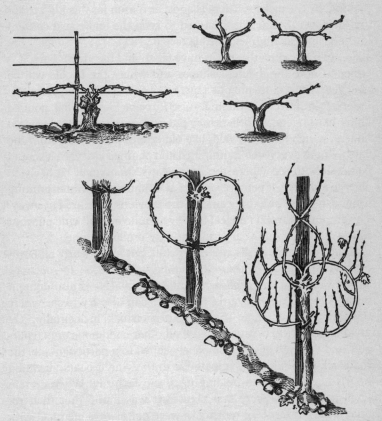

A method of training on the very steep slopes in the Mosel, the vines being attached to stakes. The canes are bent so as to angle the fruit to light and air, and, after the vintage, the new canes are trained up the stake and main vinestock, as shown in the centre.

usually separate too, but low on the ground, like a small shrub. Other methods of pruning and training that are easily noted are the bush method, when the various shoots are bowed outwards and then pulled together at the top; trellising, such as is seen in parts of Italy and in Madeira; also the very high cultivation, common in the Minho region of north Portugal, where the vines that make *vinho verde* literally grow to the height of trees – in older vineyards they may even be trained up trees – and tall ladders are required by the pickers. There is another reason for this high training, however, because it is wished to keep the malic acid content in the grapes as high as possible (see p. 181).

Sometimes, when the leaves have fallen and the vine is bare, it is easier to note the different shapes and where the shoots will be next year: some vines put out a mere two or three sideways strands; others, from lower positioning, raise three or four twisted, pointed limbs, like fingers; yet others may put up a number of these gnarled fingers, which look very odd, like old crones pushing up from the earth. But in every well-maintained and planned vineyard it should be possible to see where the next year's shoots will be likely to emerge and also, if you are visiting at a time when winter pruning is done, to note how the canes of the previous year are cut away. The amount of wood and leaf that even quite a small vine puts out in the course of one year is surprisingly prolific.

Grafting cannot be discussed in detail, but as in nearly all European vineyards the vines will have been grafted on to rootstock suitable to resist the *phylloxera* aphis, and as this is also done in many New World vineyards, the visitor can also try to see where the graft has been done. The choice of rootstock, incidentally, is of great importance, because, even if all other conditions are favourable and the type of vine completely suited to a particular site, the rootstock must also be sympathetic to the vine it bears, directing nourishment to it and holding it up satisfactorily. When certain English vineyards were first planted it was found that their requirements in terms of rootstocks were not always identical with those of many established and famous vineyards of Europe, and some owners had to uproot and replant before their vines could yield adequately.

The graft will, of course, be low down, near the soil; in some vineyards the topsoil may even cover it. But it is not usually difficult to see the join of the *vinifera* vine to its sturdy relation. With ungrafted vines there is no join and the enormous weight and spread of a vine above quite a slim stem is something that always amazes me, even though the plant is supported by wires or posts. Old vines develop thicker stems, especially near the ground, and, just as the rootstock of an ungrafted vine is supposed to be thicker than that of a pest-resistant rootstock, so the wood above ground of an elderly vine – twenty-five to thirty years for many varieties – becomes ridged, dark and convoluted. But a really old vine, such as may be kept mainly for show in some classic vineyards so that visitors can see what a century means in terms of a vinestock, will be very thick-stemmed, with deep ridges in its outer bark, more like a little tree.

CLIMATE

The vine can, even in its now highly-bred and sensitive form, resist many extremes of weather. It can survive drought, although it cannot, without some moisture, yield in quantity; this is when its deep roots can continue to feed it. It can survive rain, although not to excess during either the spring flowering or vintage periods, when satisfactory fruit set is prevented in the first instance, and rot and battered, split grapes can occur in the second, with a general weakness in the resulting wine if picking has to stop once it has begun and, sometimes, so much rainwater in the must that certain red wines of particularly bad years have, even though carefully made, looked more like *rosés*. The vine can stand being snowbound, as frequently happens in Germany, but it can be destroyed by frost; the terrible spring frost of 1956 in Europe gave a type of 'cold burn' to many vineyards, especially that of Chablis, where the blackened vines never recovered and extensive replanting had to be undertaken. The spring period of mid-May in Europe is known as that of the 'Ice Saints', because of four saints' festivals coming at the time when the risk of the last frosts is still dreaded.

Rain getting into cellars and wine stores can also prove hazardous – modern wineries are not likely to risk much damage from this, but in one sodden year a great Burgundian grower had to get around in his cellar by swimming – and when casks are floated off the scantling or racks where they have just been filled with the new wine, not much good can be expected of the contents.

There are, however, many who suppose that a very hot summer is likely to result in an outstanding vintage. This is not so. Great heat can, in a way, scorch grapes as well as depriving them of moisture; this is why, in the Rhône Valley and many other hot vineyards, the vines are pruned so that the leaves act as a protection for the fruit. Too much sun can bring out various elements in some wines that throw them out of proportion – too much tannin extracted by hot weather from a grape is as bad as too much acidity being present because the weather has not been warm enough for the grapes to ripen. What growers like is a good set, then a moderately warm summer, with a little soft rain – torrential downpours damage both vines and grapes, and as hailstones the size of walnuts can hurtle out of a suddenly black sky, it is not surprising to find many vineyards equipped with rockets to loose off at storm clouds before they can reach and break above vineyards; it is also not unknown for growers to go out with their guns and shoot at the clouds, to break them.

As far as many classic regions making fine wines are concerned, the vines tend to be cherished and special, not quite as robust as some varieties cultivated for more everyday wines in the huge vineyards of certain southern vineyards – the south of France, North Africa, some of the mighty wine regions of the New World. But the wine vine, even at its most aristocratic, is not really a delicate plant and, in the regions where it gives of its finest quality, it has to be definitely tough: the Douro Valley in winter is bleak, the vineyards are mostly granite, the peasants wear huge cloaks to keep out the weather. In the Mosel, the snow piles up on the precipitous slopes of many of the bends in that tortuous river, where a foothold is quite hard to get, even in fine weather. In the course of a year the vine runs many risks, but it is surprising how well it survives many kinds of bad weather. It is warmth rather than continuous sunshine that the vine likes – soft, sunny days, maybe with a little gentle rain to swell the grapes just prior to vintage or at night, with no hint of sharpness in the air until the harvest is finally in.

It should also be remembered that the exact 'climate' prevailing in one vineyard may be very different from that of one almost adjacent. There are 'pockets' that get frost (these exist even in the home counties in the UK during summer), and in the wine world it is not strange to find one vineyard suffering from rain or hail damage which has completely missed its neighbour. These micro-climates account for some of the great variations in quality – and price – of wines made within the same smallish area, all bearing the same name. It is strange to drive along a road in a wine region and find that it is raining on one side of this and not on the other, but it frequently occurs. There is at least one 'channel' in a mountain range in the Cape vineyards of South Africa through which freshening winds blow and, passing by way of this dip in the peaks, cool the vineyards on the further side; to the onlooker, the gap may seem merely a slightly lower point along a series of crests, but the vineyards located where this wind tunnel will reach them benefit to an extent that is remarkable when their yield is compared with that of those alongside them.

Although generalizations are risky, it is possible frequently to say that wines made in very hot vineyards usually lack finesse, tend to be high in alcohol – unless very strict control is observed throughout – and do not possess the beauty of bouquet that is so marked a characteristic of some of the wines from chillier northern vineyards. Modern technology can do much, but cannot radically change the material with which it has to work – grapes coming to the winery. It should not, however, be forgotten that water or its proximity can have an effect that is not immediately obvious. Desiderius P. Pongrácz, advising viticulturalist to the Distillers Corporation at Stellenbosch, pertinently notes that 'seas, large lakes, and large rivers exert a moderating influence upon the climate in their adjacent areas. Water acts as a "regulating reservoir of heat" far more than soil or air does.' The curious modulations of the sea mists on the coast of California, the coastal sherry vineyards at Sanlucar de Barrameda, where *manzanilla* is made, some of the Italian vineyards, the difference in vineyards at the Cape in South Africa where the vines can 'see the sea', or the New Zealand vineyards and many of the most famous Médoc vineyards, where the saying 'the vine likes to see the water, but not to get its feet wet' is proved by the view from many over the Gironde estuary – all of these, being near either water or rain forests, make an effect on the vines that science is only just beginning to understand, interpret and document.

In some vineyards, such as certain of those in California, where the temperature drops fairly low at night even in warm weather, the overnight coolness will certainly have an effect on the grapes, so that they eventually yield a different type of juice from that of vineyards where the night temperature is only a few degrees lower than that of the day, as prevails in some European vineyards at vintage time. The speed at which the temperature encourages the ripening of the grapes is obviously of importance and this must be related to the variety or varieties of grape being cultivated. If the autumn in the vineyard approaches gradually, the air cooling slowly and some mid-day temperatures being quite high, then certain differences in making the wine subsequent to the differences in picking the grapes will be inevitable – as happens in the German vineyards when a long, warm, even sultry autumn enables the harvesting of late-picked grapes. If, however, autumn rains and a sharp drop in temperatures are usual following the vintage, then wines made by the action of *botrytis cinerea* (noble rot) or simply late pickings will be difficult to produce (see pp. 168–74).

It is sometimes not realized that vineyards are subject to the practical considerations that govern other businesses: if people have been engaged to pick or machines hired to do the job, then it is costly to suspend operations or postpone starting the harvest simply because weather conditions are not ideal. Nor is it always possible to make what might be a fine wine even in a suitable year, when what the estate or vineyard owner really aims at and needs to make is something of good quality for everyday drinking. In some German regions it is not possible for pickers to be engaged to pass several times through a vineyard knowing how to gauge the exact ripeness of individual grapes and picking them late, so, with an eye to the sky and another on the falling barometer, a grower will pick his entire crop, flinging in grapes with some *Edelfäule* (noble rot) on them with those that are simply just ripe. On one occasion I was in a vineyard in New Zealand watching the approach of a mechanical harvester along lines of Chenin Blanc vines: on some of the bunches of grapes, all in prime condition, the beginning of the *botrytis* was to be seen. But the machine can't differentiate and the farmer couldn't bypass certain bunches of grapes and, later, engage experienced pickers to go out and glean the over-ripe and, even, too-shrivelled grapes; all had to go into the crusher at one time. It is fair to say that the inclusion of such special elements will usually boost the overall quality of the wine, although the outsider sometimes may feel it is a pity that no one could have waited ... but then, maybe, there might have been a sudden downpour or drop in temperature that would have destroyed the remnants of a fine crop.

If money were no object, then of course all vineyard owners would postpone picking their grapes until maximum ripeness or, in certain special areas, over-ripeness and 'noble rot' might be achieved ... or the whole crop lost. But nobody can operate in this way, the risk is too great and the absence of a wine's name in lists for one year can damage its future in terms of sales, just as its destruction in a storm or by frost can damage its vines for a decade. There are many visitors to wine regions who, with benevolent intentions, frequently ask 'Why don't you make so-and-so?' quite unaware that, although the production of the wine they think they would like is *technically* possible, it is both uneconomic and possibly uncommercial. Realizing the problems that the wine-grower faces can enable the wine lover to acquire a more realistic attitude towards wines and deepen the respect for those who do achieve good and great wines in spite of all difficulties.

So – vines and the wines they are to make and the wines that it is economic for them to make must all be adjusted to individual conditions and requirements. They must also be chosen to suit the soils of available vineyards.

SOILS

The vine will grow in a variety of soils, many of these very poor and virtually useless for the cultivation of other crops. Although it is technically possible to change soils as far as the topsoil is concerned, there is far more to soil in a vineyard than the eye can see. Years ago one was taught that certain vines flourished in light-coloured soil, making light, brisk, vivacious wines – as in the *albariza* region of Jerez, in Champagne and a point in Burgundy where the soil turns pale and the Côte de Beaune vineyards begin. But this and other generalizations were misleading; a light or dark soil *does* have an effect on vines, but not necessarily that of making *only* light, crisp wines or firm, weighty ones. This is something to be mentioned later, but anybody looking at a vineyard should consider, first, the appearance and type of topsoil, then, if possible, know something about the subsoil or, ideally, subsoils, for there may be many layers below ground. In addition, the flatness or slope of the land itself should be appraised and its 'aspect'; this last term is specialized in the context of wine, because it means the outlook of the vineyard – the way in which it faces the sun at a particular time, the way in which it is sheltered or exposed, the vulnerability to winds or liability to rain (if near mountains).

Vines for wine seem to flourish best in soils that are lightish in consistency. This need not be the topsoil – there is a streak of gravel running through the Pomerol vineyard, for example, that lightens these wines and differentiates them from the more earthy, even fleshy wines of adjacent St Émilion. But, to the uninformed eye, both vineyards look much the same on the surface, fairly dark and with an odd, slightly sticky type of clay that dries hard and powdery on the shoes. Under Pauillac there is a virtual plateau of *alios*, a type of sandstone, which is rarely found anywhere else; it must contribute at least something to the special quality of the wines of this parish. Knowledge of what is underneath as well as in the vineyard is now an essential preliminary to the laying out of any vine plantation. Analyses of soils are taken at various places and the subsequent reports carefully studied.

As wine is, essentially, water that has been passed into the vines and thereby reaches the grapes – their fruit – on which subsequently crushed material the process of fermentation will operate, the soils relevant to satisfactory vine growing must be able to contribute to the water flowing through and being absorbed by them. This is more important in the subsoils than the topsoil, because, although rain falls upon the vine and the topsoil, the vine's roots take up water from subterranean sources, often at times when there is either no rain or not much and when – as during a long dry spell in the summer – the grapes must be plumped out to ripen properly. Anybody who has kept indoor pot plants will realize the importance of watering from the bottom rather than simply pouring water on the top of the plant and its topsoil!

The layers of the soil and subsoil are like solidified waves, undulating below the vines and accounting for the differences between one plot's wines and another's. There can be many layers and, if water passes through several of these, then the moisture drawn up into the plant is complex, each layer of soil affecting the water. Once I met a geologist who said, without pretension, that he could identify many of the wines of the Mosel blind, simply because he knew the soils and rock formation of that sinuous river and its tributaries and, therefore, could detect the difference in the original water supply taken up by vines in certain vineyards along its banks. I am sure that this was no boast.

Naturally, the vine's roots start by going straight down. Then the auxiliary roots explore the areas around the taproot. If any of the roots is unable to penetrate the soil or subsoil with some ease, then it can go no further and, if water accumulates underground in the layer of whatever is halting the roots – usually dense clay – whether because of ordinary rain or irrigation, then the vine cannot develop. Vine roots do not thrive, either, in waterlogged, badly drained ground, so such a situation is undesirable.

Should a vineyard consist of various layers humped up and down – possibly by previous volcanic action or some prehistoric upheaval – then the grower must know something about the placing of these. The almost undetectable hillocks and ridges in certain famous vineyards are the subject of pride, often considered as accounting for that particular wine's individuality.

Until quite recently it was generally supposed that the finest wines could only be made from vines grown on slopes, however slight; where a vineyard was on a slope anyway, it was usually noted that it was the vines two-thirds up the slope that would yield the best grapes, being both sheltered by the top of the slope and unlikely to be waterlogged at the bottom. But some New World wine makers find this insistence on vineyards being planted on slopes unnecessary: in a recent article by Simon Loftus in *Wine and Spirit*, Joe Heitz, maker of very fine California wines, is quoted as saying, 'It's a lot of hokum that vines have to grow on a hillside to grow good wine.' Simon Loftus goes on: 'Most California wine makers rate micro-climate above soil (the zonal classification of vineyards is based on climate) and consider clonal selection more important than the age of the vine. Others take the traditional view that in poor, well-drained soil, the vine is forced to send its roots deep in search of nourishment and that an old plant, reaching over fifty feet underground for its sustenance, can bring up mineral trace elements from the subsoil that affect flavour.' A comparison of yield is made between certain mountain vineyards in California and top Médoc estates, which appear to be about the same, and the writer makes the relevant point that some of the finer wines of California do come from mountain sites – some of them originally planted by Europeans.

Much must depend on both the variety of vine planted and the resources of the vineyard; steep slopes require either more workers to tend them or more expensive machinery to work them, sometimes both. Flat vineyards are comparatively easy to run but can only yield good rather than fine wines. The Hérault region in the south of France is one wine region producing abundant quantities of wines, but these do not achieve more than moderate quality. Even if a vineyard looks flat or flattish, there may be some small undulations of the topsoil or, possibly more significant, beneath the surface, which can – according to the theories of many –

account for the circumstance of one patch of vines being capable of producing truly fine wine, whereas an adjacent patch will, no matter what care is bestowed, produce only medium to good wine. The striking and, possibly, unique exception is Coonawarra which is completely flat – yet from here come some of Australia's finest Cabernet Sauvignon wines. The ruler-like road that runs through the region is parallel to a strip of very odd, dark reddish soil running like a red carpet a short distance away – this is the *terra rossa* which, it is thought, gives the special quality to the wines. Coonawarra may be the outstanding exception to the 'vineyards should be on slopes for fine wines' theory, but it is beginning to look as if there may be some others, especially when mechanical cultivation and knowledge of what grows best where inform today's vineyard owners more than in the past.

The other strange thing about soils is that what seems to be an ideal soil for a certain vine in one region does not necessarily prove equally satisfactory when that vine is planted in a similar soil elsewhere – all this giving substance to the theory of importance of climate rather than soil. However, there are certain soils that the vine does like. These tend to be light in consistency rather than heavy, even if the components are solid.

Clay, as has been mentioned, can prove a barrier to water, although some types of broken clay need not be an obstacle. Some substances, such as alkali salts, or boron and similar elements, do no good to the vine, and nor does any soil that simply holds water – proper drainage is essential to vine health. Salt water, if it stands around the vines, also harms them, although it is now possible to reduce the saline content of some soils, so that there are regions where vineyards have been successfully planted almost on the seashore, on reclaimed soils, as in the south of France.

Chalky soils and those high in lime seem to be liked by many vines, as witness the huge blanket of light-coloured soil that spreads over the Champagne region, plunges under the English Channel and emerges on the Isle of Wight and at the white cliffs of Dover. If a visitor to a vineyard region sees very pale soils it should also be remembered that these play a part in ripening the grapes by reflecting the light upwards on to the fruit. This is a two-way warming up of the vine at vintage time: in the sherry vineyards around Jerez the *albariza* soil is so dazzling white as to make one blink – and heat is reflected.

Stones, likewise, not only drain a vineyard – anybody walking round an estate will kick pebbles on to the vineyard instead of off – but also reflect light and heat. This of course applies to those on the surface. In the Rhône Valley one of the most remarkable sights is certain vineyards that appear to consist entirely of truly giant pebbles, some of them the size of a human head or even larger, orangey in colour and slightly rough in appearance; they look exactly like potatoes baked in their jackets. These stones drain away the torrential downpours of some of the spring storms, they hold the vine firm and, in the summer, their sponge-like texture serves as a type of night storage heater, because they retain the warmth of the day and direct this heat upwards to the vines – which have to be pruned so that their leaves shelter the grapes from the direct rays of the scorching sun.

The pebbles in the vineyards south of Bordeaux have given the region its name – Graves, or gravel. Gravelly topsoils also serve to drain and retain the vineyard soil. Sand often goes with gravel and in several well-known vineyards the two types of soil are found together. There are various types of sand, some hard, some very soft and porous; in subsoils certain sands can pack hard together, but some silts and light sand can remain fairly friable and loose. Sand does not hold water well, which is why some gravel is usually desirable in both top and subsoil, but sand does retain heat – think of sitting on a dry sandy shore even after the sun has gone down – and therefore can be useful 'packing' around a vine.

Humus is an important part of the soil of any place in which plants are to be cultivated and, as Desiderius P. Pongrácz notes, it 'can be considered as a comparatively permanent constituent of every agricultural soil, but it also undergoes a further slow decomposition by new generations of soil microbes'. Every form of animal and plant life that dies and decomposes in the soil becomes a form of nourishment for the future – the plants on which animals feed pass through them and become manure and this occurs even with carnivores. So everything that dies and remains in the earth adds to it, in a different form, in order that other forms of life may be fed later. This is why the soil of any vineyard must be turned, aerated and, at intervals, rested by having vetch or similar plants containing valuable nutrients sown and then ploughed in. One cannot go on indefinitely – even with all the resources of the laboratory and modern fertilizers – growing one plant from one patch of soil. It must be refreshed.

Other important basic soils – the whole subject is, as may now be realized, far more complex than it at first appears – include schist, granite and slate. These seem highly unlikely soils for any plant, yet the greatest German wines and the wines that make port originate in granitic, schistous vineyards, where it is difficult to walk without sliding on the sharp, hard, irregular surface chips and slivers and where, in the Douro, it was and still is sometimes necessary to blast to get a vine planted in the otherwise impenetrable hard 'soil'.

The vine requires certain things to nourish and keep it healthy, and these are the same as the requirements of many other plants. The important chemical elements are: carbon, for about half of the dry matter of any plant is carbon; water – which is hydrogen and oxygen, essential for any plant; nitrogen, which is of particular importance to the vine; phosphorus, which enables a plant to 'breathe'; potassium, highly important to ensure healthy growth; calcium, magnesium and iron. These make up the 'diet' of a vine, just as certain things compose a diet for a healthy human. If it cannot obtain its basic needs from natural sources, then it needs the help of the scientist and soil expert. It has been known for certain vineyards to be virtually 'resurfaced' like roads, when it has been considered necessary to correct any deficiencies or undesirable elements in this topsoil, but of course this sort of thing is only possible where a vineyard is going to be started – and where there is a great deal of money behind the operation. In established vineyards, simply because they have been under vines for so many years, certain elements will have accumulated, notably humus and marl, and this is why I have a personal theory – at least not contradicted by any specialists with whom I have been able to talk – that a vineyard needs to 'mature' before it will give of its best, very much as a vine and certain wines also need to 'grow up'. This is something that I have noticed in the wines from certain English vineyards: even with well-established vines and the most informed methods of cultivation and wine-making, it seems to take the vineyards several years – sometimes a decade or more – to settle into wine production. This, of course, may be due to various elements in the air as well as the soil, as will be noted in a subsequent chapter.

However, just to be fair, it is within the same week of writing the former statement that I have also read equally interesting comments by Bill Jekyl, of Jekyl Vineyards, in *Decanter* magazine. He makes the following points: '. . . the mineral components of the soil contribute little or nothing to wine quality, but the physical structure of the soil that determines the environment of the roots is vitally important to making fine wine.' He further makes a point that will probably be as new to readers as it was to me: he says that the French AOC system of controls 'grew out of a history of dry-farmed vineyards. Curiously, many French vineyards, for that very reason, are probably not on the soil best suited to their roots. When vineyards are dry-farmed the soil must be heavy enough to hold water and carry the vines from the cessation of rain in the spring, until the grapes are harvested in the autumn. Clay soils hold water much longer than sandy, gravelly or loam soils, and so many French vineyards were established on soil that is heavier in clay than is ideal in order to survive under dry-farming conditions.' This seems a sound piece of reasoning – if it were true that rain, in European vineyards, really does 'cease' in the spring – would that it were always so!

However, Bill Jekyl makes another point – soil structure, he says, can affect 'the micro-climate of the vine by increasing the warmth both above and below ground . . . Well-drained soils, being low in moisture-holding capacity, also warm up more rapidly in the spring so that early growth is advanced by speeding development of the essential root system' and, further, 'There is no correlation between the level of mineral elements contained in the soil and in the must or wines grown on it. Thus, the different quality characteristics of various wines cannot be attributed to specific elements in the soil. It is rather the organic constituents – alcohol, acid, esters, colour, tannins and aldehydes – by which wines are distinguishable because they directly affect the appearance, aroma, bouquet, flavour and body of the wines.'

This straightforward argument is of great significance today and, although British readers of this book are unlikely to fling themselves into details of chemistry and oenology at the higher levels, as some American enthusiasts enjoy doing, it is worth while being aware that there are several views about soil, as about everything else to do with wine, which differ a great deal throughout the world, yet are held by some whose achievements and qualifications inspire respect.

THE VINE THROUGHOUT THE YEAR

It will be realized that the terms 'spring' and 'autumn' in this book refer – unless otherwise stated – to those seasons in the northern hemisphere. In the southern hemisphere, of course, the seasons are reversed, with the vintage in, say, Australia, occurring in what would be the European spring so, in consequence, putting the age of wines vintaged then six months ahead of those of the northern hemisphere, although both will be dated as the same year.

A resumé of what goes on in a vineyard and a winery must be very general, as all establishments have their individual methods of working and may observe specialized time-tables, but it will be noticed that the different seasons tend to stress indoor and outdoor activities. If every wine installation had a large permanent staff, able to carry on tasks in vineyards and the winery as and when required, this would make everything simple, but very few are able to do this and today, when machinery is of such importance in wine making as well as labour, the economics of the work involved in making wine are complicated. When you are taken round a winery and see the large and expensive equipment, some of it only in use for a matter of weeks in the entire year, it will be realized that the amount of capital required on outlay and maintenance is considerable – it is not just the greedy peasant farmers or the owners who exploit their estates who are responsible for the rising prices of wines: far more money, whether in the form of capital, interest, equipment or simply running costs goes into the production of even a modest bottle today than occurred in the past.

The following are the main activities that the vineyard visitor may see in a northern hemisphere vineyard where the production is organized on either a slightly or substantially larger scale than that of a fairly typical small family holding, where even grandparents and infants chip in with the work. As, from the southern vineyards in the south of Spain and North African coast to the northern German vineyards, the progress of the grapes can vary enormously, this too must be taken into consideration: a vintage may be in full swing in Jerez by mid-September but picking may not begin in Germany until late October. The information here is, therefore, based on a Bordeaux calendar, being mid-way.

January: In the vineyard, pruning will probably have begun around Christmas, although it is a tradition that it starts on 22 January, St Vincent's Day (he is the patron of vine-growers). Modern methods have brought this operation forward without harm. In the winery, wines in vat or cask will be under careful observation, regularly topped up, bungs cleaned if required, the health of each container reported. With any older wines than those of the previous vintage not yet in bottle, the technicians' reports on these will indicate progress and suggest bottling dates and procedures, plus any necessary treatments.

February: This is when the process of racking usually begins – the transference of wine off its lees in cask to fresh casks. If a vineyard consists of various different plots (parcels) – it is surprising to discover how many do – and, certainly, if there are a variety of different grapes in these, then, because the grapes will ripen at different periods and possibly the wines from different sites will develop at different rates, this is the time when the 'assembly' of all the wines of the previous vintage will be made, putting them together in a large container before transferring them back into casks or, with large-scale production, into other vats or tanks where they will remain prior to bottling, according to whether further maturation is required.

By now the second stage of fermentation is taking place or has finished in many wines, so that certain of them will soon be prepared for bottling. As the weather becomes a little warmer, the wine starts to come to life again, 'murmuring in the gloom' as one writer describes it 'because it knows the spring has come'. The vine, too, begins to show life.

Out of doors, the process of taking cuttings for grafting begins; the grafts and rootstocks are kept in sand until required. Sometimes they will be made from the estate's own vineyards, often they will be supplied from special vine 'nurseries'. Any pruning that has not been completed must now be done and, with the prospect of lighter days and – with luck – milder weather, any tools and equipment required for vineyard work should be checked ready for using outside.

March: During this month many things happen. The spring rackings should be completed and, with wines that are to be bottled after they have completed their fermentation, the bottling line should be prepared to receive them and final samples checked to ensure that they are in prime condition for going into bottle. The same applies to any older wines that have remained in cask or vat for more than a year, although some of these will not be bottled until the autumn. The season is curious because, as the vine begins to come to life again after its winter sleep and the sap starts to rise, there seems to be some affinity between the vine and the wine – some say that it is this that starts the wine off on its second period of fermentation. It is certainly odd the way in which even wines in bottle for years tend to be a little strange at this period, especially around the spring equinox (21 March), sometimes going somewhat 'dumb' or being very slightly disturbed; if you are tasting a wine round about this season, do not judge it too severely should it be less satisfactory than expected.

In the vineyard, the soil around the vines must be thoroughly turned up, so as to aerate it. The vines do not now need it banked up around their roots to keep these warm – at least, growers hope not.

April: Work in the winery continues, with careful supervision of all wines not yet in bottle. Bottling should be finished and wines in casks be topped up – air on top of the wine means that various infections can get at it. This is a time when trade visitors begin to sample wines they may be buying – some do this even earlier, but the wines should, ideally, be given time to settle down after the spring rackings before being appraised.

In the vineyard, cuttings are planted, any turning of the soil or ploughing should now have been done, but growers tend to prowl anxiously about the vines, because, if the vegetation comes on too fast due to warm spring weather, there is a great risk of frost damage – frosts are still a definite hazard. Forms of heating the vineyard, such as smudge pots, may be prepared and, meanwhile, vines are trimmed and spraying may be started.

May: Wines in cask are racked for the second time in the year and, by now, the business of buying and selling the bottled wine begins to be brisk – or should be. However, wines drawn from the cask are not always satisfactory samples at this period – May seems to be a time when many of them are extremely reserved, so that it takes experience and skill to taste them well.

In the vineyard, work begins to be well under way – weeding, spraying and trimming the vines must be done, and the time of the 'Ice Saints' (Pancras, Servatius, Boniface and Sophid) in the middle of the month is an anxious one, because now the vine is fairly well advanced towards the period of flowering and a frost can cause lasting and irremediable damage if it occurs so late.

June: The second racking of last year's vintage wines takes place, also any other wines in cask must be racked off (in Bordeaux the red wines are generally racked four times, but this naturally varies in other regions). Out of doors the vines are continually being tidied up – care being taken to see that they are settled as they should be on wires or however they are arranged, and spraying may also be done. This is the month when the vine should flower and, ideally, this should take place in warm, dry weather, the process lasting only a few days, so that the subsequent set of the fruit is equal and healthy. After the flowering, the shoots are also checked to see that the eventual grapes have space, light and air in which to grow.

July: Weeding and spraying occupy much time in the vineyard, with vine shoots being 'topped' or trimmed, so that they do not deprive the forming grapes from getting maximum nourishment. It may be necessary to weed the vineyard, to keep any unnecessary vegetation away from the vines, but nowadays there may be plastic covers laid between the rows to keep the weeds down and the moisture in. It may also be necessary to spray the vines, and a sharp look-out must be kept for all types of pests, including small animals – rabbits are capable of doing much damage to vines – and birds. Some vineyards are able to net the vines against these, but this naturally costs a great deal; oddly, it has been found that the coarse plastic netting, which casts a blue veil over many German vineyards when these are viewed from a distance, raises the temperature inside, like a string vest keeping a human being warm, so use of this can bring on ripening in advance of vines protected only by bird scarers (human and artificial), such as appliances that bang at intervals, as well as those that flap, turn and imitate the cries of predators, such as hawks.

August: This, in many European countries, is the great holiday month, when most people go away and even large businesses shut down. Many vineyards are not open to visitors at this time, but a skeleton staff have to keep an eye on things. Wines should, ideally, now have been bottled, although some may be left until September, but, if the temperature rises, there may be trouble in anything still around in the winery, although these days cooling devices protect most of the great wines. Great care in keeping the winery clean must be observed and, in the vineyard, progress will be surveyed. This is the period when grapes swell out noticeably, when certain white grapes turn faintly pink or bronze, and black grapes take on some of their eventual colour – 'The painter has been round,' say the Douro growers, where, of course, this will probably have taken place in July. But the vineyard now has to be left to its own efforts – in some, spraying is prohibited after early July.

If anyone has time for indoor work, this is when vintage equipment must be prepared – both for use in the vineyard and in the winery. Casks to be used will be checked and cleaned, sometimes by burning a sulphur candle inside, or they may be filled with water and left for some days so as to get the wood swollen and the staves tightly aligned. Anyone able to do so will start to prepare the winery for the vintage, because scrupulous cleanliness is essential at this period, the grape juice and the new wine being vulnerable to infection, as well as attracting flies and similar more obvious pests.

September: The preparations for the vintage are continued and should be completed. The vats are cleaned out – often the tiny doors in their sides appear so small as to make it impossible for anyone except a boy to get in, but grown men do – and if a winery or an estate engages outside workers for the busiest season of the year, then arrangements for their reception must be made. Sometimes – as in Champagne and the port region – special hostels or dormitories are prepared. Extra help must often be arranged so that workers can be well fed during what can be strenuous sessions.

In the vineyard constant observation of the grapes continues – also attempts to keep birds and other predators away from the fruit. It is ideal if warm weather continues, although a little fine rain for a short time is not necessarily harmful and will plump out the grapes. In some regions there are various festivals and ceremonies heralding the start of the vintage, but, for those who really do the work, the celebrating tends to be at the end of the harvest. However, vintage time is usually a period when estate and winery owners do a lot of entertaining of visitors, such as trade buyers and those of importance in influencing buying.

Once picking begins it should not stop – grapes should be brought to the winery as soon as they are ripe, both to avoid the risk of the weather changing and so that they do not – unless specially required – become over-ripe and split or develop rot. In their filled-out state they are of course at risk from even a moderately heavy downpour of rain, and rot can set in if the weather remains hot. If mechanical harvesters are in use they can speed up the picking enormously, and with these it is also possible to vintage at night – when the slightly cooler temperature facilitates working and also means that the grapes arrive at the winery in good condition; this cannot be done, of course, if there are very heavy night dews, but certainly the use of mechanical pickers can enable work to go on outside the normal hours when human beings could be engaged to pick. There are some vineyards where, by the light of arc lamps, vintaging goes on non-stop for the entire period of picking – winery staff sleep in snatches as and when they can.

At the vintage time the curious link between the vine and wine in bottle is sometimes once again manifest, as some wines show a difference in character at this period, as if they were 'working'

with their family. This is seldom more than a briefly passing phase, but it is not fair to judge a wine once and for all at such a time.
October: Picking continues, and in the winery work is non-stop. Visitors receive apologies for untidiness, but in fact a well-run winery is seldom truly untidy. Flies can be very troublesome, and modern devices to keep conditions as hygienic as possible are used, floors are frequently washed down, all appliances disinfected and kept as clean as may be. As the new wine will now begin to occupy the cellar, other wines still here and not yet bottled must be moved to another place of storage. The laboratory also continues to work hard, checking on the condition of the grapes, the must and the newly-made wines. If any farmers have been supplying grapes, payments have to be made for these as they come in and are weighed and accepted.

Once a section of vineyard has been picked, it will be tidied up even before the leaves fall, and often the debris from the final pressings of the grapes is used as fertilizer. Plans are made for any new or extended plantings and, if labour is available, some ploughing may be done. In vineyards where grapes are picked late or where the 'noble rot' is developing, the harvesters pass several times through the vineyards, selecting the bunches or, even, single grapes at the correct moment of ripeness. This is skilled work and is usually done by the regular vineyard staff rather than by temporary pickers.

At the end of the vintage there is usually some kind of party for all concerned, often with the estate or winery owner presiding – and, frequently, distributing largesse in various forms.
November: The weather becomes cooler and, in many wineries, the wine will have completed its first and tumultuous fermentation and begin to be quiet. It will now all be in cask or vat, having been run off from the vessel in which it underwent fermentation. The vats and any equipment used throughout the vintage will be cleaned and put away for next year. Any mature wine not yet in bottle will now be bottled and, prior to this, be fined, although exactly when this is done depends largely on the character of the particular vintage. The cellarmaster also decides the time for the new wines to undergo their first racking and their progress is very

carefully studied, wines in cask being regularly tasted, cask by cask, at frequent intervals. It is possible to have some notion as to the character of the vintage – although only a fool would be definite at this stage! – and decisions of policy, such as whether a particular lot of wine will be part of the *'grand vin'* of an estate, or a lower classification, must also start to be made. The business aspect of wine assumes great importance – customers are beginning to be informed as to quantities that will be available and possible prices, promotional activities in the run up to Christmas are planned and, as far as the producers are concerned, everything possible is done to encourage the consumers to sample their wines at this, the year's main boom time in the shops.

Out of doors, the ploughing continues, the vines are trimmed and generally tidied up, and their roots have earth heaped up over them so as to protect them from the cold weather. During the autumn, the vine leaves turn a variety of rich colours, making them a wonderful sight on a sunny day.

December: The winery is cleaned and put in order, bottling may continue and the new wine is watched, casks being topped up. In the vineyard the leaves fall and the vines look virtually dead. Some pruning can be done at the end of the month, but this depends on the locality, the vine and the judgement of the manager. The frenzied business activity carried on in earlier months is now dying down as far as growers are concerned – it is the merchants who work the clock round just before Christmas – and plans are made for the New Year, assessment of past achievements reported and views on possible future policy and projects are talked over, as sales reports come in.

VINEYARD LAYOUT

The way in which the vines are arranged in the vineyard is usually impressive – the regularity of the rows in a classic and well-maintained region, with the vines sometimes following the contours of the slopes, sometimes extending almost as far as the eye can see towards the horizon, makes even the casual traveller reach for a camera. (Few pictures truly capture the detailed beauty of land under vines, the variations in the tone colours of the vegetation, the texture of the topsoil, the surrounding landscape framing the vineyard.)

The layout can be varied, according to the resources and, in some European vineyards, the traditions observed in the past, but the arrangement of the vines is primarily done so as to achieve both quantity and quality in the yield. In the past, rows of vines were closer together than they are today: a worker could pass between them and if horses were used for ploughing they too took up little more space and also provided manure *en route*. But with increased knowledge of viticulture, it was realized that to crowd vines too much into a particular area was to risk exhausting the soil; much depended, also, on the way in which the vines were pruned – if a vine is grown high, up trellises, on wires or up stakes, then there is, obviously, more air down at ground level than if a succession of low-pruned bushes are cultivated.

The real change came with the use of machines in the vineyard. The 'tractor' can be of many types, some, almost like playthings, being small enough to crawl along narrow terraces a few feet in width; other tractors are giants, straddling the rows of vines and able to get along even in the worst of muddy conditions. For the tractor performs many tasks – spraying, topping and even pruning in some vineyards, ploughing and hoeing of course, and, now, picking. To enable a machine to work, adequate space must be provided, but many growers soon realized that, even if they had to replant and space out their vineyards and buy what might seem to be highly expensive machinery, the saving on labour and time could soon pay for such outlay. Labour, even if it is easy to obtain – and there is a drift from the land in many vineyard regions today – can never compete in terms of hours and speed with the machine, if it is possible to use this in the vineyard. There are, of course, some classic vineyards which can only be tended by hand – the terraces along the Mosel, for example, where sometimes only half a dozen vines occupy a few feet in the shelter of a rock on a ledge above a virtual precipice; even such vineyards may, however, sometimes get the benefit of the mechanical age by spraying from the air, by helicopter. Picking grape by single grape is another task that can only be done by the hand of man at present, although I have seen the beginning of experiments that enable grapes to be mechanically sorted from the ordinary degree of ripeness to those that have the 'noble rot' on them, all of them being picked at one time.

The spacing of the rows of vines, therefore, is something that varies according to area and, in addition, to the resources of the soil – drainage and so on. Controls are exercised in many countries and regions so that a vineyard does not risk being exploited by over-cropping. At the same time, it is sometimes difficult to convince someone whose family have farmed a particular patch for several centuries that, by planting fewer vines and by spacing these further apart, the ultimate yield of grapes will probably be well up to or even exceed the amount produced in a more crowded plantation – and the overall costs may be much lower per hectare. One estate owner recently announced that he planted his rows of vines close together because he believed that this resulted in greater quality in the ultimate wine; the reported comment caused some amusement – it was really a justification for his not having bought a tractor!

Then, the terrain itself must be both workable and suited to the types of vines to be planted. In the Douro Valley the remarkable terraces, which are like layers among the banks of the 'Golden River' and its tributaries, are still thought one of the most satisfactory forms of vineyard there. From the earliest history of vine cultivation, the plants have been arranged in rows; just outside St Émilion one can see the lines of stone, rather like earthbound windowboxes, in which the Romans planted their vines. The vines must have light, air and be reasonably easy of access; also they must either have good natural drainage or, if irrigation is permitted, then this must also be a workable and economic thing to arrange.

To plant vines on terraces, therefore, so that they can benefit from maximum exposure to the sun, has long been traditional in many cool or cold vineyards. Often one can see the traces of such terraces – used for other crops as well – in land that is now scrub or used for grazing. To look down on some of the vineyards of the world is to see a remarkable series of patterns, the terraces curving around hillsides, meeting and fanning out, striping the countryside in a warp and woof as of tufty candlewick. But terraces have to be maintained and, as anyone with experience of building or keeping up a dry stone wall will appreciate, this is a skill that is not always at the command of the farmer – including the wine farmer – of today. In Sicily, the Barone de Villagrande, at Faro, made some important alterations in his Etna vineyards some years ago, converting the traditional terraces to a series of slopes where machines could work as well as men and without the walls that, previously, had retained the soil. This has also been done in some of the Douro Valley vineyards; the banks of the 'Golden River' and its tributaries are still intricately terraced, but, especially if a vineyard has been allowed to decline and has not been given constant care, the rehabilitation of such a plantation is far too expensive to undertake today. Again, the curvier sloped type of vineyards are proving suitable for many machines and there is at least one plantation here that has altered the entire concept of planting, by doing away with the whole concept of terracing, planting vines vertically up and down the slope of the vineyard, so that a machine can work vertically – being hauled from the top – rather than horizontally; this adaptation of the late Lenz Moser's remarkable achievement in Austria is not yet wholly proved, but, whereas no human picker could work for long on a slope as steep as a railway cutting, a machine can.

On flatter vineyards the problems of adaptation to the latter part of the twentieth century are not so difficult. But details must all be considered. For example, if a full basket of grapes, picked by hand, has to be tipped into a larger basket, which must then be loaded on to someone's back, on to an animal, on to a lorry, which then takes such loads to the winery, time is taken up and much energy consumed. If the grapes can pass from the vine to the method of transport direct, then obviously the saving is great: some mechanical harvesters operate in company with another vehicle, passing alongside them in another row of vines, or behind the picking machine, so that, as the grapes are picked, they are passed across to this; when the container on the alongside vehicle is full, it disengages itself from the harvester at the end of a row and goes off to the winery, while another takes its place. One friend of mine in New Zealand operates a 'stripper' – the machine that takes the grapes off their stalks – actually in his vineyards, so as to save even minutes before the grapes get to the nearby winery and are crushed. He makes admirable wine!

In vineyards concerned with making large quantities of inexpensive wine, the costs throughout must be cut, and, on one visit to Sicily, I was told that the concrete posts that sustain the wires on which the vines are trained do cost more than ordinary stakes or canes, but that these last, in this poor country, would be at risk from pilferers. It is certainly the use of machines and cutting costs of basic materials as well as labour that has enabled many people to drink wine regularly today and for some areas to make wines that, in the past, would have been purely for local consumption; nowadays they can operate on a larger scale and reach distant markets.

In looking at a vineyard, its 'aspect' is of great importance. As we have seen, this term means its outlook, not what it looks like. Everybody will know that, when they are beginning to acquire a suntan, it is the morning sun, rising, that risks burning them; in the afternoon it may be hot, but the risk of the burn is less or negligible. So with vines. The story of how the Emperor Charlemagne, in his palace at Ingelheim, noticed how the snows melted first on the southwards facing slopes and was prompted to suggest that these might be put under vines, exemplifies the importance of aspect. Today, there are some vineyards that make very good wine, thanks to knowledge and technical resources, but, in the great vineyards of the world, it is usually those that get the morning sun that tend to be outstanding; although it is no longer fair to say that Montlouis, on the south bank of the Loire, with many of its vineyards facing north, north-east or north-west, is 'the poor man's Vouvray', a direct comparison of these wines with those of Vouvray, on the north bank, where most of the vineyards enjoy a southern aspect, will show the way in which the wines are 'different'. In vineyards enjoying fairly regular seasons of sun, of course, there are not such appreciable differences, but among the finer wines the aspect has considerable influence. When tasting, it may be helpful to see if you can detect whether the wine comes from a cool or hot vineyard – and also if it has the particular 'smile' that, to me, characterizes a vineyard ideally situated and, therefore, as sure of itself as a perfectly healthy, confident human being.

Because so many of the world's vineyards are irrigated today, something about this process is possibly helpful. Irrigation in the context of growing wine grapes does not mean – as I used to think – vines being lavishly sprayed with water from the sort of devices that water lawns, nor does it involve canals flowing between the rows, making the soil soft and spongey. There are reasons why this sort of irrigation is necessary in certain circumstances, but, as far as fine wines are concerned, it may usually be discounted.

If a vineyard is likely to have to be irrigated, then of course this must be planned when it is laid down. If, except in special circumstances, it will not be 'watered', then not so much attention need be paid to this. But in what may be termed 'modern' vineyards, such as certain of those in the New World where droughts can last for several years and dryness can be as serious a hazard as frost and hail in colder wine regions, there are various methods of providing the vines with moisture. It may be dripped, literally drop by drop, from pipes passing below the main foliage, so that the roots are gently moistened; there are even systems where pipes are laid below ground to achieve this. There are vineyards where plastic sheeting is laid between the rows of vines, keeping down weeds and retaining moisture that would otherwise evaporate. There are schemes by which water is released at the top of a sloping vineyard so that it gradually permeates the land lying below.

In Old World vineyards irrigation has often been viewed with suspicion and contempt, and sometimes it is forbidden; whether or not this prohibition is always observed in certain years is possibly open to doubt. But European vineyards seldom face the sort of dryness that is common in other areas. Nor do they always have to consider the variations of subsoil and drainage that concern owners of vineyards of enormous size and extent; somebody whose ancestors worked out which particular patches of a property would grow vines has different problems from the owner who has bought a piece of land the size of a county and, acting on the advice of soil, climate and grape consultants, is going to start growing vines. Although it was taught, when I was a student, that wines from irrigated vineyards could not achieve more than modest quality – plumped out grapes, like champion vegetable marrows, were not comparable, it was said, with the smaller-bodied and often tight-fleshed aristocrats of the classic vineyards – this is no longer true, if it ever was. On visiting Backsberg, where some of the finer wines of the Cape are made, I was shown over some of the extraordinarily varied terrain by the owner, in his Land Rover; even so, there were some slopes, gullies and outcrops of rock that would have made many European wine growers reject the land as almost impossible to cultivate, just as it was almost impossible to drive over. On being asked whether he irrigated his vineyards, Sydney Back roared with laughter. 'Of course I do – but not as much as in the Bordeaux vineyards.' And he explained that, although irrigation is not legally controlled at the Cape, he adjusted the amount he irrigated according to the different plots within his estate and, in fact, compared with the rainfall in the Gironde, his vines got less moisture than those of Bordeaux that are 'irrigated' by the rainfall! So such apparent alterations in 'climate' should be viewed with the same respect – when they are wisely used – as any different methods of training vines and picking grapes. A grower who is informed and not greedy (although naturally wine must make a profit) may well achieve the aim of quality, adequate quantity – and at not too great a cost in too long a time.

In any conversation about soils, the term 'pH factor' is nowadays sure to be mentioned. This, which was unknown on this side of the Atlantic until very recently among lay people (I think the first time I heard it was in the late 1960s), is not always really understood by those who fling it into what they hope is wine-informed talk, and I sympathize with one friend in the wine trade who, on sitting down to an important wine dinner, was breathlessly questioned by his neighbour as to the pH of certain wines set before them. 'I do prefer,' he said afterwards, 'to leave that sort of thing behind me at the end of the day – in my laboratory.' It may be noticed that various cosmetics now involve themselves with this, in products aimed at restoring the texture of the skin.

In relation to wines, however, one thing should be immediately understood. Although this term is related to certain acidity content, it is *not* to be equated with the acidity noted by the drinker in a wine. This is as misguided – and can be as foolish – as those people who suppose that a wine designated as '*Spätlese*' is 'less sweet' than one designated '*Auslese*' (see p. 170). Because my friend Julian Jeffs, QC, is also a qualified chemist, I will quote his definition:

The term pH stands for hydrogen power and is the measure of the acidity or alkalinity of a solution . . . Water, of a completely neutral solution, has a pH of 7. If the pH is below 7, it indicates acidity and if it is above 7, alkalinity . . . The measure of pH will indicate either volatile or fixed acidity, or both – and of course both are always present in any wine, since the volatile acids include not only acetic (which is produced to a limited extent even in a healthy fermentation) but also lactic and others . . . but I urge you not to simplify the matter by suggesting that the pH is determined by the amount of acids present. There is always a substantial buffering effect in wine, that is to say a mechanism caused by the presence of salts and the like which helps to keep the pH steady, so that the actual pH is brought about by a number of factors. The pH of wines varies in the course of the fermentation, for instance, when the malo-lactic fermentation takes place, when lees falls, and so on.

So – understand the significance of this if you hear or try to make use of the term. And bear in mind that two wines with the same pH factor can taste quite different – one perhaps even having a tart, acid taste which is not present in the other.

This is the end of basic information about vineyards. Never forget that behind any wine there is the vineyard and its vines – and grapes. There is, to the wine lover, always something wonderful about seeing even the most modest vineyard: to have one's own is often a dream surpassing the mere acquisition of other material things. But, as will have been seen, even the 'home wine maker', following the instructions as to how to make an alcoholic beverage from a pre-prepared kit, or the gardener working in window box or sheet-sized plot, can share in the interest in the stages along the way and, I hope, appreciate more of the beauty of any view of the great vineyards of the world. It is not unusual for even the most matter-of-fact wine farmers to admit to an excitement at vintage time, for the most businesslike merchants to sigh in satisfaction at the view of a panorama of vines in prime condition; we, the wine lovers and drinkers, can make contact with them at the point where we look at a vineyard and know something more than what the casual eye sees – being aware of the beauty in the bottle at the end of the often difficult but always interesting road. Wine is, when one thinks about it, rather like life – for those who can see and learn, there is so much more richness in terms of enjoyment. This certainly applies to visiting vineyards.

It is now appropriate to study what happens at the most important time of the year – the vintage – and the contribution of the great grapes.

[TWO]

THE VINTAGE

This, the high spot of the wine maker's year, is one of growing anticipation and excitement. There are, however, more activities going on than the ordinary visitor may appreciate, sometimes obvious, often behind the scenes, and more advantageous or adverse factors involved throughout.

Because the subject tends to be outside the ordinary studies of even the keenest lover of wine, I have, for this and the subsequent section, had the privilege and benefit of the advice of Mr A. C. Simpson, of Group Technical Services of International Distillers and Vintners. Because IDV represent, handle and sell a range of wines made in many countries, in the New as well as the Old Worlds, his experience has been invaluable in clarifying many technicalities with which I was not wholly familiar and therefore I have no hesitation in quoting him.

Mr Simpson suggests that it is important to distinguish clearly between the aspects of crushing and pressing, also, to point out the basic differences between red and white vinification. He summarizes the processes, described further in detail from what I know about them, as follows:

Most grapes are crushed – both red and white. Some exceptions occur in the Beaujolais and Rioja regions, where Mr Simpson considers traditional vinification to be, for the most part, somewhat primitive; exceptions also include places where the relatively new *macération carbonique* method (see pp. 165–7) has been adopted.

At the time of crushing, the stems are either removed or allowed to remain with the grapes. In the case of red wines, the stems are, nowadays, mostly removed although, in some traditional vinification, they are retained either wholly or in part. With white grapes, the stems are wholly removed in California, whereas in Bordeaux stems are retained in the press, where they facilitate the draining of the juice. Crushing and 'stemming' (removing the stems) is most frequently combined, in machines such as the *fouloir-égrappoir* (see p. 272). It is important to make the distinction between red and white wine vinification: in the former, the crushed or squeezed grapes are fermented before a final pressing of the debris, in the latter the pressing is, normally, undertaken before fermentation.

The mechanics of pressing and the different types of presses in use – which may vary considerably – need not be understood in detail, but it should be realized that the variations and differences exist.

Bearing these points in mind, I hope that the following may enlighten the visitor to a vineyard at vintage time as to what there is to see and, possibly, to interpret the conversations between those making the wine. It may be worth my stressing that, until you feel fairly sure of understanding this kind of semi-technical talk, it is always wise to listen rather than to propound personal opinions or, even with the most indulgent hosts, insist on answers to numerous questions. If you can study even a little in advance, certain matters may be made quite plain once you see wine-making in action and hear of the matters that make the highlights of conversation. Impetuous comment or, worse, discourteous and uninformed criticism can be unwise. So – to a vintage commentary.

PICKING

Grapes are carefully watched until they attain the correct degree of ripeness with which to make satisfactory wine. But, in certain vineyards where sunshine and no rain cannot be counted on, risks may have to be taken: does the wine maker wait another day or so, until the maximum ripeness is achieved naturally, or does he – looking at the sky and hearing the weather reports – decide to get the harvest in anyway and hope to be able to compensate for any lack of ripeness when the wine is being made? To leave grapes on the vines may mean that a sudden storm or night frost can destroy the whole crop; to pick too early may result in a green, unripe style of wine being made – and it is infuriating, if this has been done, to see that the apparently less provident neighbours (and competitors) continue to bring in perfectly ripe grapes and achieve higher quality in the ultimate wine. (Weather forecasts are not always accurate.)

In vineyards enjoying fairly constant conditions, throughout the year as well as at vintage time, these are not matters for too much speculation, but, in the finer wine regions, invariably at the edge of the areas where the vine can yield satisfactorily, a delay even of hours can make a great difference and anticipating the ideal period in which to pick can result in disappointment. There is one Bordeaux estate which, traditionally, tends or tended to pick early: the wines were always well made and agreeable but some found them to lack a certain finesse and generous, ripe character as a result. One year, in the autumn of 1964, the weather changed abruptly and it rained hard during the vintage, so that most picking had to stop for about a week – but the property that had started and finished early, before the rain, made a successful and fine wine.

In vineyards where the grapes are picked little cluster by cluster or even grape by overripe grape, the pickers may have to pass through the vines up to a dozen times, day by day, picking only when the particular grapes required are sufficiently developed to go into their basket. This is one of the reasons why late-picked wines inevitably cost more – because of the labour as well as the skill of whoever makes them (see pp. 168–71).

Where labour can be hired or is locally available, picking is still often done by hand. For those who bend double or, in trellised vineyards, stretch above their heads, often under baking sun, it is extremely hard work. When I returned from one southern hemisphere vineyard and reported that picking ceased over the weekends during vintage, I shocked many European friends: once grapes are ripe, they *must* be got in. At the first general election in Portugal since the 1976 revolution, the date was fixed for voting to take place during the vintage period. Electors were required to return to wherever they had been registered to cast their votes and, so as to disrupt the working week as little as possible, polling day was a Sunday. The port vintage was in full swing and, in the ordinary way, would have continued throughout the weekend. Because of so many establishments taking on extra labour at vintage time, it was agreed between all the port firms that, after mid-day on the Saturday before polling day, no grapes should be received at any of the wineries in the Douro Valley, so that no accusation might later be brought that workers were unable to travel to their homes and vote. Much anxiety was expressed as to the conditions of loads of grapes picked after the crucial date, Monday was a heavy day – but it is pleasant to record that a particularly fine vintage has since been declared by most houses for that year!

Usually, pickers work in bands, supervised by overseers either from the estate or those who have much past experience in this work. The ultimate decisions about what to pick when are of enormous importance, and in some vineyards a type of mini-vintage may be tried, a few bunches of early ripe grapes being picked and crushed in a tiny press, the result being appraised in detail, the laboratory working hard on the analyses.

The grapes are cut in bunches, being put into the baskets carried by the individual pickers, who usually subsequently discharge them into larger containers, which will later be heaved on to lorries. Grapes are heavy. The overseer will have been directed where to employ his band by those who have been watching the progress of the grapes, often measuring their ripening morning and evening by using a device called a refractometer, by which a needle extracts a drop of juice from a grape; this can be calibrated on a scale within the instrument to indicate the amount of sugar in this juice. Or, of course, someone simply goes and appraises the grapes by eye – and by what grandfather used to say – and decides to start picking.

The transfer of grapes to the transport that gets them to the winery is significant. If, once picked, they have to stand about, especially if they have to remain in the open under the daytime sun or at least in the heat, they may start to undergo a certain type of fermentation; the grapes at the bottom of the basket will be pressed down and slightly crushed by the weight of those on top and the wine yeasts begin to work. This pressure is important in the method known as *'macération carbonique'* (see pp. 165–7), but in general it is not desirable if it starts in the vineyard, because grapes ought to reach the winery in the same condition as they were taken from the vine and, ideally, be as cool as possible. If tons of grapes are simply tipped into a lorry, then, by the time the tailboard is let down later at the winery, at least a significant proportion of the juice that runs out will be on the way to being wine – of a sort. This uncontrolled fermentation is frowned on, because all kinds of things can go wrong in wine made in this way. It can often take more time and cost more in terms of resources and skills to put right something that should never have gone wrong than to make the wine properly from the beginning.

Because of this, timing and sometimes speed are important in vintaging. The mechanization of wineries which can work all round the clock is wholly to the good as far as the quality of most wine is concerned. A mechanical harvester, which can pick faster than any band of human beings and go on doing so, if necessary, at night by arc lamps, can get in the harvest when grapes are in prime condition. If grapes have to be transported some distance to the winery, they can then travel in cooled containers, by night, and arrive without any deterioration. If one plot in a vineyard or one variety of grape takes longer to ripen, this is not necessarily a disadvantage, because obviously there is a limit to the amount of grapes that can be received by the winery at one time, even by the most modern and large installation, but generally grapes must not incur delay in being 'processed', else they risk being attacked by flies and becoming liable to contamination. This is why it is essential for a winery, even at its most hectic working time, to be kept as clean as well as orderly as possible. (Fly repellent devices are useful assets.)

The containers in which the grapes are put are, these days, more likely to be plastic holders than the picturesque baskets of former times, such as the *'paniers Beaunois'*, the double-bellied Burgundy baskets, with a hole through which a pole could be slotted so that it might be slung between two carriers, or locally made shaped wider receptacles. But a basket is difficult to keep clean and disinfect, whereas the plastic container is of neutral material and can be swilled out, instead of having to be scrubbed hard with a protective solution; this type of progress is beneficial, even if it doesn't look so attractive in a photograph. The huge *'hottes'* of Alsace, giant triangular baskets held on shoulders or braced by a headband on the backs of tough labourers, are becoming museum pieces, bright-coloured plastic paniers taking over.

Although practices naturally vary, both from winery to winery and from country to country, it is usual for loads of grapes to be weighed as they come from the vineyards to the winery; this is both to assess the quantity to be handled and, if a co-operative is concerned or if grapes are being supplied under contract, to pay at once or note on an account the amount coming from a particular source. It is also the practice, in many instances, for someone in authority to take a sample of the juice from various loads as these arrive, so as to ensure that the quality of the picking is exactly as required. When wine is made on a single estate, of course, there is no need for this, because the manager will have watched the quality as the grapes have ripened.

It is still being debated, in some classic vineyard areas, whether the use of mechanical harvesters is, long-term, a good thing, because of possible damage to the vines; however, if the immediate saving in labour and time is satisfactory and if the quality of the wine is maintained (or even improved), then the (huge) initial cost of the machine would seem justified and even some shortening of the vine's life need not be considered a serious drawback. Although maturity of a vine is desirable, it would seem, from opinions expressed in California, that longevity (of a vine) – which goes hand in hand with progressively lower yield – is not necessarily or even frequently expressed in terms of quality. I do not think that certain owners of great vineyards would all agree with this, but it is not necessary that they should: their vines, carefully planned for systematic replanting as and when required, are not likely to be subjected to mechanical harvesting unless their vineyards are fairly flat; their production anyway is not so large – unfortunately – as always to warrant the use of costly machines and more frequent replanting than is currently done, when hand picking – which is sometimes mentioned with a certain pride on Australian labels – can still be the method of harvesting.

The quality of any wine is established in the vineyard. The laboratory and the winery cannot create the great wines from mediocre grapes. It may be difficult for the visitor to realize this, while watching motley bands of pickers working up and down the rows of vines, possibly with an infant or two parked alongside the piles of coats and any bottles for quenching thirst, many wearing rubber boots and, sometimes, plastic raincoats to give some protection against the weather; it is possibly even harder to appreciate when, in a vineyard without people, a huge machine prowls across the rows, grapes flapped off by its fin-like paddles on either side, then dancing over a moving band to a container before being driven to the winery. It may seem, to the uninformed, that the sort of vintage scene where sturdy peasants laughingly lift huge baskets on to mule or donkey back as they receive these from full-skirted girls, wearing coloured kerchiefs bound round their hair, where the odd dance on top of grapes piled on to a cart to get even more into the panier can still be seen, is more 'genuine', resulting in the sort of wine that evoked the purpler passages of wine appreciation around the decanters of our ancestors. Not necessarily so!

Grapes in perfect condition make good wine. The satisfaction of the wine maker, viewing such loads coming to the winery, is enormous. But perfection is not haphazardly achieved and is the result of at least a year's care and surveillance. The important thing is that, if the grapes are in prime condition, it will not be difficult to make good wine from them and, equally important, the likelihood of anything going wrong is less. It is rather as if somebody in good health is required to tackle an important job – they will do so with more vigour and lasting strength than anyone who is enfeebled or handicapped by some illness or deficiency. A load of grapes showing some bunches attacked by grey rot, damaged in any way, or shrivelled and imperfect cannot make good wine. Ideally, any bunches that are in a poor state should be removed before pressing, but of course this is not possible with huge loads being sent to be crushed. In certain fine wine vineyards not only will the person supervising the work watch to see that the pickers select only ripe bunches that are without any damage or imperfections, but there may be some sorting out of the grapes even before they go to the winery; in Champagne, this process, known as *épluchage*, is still sometimes done on wicker trays actually set up in the vineyard, all imperfect grapes being rejected. But, as can be imagined, this sorting costs money, takes time and requires the skill of experienced sorters. If the grapes can be supervised so that damage does not occur, then the bunches will come in without blemish, although, even with today's sprays and protection against pests, it is not unusual to see a grower or even an estate owner, standing alongside the reception area in a winery, lean over and pick out a bunch showing incipient signs of rot or similar imperfection and throw it away.

CRUSHING

How the grapes are crushed is a more delicate and complex procedure than is generally imagined. The method used to extract the juice depends both on the individual grapes – some varieties are much tougher to squash than others – and the resources available, also, although this was not fully realized until comparatively recent times, on the type of wine that is ultimately to be made.

Treading by the human foot has been the time-tried method of crushing: the weight of a human being will not split stalks and pips and, although the early wine makers may not have realized this, the contact with the human body during the beginning of fermentation could have helped the process in cool vineyards, where the drop in temperature at night could make it difficult for fermentation to start or continue. One Burgundy estate is still said to tread its grapes. But the work is very hard – not for nothing do those Douro estates that still make port by having the grapes trodden pay musicians to play alongside the *lagars* or troughs in which the grapes are crushed. The accordion player, who will go on playing all night, is paid the highest rate. The scriptural reference to one who has 'trodden the wine press all alone' is a vivid description of a drearily hard task – anyone who has seen the treaders continuing hour after hour, pushing down the sticky pulp, will not henceforth associate this with Keats's 'dance and Provençal song and sunburnt mirth', although there is good humour, from time to time a little singing and – but often outside the *lagar* – dancing around. To start the 'cutting' of the port *lagar*, men link arms and march firmly about and, although nowadays there are some women and girls occasionally to be seen treading in remote farms, it is a job only for the tough.

The aim of this first stage in making wine – any wine – is to extract the juice from the grapes so that fermentation can proceed, if it has not already started. This is why the New World term 'crush', used as a noun, is sensible. But when the grapes are picked their stalks are usually included in the bunches and, sometimes, at least parts of stems also get picked. In addition to the actual pulp of the grape, which contains the juice, there are the skins and pips which get into the crush. All of these can contribute various things to the grape juice and, therefore, to the ultimate wine. Sometimes these contributions are welcome and required, sometimes they are undesirable. So it is essential to 'process' grapes in various ways, not simply by stamping on them to release the juice, or 'must', as this is called in wine making. Therefore, depending on the type of wine being made, after the grapes are received at the winery they are subjected to crushing by various methods.

If, however, it is wished to strip the grapes off their stalks and any stems first, the bunches are directed on to a device that strips off the fruit, leaving the stalks; this debris is sent off away from the grapes. This de-stalking device is often one that consists of a perforated drum, whirling round, into which the grapes fall and where the stalks are detached from the fruit by a series of spikes inside the drum. An old-fashioned procedure, still in use until fairly recent years in parts of the Bordeaux vineyard, was for the grapes to be tipped on to a huge wooden table with slats in it and for teams of men to rub the bunches on this, forcing the juice and pulp through the slats, then throwing away the stalks. The stems and stalks are, sometimes, put for a brief period into the fermentation vat, if the grapes seem likely to be lacking in tannin in that year.

The grapes having been separated from the stalks and stems,

these may be thrown out and kept for final hard pressing, probably by a device rather like a meat press. Any juice that comes out may be used for wine – although, with the finer wines, it is seldom added, but is kept apart for domestic use, or for distillation. The final debris of vegetable matter that remains of the stalks is completely removed – in some wineries one sees a huge pipe blowing it out of the press house – and is sometimes sold for possible use as manure, or simply put on to the vineyard or added to cattlefood. Some vineyards, therefore, literally consume their own waste matter.

By these and other variations on the basic means of crushing, the grape juice or must gets into the fermentation vat where, if the wine is made with black grapes, the skins and stems may also be. For certain wines, all this solid material is allowed to rise to the surface of the must and collects there, looking somewhat like the 'cap' or *chapeau*, which is its name in wine making. There are then various procedures, according to the wine maker's ideas and the type of wine he – or she – is making: the cap may be pushed down into the must at regular intervals – wooden rakes generally being used, so that there is no contact with metal at this critical stage of the wine's evolution; or else the must is churned up by paddles, or circulated by a pump pushing it through a pipe – this may work from the bottom of the vat, or be pumped over the top, saturating the cap. There are also fittings whereby the cap is kept down mechanically, so that, as the fermentation proceeds, it is submerged and kept in contact with the must.

The skins of black grapes will be giving colour to the must in this period; stems and any stalks and pips will be contributing tannin and various other elements. But the type of wine to be made and the potential of the combined forces of vineyard, vines and weather will be appraised by the maker to determine individual variations on this basic procedure. In different parts of the world some elements are considered more important than others and different methods are adopted or adapted. This is only one of the many aspects of wine about which it is impossible to generalize.

The length of time that the skins remain in contact with the must is, as may be understood, important; in former times, in many regions and certainly in the Bordeaux area, the cap might stay on the top of the new red wine for three or even five weeks. This resulted in a very deep-toned wine and also one that was very hard, astringent and impossible to drink until it had passed a considerable number of years maturing in bottle (after far longer than the customary time in cask that we should expect today). This type of wine was certainly long-lived, but, although it is wonderful to be able to drink an example of a wine older than oneself, it is misguided to suppose that such a wine will inevitably be 'better' than something that is highly enjoyable when only a few years old. As the purpose of wine is to provide enjoyment and as wine makers have to live, there seems nothing wrong with making wine that is enjoyable while young or youngish, compared with its life in former times, providing that the traditional character is not distorted; this, however, applies to the finer wines of the world. They 'peak' at widely different ages. The more everyday wines, available these days to everybody, are not intended to have long lives, certainly not if they are non-vintage (see p. 99).

PRESSING

For most wines, different methods of separating the juice from the pulp and skins involve machines that are usually referred to as presses, although the way they 'press' is quite different from what may be imagined by anyone who has previously supposed grapes to yield their juice only as the result of some form of fierce squashing. With white wines, there is usually no point in allowing skin contact with the must, so the grapes are destalked on arrival at the winery and a different method is generally employed: the grapes are tipped into horizontal cylindrical containers, which are 'presses'. In one type, there are loops of chain around inside, with a slatted or perforated cylinder to which they are attached and a receptacle underneath. When the press has been filled to the required extent, it is set in motion and revolves, the chains inside breaking up the grapes, the must running out from the inner cylinder and draining away below the press, subsequently being run off into the fermentation vat, or, for certain very special wines, directly into casks to undergo fermentation there. (This applies to many of the great sweet white wines of Europe.)

Another type of press, also a long cylinder in shape, contains a bag which is inflated and gently squeezes the grapes against the sides of the cylinder, so that the juice runs out. Sometimes there are two plates at each end of the cylinder that can be powered to advance within it, pressing the grapes in a concertina-like action, so that the juice runs out.

The ancient Egyptians used to put a load of grapes in a long, hammock-like bag and then twist the ends, so that the grapes were squeezed and the juice trickled out from the bag. A board exerting pressure on a vessel holding the grapes, brought down on to them by the operation of a screw, is another very old method; sometimes an animal pushed or pulled the beam turning the screw, sometimes this was done by human beings. With both these and similar primitive methods care had to be taken not to exert too much pressure, because this would crush the stalks included in the load of grapes and even split the pips – this made the wine harsh, astringent and bitter. So some control always had to be exercised on the pressure, and it had also to be possible to arrest the process at any given moment, if someone should decide that enough juice had been extracted.

There are not many places nowadays where a heavy lid comes down and simply squeezes out the juice, although this does occur in the traditional method of making Champagne (see p. 182). In many big wineries concerned with producing inexpensive and medium priced wine, also in some that are concerned with fine wine, the grapes, after being checked and weighed, are tipped into a huge bin, through the bottom of which passes a continuous screw – an Archimedes screw; the grapes drop on to this and are carried along, being squashed on the way, until they are directed into various containers or vats, where fermentation will start. If the only form of 'pressing' is done by the Archimedes screw, then the rate at which this turns is relevant: if it goes fast, then obviously the pressure is harder and more juice will be immediately extracted; if it goes fairly slowly, then the grapes are squeezed more gradually. This, of course, depends on the grape variety as well, some grapes

WINE PRESSES

Top, a vertical hydraulic press. The debris of grapeskins is wheeled under the fixed press, then the round container is raised so that the contents are squeezed against the disc. The juice flows between the slats and is channelled away. It is not always added to the other wine.

Bottom, a horizontal hydraulic press. There are two types: in one, there are chains slung inside which break up the grapes when the press revolves. The juice runs out and is channelled away from below. In the other, the two ends of the press advance to squeeze the fruit, or, for gentle pressure, a bag is inflated to squash the grapes against the sides of the press.

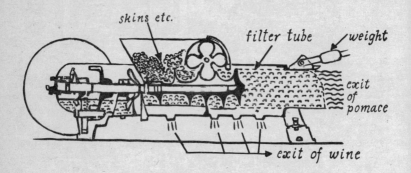

skins etc.

filter tube

weight

exit of pomace

exit of wine

THE CONTINUOUS PRESS

This shows in section one version of the type of press that may be used in a winery handling large quantities of grapes. The fruit drops into a receptacle on to a continuous screw, and may be whipped off the stalks and stems by a spiked wheel. The juice is extracted and pumped into vats to ferment, while the pomace or compressed debris remaining behind is pushed out of the press, for distilling, manure or cattle food.

having much tougher skins than others. Black grapes tend to be firmer, many having thicker skins, than white grapes, but some white grapes do have thickish skins.

If pressing is done in several phases, generally the initial 'free run' juice that simply runs from the mass of grapes, also the juice from the first pressing, are both considered superior and may be kept apart.

With the white wines, the fermentation continues as with the reds, without the presence of the skins in the vat. There is, however, quite a lot of general debris even in the must of white wines and at this stage the must or even the new wine looks cloudy, totally unlike any beverage that might be good to drink. However, freshly pressed grape must can be delicious and, in some wine regions, it is a vintage time speciality, often being served with the new walnuts that are beginning to be available at the same season. But anyone invited to drink grape must straight off the press should be careful not to be greedy – if fermentation is about to start or actually has begun, then it will continue in the stomach of the drinker, having the effect of a mild purge.

It is important to stress that, in a vineyard where several varieties of grapes will make up the wine, these different grapes will be picked at different times – because they will ripen at different times – and the must of each variety will (as far as the fine wines are concerned) be subsequently kept separate until after the fermentation is complete and the different wines are combined. This does not take place in all vineyards, however; the peasant or small-scale grower may not be able to prolong the picking of several plots and grape varieties over more than a few days, so he will put them all into the vat together. The classic example of this is the red Burgundy called Passe-Tout-Grains, which expression literally means 'process all the grapes' (at one time); the Pinot Noir and the Gamay are therefore processed or crushed together and a very good wine can result. But such processing is not done, for example, in Bordeaux, where the different grape varieties are picked and made separately and only combined in the spring after the vintage, when the 'égalissage' or blending of the new wines is done from these varieties that have been kept apart up to this point.

The taking on of colour from the skins of the black grapes is subject to many variations. Champagne, which is mostly made from several grape varieties, can sometimes seem very faintly bronze-pink – this is because the skins of the Pinot Noir (usual in all but the *blanc de blancs* styles) have been left in the must just long enough to impart a very slight tint. Sometimes a white wine will be made from black grapes and be described as 'processed as white'. In the past, for example, this might be done if a maker simply required a white wine.

Rosé or pink wines can be made in various ways. The traditional method for the finer examples is to leave the black skins in the must long enough to turn this pink; sometimes, in the south of France, a wine may be described as a *'vin d'une nuit'*, meaning that it will have been made with the skin contact lasting for twelve hours or thereabouts, and it is usually a light rosy tone, rather than a colour verging on red. But the difference in the colour of pink wines can also be accounted for by the vineyards from which they come: a wine made with a proportion of black grapes ripened in a northern vineyard, where the climate is definitely cold, will be paler than the *rosé* of a Mediterranean or hot vineyard, simply because, in a cool climate, the pigments in the black grape skins will not have been loosened so much by the sun; in a warm vineyard these pigments may tint the must almost to the colour of red wine. Pink wines can also be made by simply mixing red and white grapes, but in the EEC it is not permitted merely to mix red and white wines. The methods of production in many classic regions are subject to controls, but acceptable inexpensive *rosés* can result from various methods of blending.

In this description of what happens at vintage time, it must be understood that the processes have been greatly simplified. Essentially, the grapes are crushed to release their juice. The skins of black varieties are allowed to remain in contact with the must for long enough to release the colour. The fermentation should, ideally, start as soon as possible after the first crushing and continue briskly, until it gradually dies down as the weather becomes cooler and the yeasts cease to work. It will not have stopped completely and the new wine is very vulnerable throughout this period, like any baby. (And this is why modern machinery, which can be thoroughly cleaned and disinfected against the various diseases that can attack wine, is better for making good wine than many of the picturesque but less hygienic devices of former days.) Throughout the making of any wine, all the resources of modern technology, inherited know-how and independent judgement are wholly involved.

THREE

GRAPES

Wine is made from grapes, but the different varieties of *Vitis vinifera* and the different styles evolved within the various branches of the great families of grapes make it difficult to generalize that such-and-such a grape makes such-and-such a wine. Controls, however, determine that, in certain areas, a particular type of grape or combination of grapes alone may be used to produce certain wines. This varies according to where you are.

The words 'varietal' and 'cultivar' occur in wine writing and they mean grape variety – or vine. I admit to a personal preference for the terms grape and vine, but a shortening of any term may be advantageous.

It is perhaps wise at this stage to indicate that, although in accordance with some regional regulations, wines may only be labelled with the name of a particular grape if they are made either 100% from that grape or at least from a high proportion of it, in others a lower proportion of the one variety is accepted. It is also relevant to say that the notion of naming a wine by the grape that makes it is rather an innovation. To those of us who can remember general labels of thirty or more years ago the 'style' of the wine, as far as wines from outside the well-known European regions was concerned, might acquire a name – Chablis, Sauternes, hock, Burgundy, claret and so on – to indicate what the maker supposed to be its character, also what the merchant or shipper might think would appeal to the customer. This was the wine required – coming from certain already well-known regions, made to please a particular export market. (In case it is thought that I am too disposed to cite British examples, I must state that I can remember when a Bordeaux grower and British shipper challenged a French authority as to the 'authenticity' of the Beaujolais then being sent to Switzerland. What the Swiss wanted was not exactly 'Beaujolais' as the UK wine man would have accepted it – but 'horses for courses', wines for a receptive set of paying customers.

There is nothing suspicious about a wine made from a blend of grapes. Indeed, it is relevant to dispose of the hesitation with which many people still use the word 'blend'. All wine *must* be a blend: a blend of the produce of a number of vines, the blend of different plots within an overall vineyard, the blend of certain grapes – as far as many classic wines are concerned; then, with the more everyday non-vintage wines, there must be blending of the different years, one vintage too assertive in, say, acidity, being balanced by the next year, in which acidity might have been low but fruitiness was high, and so on. If the extreme is noted – that from one vinestock about one litre of wine may be produced in a favourable year – then it is obvious that, if wine were *not* blended, most people would go very short! The way in which, for example, a blender will compose the *'cuvée'* (see p. 183) for a particular *marque* of Champagne, or work out how to keep style and quality continuous in a brand of table wine or sherry selling all over the world and requiring huge supplies to satisfy demand, or the way in which an oenologist will arrange a vineyard in different proportions as to the grapes planted, or choose from grapes grown under contract over a wide area to satisfy (both as regards quality and price) the requirements of his winery – all these are delicate and skilled tasks; the blender's work is an art at every stage.

Indeed, one much respected wine merchant of one of the great families active in the British wine trade over several centuries once remarked to me that he wouldn't have been surprised to discover that his own father hadn't much idea as to which grapes were grown where. Would he, my friend wondered, even without any implication of criticism, have known that it is the Pinot Noir that makes the great red Burgundies? And we were both in agreement that my friend's grandfather wouldn't have recognized the names of many of the classic wine grapes if he'd heard them! Before 1914 and, I think, even later, a man ordering wine in some quantity from his wine merchant would specify merely 'three dozen of your claret'; for very special occasions, perhaps an estate might be mentioned – but it was essentially the *type* of wine that the nineteenth-century and even early twentieth-century customer ordered; he knew it came from grapes but hadn't the slightest knowledge of which. And, because he bought his wines from the Bordeaux and Burgundy regions of France, from the Rhine and Mosel districts of Germany, sherry from Spain and port from Portugal, plus some Madeira if he happened to like it, and limited his regular drinking to these classics, it wasn't necessary for him to know much more about wines. One of my late dear friends, a well-known wine writer of his time (H. Warner Allen, 1881–1968), wrote an entire book about white wines, including those of Germany and France, without ever mentioning the action of *botrytis cinerea* (noble rot, see pp. 171–5) – yet he was a scholar and most accurate reporter of facts!

Grape names have only become known to wine drinkers with the opening up of the world of wine – and the experiments and successes with many established varieties in new vineyards and evolution of new varieties in old ones. I can recall when the Bordeaux wine makers thought it would be impossible to make and market a wine made solely from the Sauvignon grape. It was my own teacher, the late Allan Sichel, who encouraged the planting of a Graves vineyard entirely with this grape; the first year they made a terrible wine, he recorded, but it then became highly successful. After that it became popular until, with the increase of other Sauvignon plantings, it ceased. As I write I have discovered a cheap, well-made Sicilian wine made from the 'Verdello' grape, which must be at least closely related to the Verdelho of Madeira – the grape that has the hazelnut aroma, according to many tasters; there is the Tintas Baroccas wine of 'Fanie' Malan, who also makes a fine port-style wine at the Cape, and who uses this, one of the port grapes of the Douro, to make a roaring lion of a gutsy table wine. Many more examples might be drawn from New World vineyards, where, for example, Château Tahbilk in the Goulburn Valley of Victoria, Australia, makes some white wines from the

Marsanne grape, which is, as far as I know, only used in conjunction with other grapes in the wines of the Rhône Valley, both white and red.

What any wine drinker should be concerned with is the ultimate character and quality of the wine. If the latter is satisfactory, then the former may be of interest. But one particular grape variety, grown outside the area in which the reputation of this grape was first made, may vary in what it produces – as has been indicated; it is therefore only fair to ascertain, first, whether the wine is made wholly from one grape and, if it is, whether that grape is a direct descendant of the classic variety. After this, one may see whether the 'family resemblance' is maintained and, where it varies, why it does so. If you plant in a hot region a grape variety that has made famous wine in cold vineyards, it will – like a human being – be confused; there was an instance of somebody planting Riesling in the Bordeaux region many years ago – but I have never met anyone who could report on the type of wine he made.

Similarly, it is fair to say, without sounding too picturesque, that vines making sound wine – providing adequate care is taken – in certain hot vineyards may not be able to make anything of top quality if they are transplanted to a plot in a world-famous vineyard region. 'Horses for courses' again. Some grapes make certain sorts of wine. Others make others – and certain of these, given the right conditions and care, can make miraculous wines, many of which will be wholly uneconomic but can make history, establish traditions – and achieve astronomic and publicized prices in the auctions.

The huge number of grapes from *vinifera*, which make the world's finer wines, takes space in learned books. The variations that evolve from the different strains make column inches in the specialist journals. Here it is only possible to indicate what the main grape varieties are – and, with some, to specify the wines that they make or to which they contribute.

White grapes: It should be remembered that these are sometimes used in blends with black grapes to make red wine – such as in the Rhône Valley, also in port, Champagne and elsewhere.

Black grapes: These can be used to make white wines – such as the *'blanc de noirs'* of Champagne – and some may be used with white grapes in certain blends, as with those mentioned above.

White wine is made mostly from white grapes and red wine from black grapes – that is an easy generalization and true. But black grapes can contribute fruitiness and fullness, plus a certain tannic toughness and acidic depth to white wine, while white grapes can give zip, liveliness and high acidity and crispness if involved with reds.

Wines from blends of different grapes may uncannily display the character of certain dominating classic *'cepages'* or grapes even if only a small proportion is used. Here I must tell how, when in Sicily years ago, I visited the Wine Institute and, after tasting several wines, asked why one had a familiar flavour – it was a Sicilian wine, but I had tried it at dinner the previous evening and recognized something about it as 'talking' to me; the oenologists around me named the various Sicilian grapes, I insisted that there was something else there. Finally, the head of the establishment came forward. There was in fact some Sauvignon in the blend of that particular wine – but only 10%. But it was *that* 10% that did the 'talking' as far as I was concerned and I kicked myself at not naming the grape variety! I have had similar reports from friends in other vineyards – the great grape varieties that have dominated wines in Europe are still the aristocrats that speak across many other combinations of local grapes and even skilled wine making. It should, of course, be realized that a vine will not be able to produce at maximum quality – as opposed to quantity – until it has reached a certain stage of maturity and, therefore, the age of the resulting fruit that makes a wine must be taken into account. The skilled wine grower and wine maker will adjust this – but the 'green' element of young vines is something different from that of the picking of slightly unripe grapes and, with experience, can be sorted out.

It is therefore helpful to become familiar with certain of the better-known grape varieties because, if one registers what they contribute to certain classic wines in established and well-known vineyards, then some link can often be perceived when tasting a less familiar wine. The following notes may help to 'fix' the styles of the main wine grapes. But don't forget that even the great grapes often have local or regional 'pet names', which sometimes confuse the traveller; these have only been mentioned here in connection with fairly well-known wines that are widely on sale.

BLACK GRAPES

Cabernet: The most famous of the Cabernet family is the *Cabernet Sauvignon*, which is the backbone of red Bordeaux and, cultivated in many of the New World vineyards, produces some of the most impressive and esteemed wines. It usually makes firm, definite wines, although, when used alone, this grape tends to make somewhat uncompromising ones. The Cabernet Sauvignon gives a slightly leafy, fresh bouquet to its wines, plus an assertive, defined flavour, which I sometimes note as 'boney', tannic until softened by time, lengthy with depth and weight and a trailing 'finish'. (I admit that I have never had even the finest Cabernet Sauvignon wines in my travels without expressing a wish that a little addition of some of the other Bordeaux grapes might be included, to add charm, grace and subtlety to the bouquet, but this may be the prejudice of a confirmed lover of claret! However, some of my friends in these newer vineyards are, nowadays, putting a small proportion of other grapes into their Cabernet Sauvignons with certainly no sign of this detracting from the ultimate quality and longevity.) This is the grape that attracts publicity, too.

The *Cabernet Franc*, however, which is also used in the Bordeaux red wines, is different in style, lighter in weight, with a crisp, zippy character; along the Loire the finer red wines are made from it and, as the acidity is fairly high, if you don't like this type of wine you may be prejudiced against the Cabernet Franc. In warm vintages, however, it can yield crunchily pleasant wines. The fruitiness and crisp style can be very charming. In the Loire the Cabernet Franc is often referred to as the 'Breton', because it was the Abbé Breton, Intendant of Cardinal Richelieu, who brought up vine cuttings from the Bordeaux region for planting in the northern vineyard and it was the Cabernet Franc that was most successful. If the single word 'Cabernet' appears on the label of a European wine – such as some of those produced in central and south-eastern Europe – then this is likely to be the Cabernet Franc; if the Cabernet Sauvignon has been used, then usually this rather prouder name is given in full. In the US, however, it is the Cabernet Sauvignon that is usually behind the word 'Cabernet' on a label, and it is this that is referred to in the sort of report that may read 'Panel judges Cabs'. The same is true to a certain extent in South Africa and Australasia, mostly because the Cabernet Franc is not widely cultivated in these vineyards. The Cabernet Sauvignon enjoys enormous prestige. In the St Émilion vineyards it is locally known as the 'Bouchet'. In central European countries it is called 'Médoc Noir', but may not remind tasters of claret.

Pinot Noir: This black grape, from which all the finer red Burgundies are made without the addition of any other varieties, is of considerable antiquity and it is thought that it is the vine shown in many examples of sculpture, carving and painting of medieval times. (It should not be confused with the Pinot Blanc, Pinot Gris and other white grapes, and it has now been established that the Pinot Chardonnay white grape (see p. 113) is in fact not a member of the Pinot family at all.) The Pinot Noir is also widely cultivated but it does not seem to have, as yet, achieved outstanding success in the newer vineyards – it appears to like a coolish climate, although it is vulnerable to extreme cold. The grape is grown in various parts of Europe as well as in France, and the particular characteristic it seems to be able to impart to the wines it makes is a soft, velvety texture and warm, alluring bouquet. A fine Pinot Noir insinuates rather than asserts itself; seriously intense, its appeal is nevertheless sensuous rather than cerebral, although the velvety refinement of some of its wines can be very beautiful. It makes the *rosé* wines of Alsace and is one of the principal grapes of Champagne.

Other names for the Pinot Noir include: Burgunder, Blauer Burgunder or versions of these names in German regions and Austria; Klevner, Schwartz Klevner and Blauer Klevner in Alsace; Cortaillod in Switzerland, also, in various places, Noirien, Vert Doré and Savagnin Noir; Nágyburgundi in Hungary.

Merlot: This is another of the claret grapes and, in certain estates, such as Château Lafite-Rothschild, the vineyard contains a fairly high proportion, giving the wines a soft, refined and yet penetrating bouquet and delicate fruitiness, markedly alluring. Many attempts are being made to grow this attractive grape throughout the world. Various European vineyards, such as those in Italy and parts of central Europe, make agreeable wines from it. The Merlot is the grape the Bordeaux pickers eat to quench their thirst, because it has a lightly sweet flavour, unlike the bitter shrill taste of many wine grapes. Some southern French vineyards have planted it with success and, with increased knowledge of how to guard it against the various forms of rot and mildew to which it is susceptible, it may be substantially on the increase throughout the world. Marked bouquet and a full flavour are fairly typical – it makes wines with a somewhat gentle but gracious style.

Gamay: This is the grape that makes red Beaujolais. Its full name is Gamay Noir à Jus Blanc and, although it was banned as a vine making quality wine in Burgundy as early as the fourteenth century, it is now appreciated in many regions, including the Loire, the Ardèche and other parts of the world. It makes mouth-filling, lip-smacking, light-hearted wines rather than anything subtle and delicate, but can give great pleasure. At present there seems to be some discussion as to whether the differentiation in California between 'Gamay' and 'Gamay Beaujolais' really is a difference between grape varieties, and some ampelographers appear doubtful as to whether either are the true Gamay of the Beaujolais. However, the use of the grape name does generally imply that the bottle will contain cheerful, fruity wine at least vaguely resembling that of Beaujolais. In Austria it is the Blaufrankischer and in Hungary the Kékfrankos.

Grenache: This vine seems to have come originally from Spain – its Spanish name, Garnacha, appears in the various grapes used in many of the better-known Spanish wines. It is fairly extensively used in southern France and is one of the Rhône Valley grapes, contributing to Tavel and Châteauneuf-du-Pape. Its ability to flourish in the most barren soils makes it popular in many parts of the world but, although it usually seems to make a fairly assertive, definite and sinewy type of wine, finesse is not generally associated with the Grenache, which is probably why it is so often used in combination with other grapes. It is planted in some New World vineyards to make wine by itself, but these wines tend to be in the lower ranges of quality and price. One name for it that sometimes occurs on the old silver labels of wines is Alicante.

Syrah: This is another grape grown in the Rhône Valley, where it seems to give particularly attractive bouquet, complexity and finesse to some of the finer wines. As 'Shiraz' it is found in many New World vineyards, often used by itself, and capable of making moderately robust but quite complex red wines that can age well, sometimes seeming to resemble the Cabernet Sauvignon as they do so – at least, this has been my experience in South Africa. To note Syrah at its best, apart from those wines made solely from it, one should sample the wines of the north Rhône, such as Hermitage and Crozes-Hermitage, where the quality is almost invariably due to this grape. As it does not yield in quantity, however, it is handicapped as a money-maker unless it is ideally suited to a particular vineyard. The variations on its name – Schiras, Shiraz, Sirah, Serine, are easy to remember, but it is thought that it is no relation to the Petite Sirah of California, which is possibly a grape called the Durif, although in France there are both the Petite and Grosse Syrah vines. Some suppose it to have originated in Persia

Cinsaut/Cinsault: This is another Rhône Valley grape, which I tend to associate with a certain stalky, tense, drawn-out character although, as it is not grown alone there, this may be a misleading comment. In South Africa and Australia, however, it is extensively cultivated. The wines it makes can be very satisfying although they require some maturation to achieve true quality. The confusing thing about nomenclature here, however, is that in South Africa the Cinsaut is called Hermitage, whereas, in Australia, the Hermitage is really the Syrah and is the major vine planted in that country, making some of the finest and most esteemed Australian reds. In addition, in California the Cinsaut is called the Black Malvoisie. So it's necessary to remember the country of origin of any wine labelled as 'Hermitage'.

Nebbiolo: This is the grape that makes some of the finest Italian red wines, such as Barolo and Gattinara. It does not seem to have had much success by itself elsewhere, although experiments in California have been made. Its wines can possess considerable depth and weight, with a firm, often surprisingly flowery bouquet. The finest, such as the Brunellos, need long aeration to show themselves well.

Carignan: This grape also had its origin in Spain where, as the Cariñena, it is still extensively planted – it is named for Cariñena, in Aragon. It will amaze most wine lovers to know that, according to grape authority Lucie C. Morton, it is the most cultivated variety in France and the second most cultivated in California! (The most planted is Thompson Seedless, usually a table grape.) The Carignan makes sturdy wines, extremely useful for blending with other varieties grown in the south of France, including many classic wine grapes, and it also makes very pleasant and useful wines when subjected to the process of *macération carbonique* (see pp. 165–7). It is not subtle but fairly firm and, to me, has a not unpleasant smell and slight flavour of tar.

Sangiovese: This is the Chianti grape or, rather, the predominant one, for straight Sangiovese cannot be categorized as Chianti. It makes a mouth-filling wine, of charm and lightness of style. Sometimes its name is shortened to 'Sangiù', or it may be locally termed the Sangioveltru. Plantations have been made in California, but, rather like the Nebbiolo, it seems to yield most satisfactorily in its homeland.

Grignolino: Another Italian grape, but this one seems to do better in California than the two previously mentioned. The wine it makes tends to be lightish and has a tawny tinge that can look pleasant. Used by itself it generally produces a pink or *rosé* wine, but it is also a useful blending variety. In the Asti region it makes both still red and a sparkling wine.

Barbera/Barbara: Italian variety, making a wide range of wines, including the slightly *pétillant* and semi-sweet versions to be found in Piedmont, where it seems especially successful, although dry, lightly fruity table wines are also made. It is used extensively for blending, both in Italy and in California, where it seems highly successful.

Zinfandel: This is a very odd variety. Extensively planted in California, in spite of possessing various weaknesses, such as irregular ripening, it was at one time thought to be a wholly native grape; then it was suggested that it might have been brought to California by Ágoston Harászthy, 'father of California viticulture', who went to the US from Hungary in the 1840s as a political refugee. But the origin of its name makes some authorities suppose it to have originated in Europe, although the Zierfandler grape, still cultivated in Austria, is a white grape. There are some small plantations of the Zinfandel in other New World vineyards now, but it is yet to be seen whether it will prove successful outside its homeland. The wine it makes is distinctive: very assertive, and, personally, I have never been able to like the edgy, strongly aromatic style, slightly 'piney' and hard, except for an example made according to the *macération carbonique* method – but this is my loss.

Malbec: This is another of the Bordeaux grapes, but it is also cultivated in the Loire (where it is generally known as the Cot) and in various southern French vineyards, where it is sometimes referred to as the Noir de Preyssac or Cahors, because it makes the Cahors red wines. It is planted elsewhere in the world and seems as if, in warm southern vineyards, it can yield satisfactory, slightly soft wines, not without length and often maturing to achieve true quality.

Mourvèdre: This is a south of France grape, especially in the regions of Bandol and the Côtes de Provence, but its origin is Spanish and its other name is the Mataro. The wine it makes is rather soft and close-textured – perhaps it is helpful to say that, although one does not often taste it as such, I surprised myself by recognizing it after an interval of some years, simply on account of its warm, yielding style, smelling slightly herby. Experiments have been made with it in other vineyards, especially for blending purposes, but it does not appear to have become popular.

Pinotage: This rather strangely-named grape was evolved at the Cape, South Africa, in the 1920s, from a cross of the Pinot Noir and the Cinsaut grapes (known there as Hermitage). The result is a black grape that makes full-bodied, moderately fruity and robust wines, very agreeable if the wine-maker is adept at his task, and capable of achieving high quality with maturation. It is very popular in South Africa, is sometimes cultivated in parts of Australia and, more recently, has proved successful in the more temperate vineyards of New Zealand's North Island, where some makers have managed to produce wines of elegance and perhaps more subtlety than in hotter climates.

Among the other black grapes making wine there are the divers varieties associated with port: Tinta Francisca (supposedly a descendant of the Pinot Noir), Tinta Cão, Touriga, Mourisco, Bastardo (this is the Trousseau grape of the Jura), Donzelinho Tinto, Periquita, Tinta Barroca (used in South Africa for port-style wines), Alvarelhão, Sousão (which seems to be acquiring popularity in California). These are only a few of the port grapes and there are numerous others in use in both Portugal and Spain, where few wines appear to be made from a single grape variety – with the exception of Madeira (for which the grapes are all white). It is often possible to place these because of their rather unusual names, obviously Portuguese or Spanish.

Then there is Lambrusco, of Italy, which makes a red sparkling wine in Emilia-Romagna, the Cannonau of Sardinia, the Poulsard (another Jura grape); Nerello Mascalese, Frappato and Pignatello of Sicily, also the Mavron and Opthalmo of Cyprus, Portugais Bleu, Tannat (France), Mali Plavac (Yugoslavia). Many of the south and central eastern European countries have their own names for the same grape: Kadarka, named for the Albanian town of Scutari, is possibly the most famous – among other wines it makes the Hungarian Bull's Blood of Eger. But there is as yet no one single dictionary or directory of all the wine grapes of the world, so frequently an apparently 'new' or at least unpronounceable grape name is found to be the local variety of something far better known. When I listen to students of the wine trade identifying many truly obscure wines made from – to me – equally obscure grapes, I admit that I have some regrets for the past when not *so* much was known! But the layman should not be discouraged and, although this may be my personal feeling, it seems somewhat easier to pick out the characteristics of many of the black grapes of importance rather than those of the whites. So if you think you can usually only manage to identify, say, Cabernet Sauvignon, Pinot Noir, Gamay, you need not be dissatisfied.

Riesling: This is one of the greatest wine grapes of the world – and it must be the one that has a longer list involving other names, many of them not referring to the true Riesling at all. Professor Helmut Becker of the Wine Institute of Geisenheim thinks that it originated from the wild vines of the Rhine Valley centuries ago. Today, it is simply termed 'Riesling', although in some other countries the names White Riesling, Johannisberger Riesling and Rheinriesling are still used, the latter being common in the US, the former in other European countries, though the names White or Weisseriesling are sometimes in use in New World vineyards where the German immigrant community is fairly numerous. Even in Germany the Riesling has another name, for it is known in Baden as the Klingelberger.

This wonderful vine makes some of the finest of all white wines, right up to the *trockenbeeren* category, as well as dry table wines, even some sparkling wines (as in the Saar, where it is used in conjunction with the Champagne method), and it makes the Rieslings of Alsace. Typical of a true Riesling – and it is not difficult to distinguish its attributes in even a medium-priced example – are the delicate but penetrating bouquet which is lightly flowery, infinitely complex, plus the superb fruity, crisp, lengthy flavour, rounded and exhibiting a delectable balance of fruit and acidity. Even in the sweetest examples this proportioned style is always there. There are plantations of Riesling in New York State, as well as California, and it is also grown in other New World vineyards, although it does not seem to like too hot a climate and appears to benefit by a fairly cold, crisp winter, which brings out its subtleties of fragrance.

The other member of the Riesling family, however, is far more prolific – although Professor Becker is firm that there are no plantations of it in Germany. This is the *Welschriesling* or *Wälschriesling* and, under various names, it is found in many vineyards. The

Wine Institute of Geisenheim, stressing that the Welschriesling has
no direct connection with the Riesling of the Rhine, lists the following names for it: Riesling Italico (Italy), Olasz Risling (Hungary),
Italiansky Rizling (Bulgaria), Laski Risling, Grassevina, Grasica,
Italiansky Risling, Taljanska grasevina, Bliea skadka grasica (all
Yugoslavia), Risling vlassky (Czechoslovakia). In my experience,
Rieslings of this type make pleasant, dry or medium dry light
wines, crisp and slightly fruity when well handled, but of direct
rather than subtle style. They are one of the most useful wines in
the 'everyday' categories on sale.

Then there are nearly twenty other 'Rieslings' that, say the
Wine Institute, have nothing to do with either Riesling or Welschriesling; some of them have other – correct – names, some being
the result of crosses of grapes. This means that, if you simply see
the word 'Riesling' on the label of a wine that has not been made
in either Germany or Alsace, it is wise both to check on its origin
and then, if possible, to consult some further work of reference to
make it clear what the grape really is. For example, in the US the
word 'Riesling' may be prefaced by the following – none of them
being true Rieslings – Grey, Emerald, Missouri, Franken: the last is
in fact the Green Silvaner; the Grey Riesling is the Ruländer, its
other name being the Chauché Gris. It is able to make pleasant
light wines in New Zealand. In Canada there is an Okanegan
Riesling. The Hunter River Riesling of Australia is actually the
Sémillon and the South Australia Clare Riesling is the Crouchen
Riesling (this is also usually the 'Cape Riesling' of South Africa).
Some of these vines can make pleasant wines, but, after somewhat
limited experience, I think only the Hunter Riesling (Sémillon) can
make anything above medium quality.

In many New World vineyards efforts are being made to overcome the inevitable confusion of the use of such misleading names
– which, anyway, cannot be used in the EEC unless qualified by
suitable labelling and explanations. But the buying public is everywhere conservative and, once it has acquired a liking for a wine
bearing a particular name, such as Riesling (which many people
still mispronounce as 'Riceling'), it continues to use that name.
Introduction of the longer but more specific name, Rheinriesling, is

often the way in which a reputable winery differentiates this type of wine from the simple 'Riesling'.

Sylvaner: The German spelling of this name is Silvaner. The grape seems to have originated in central Europe, possibly in Austria or Transylvania, and it has been extensively grown in Germany for centuries. Franconia is the region where it seems to produce its best top quality. It is also grown widely in Alsace, but it seems more suited to European vineyards than many of those in the New World, although experimental plantations in various other regions have reported some success. It makes light-bodied, fresh wines, my tasting tag for many being 'cool'.

Sauvignon: This is another of the great wine grapes of the world and it is widely cultivated, although probably the French examples are the best known. It is one of the grapes used in Sauternes and, in the upper Loire, it makes the Sancerres and finer Pouilly wines – here its local name, Blanc Fumé, is added to the wines of superior quality as in Pouilly Fumé. Other French names include Fié, Surin and, outside Europe, the suffix *'blanc'* is often added to the name – Sauvignon Blanc – possibly to distinguish it from an odd and rather obscure grape called the Sauvignon Vert, which does not seem to be making wine these days. In California the Loire name is often reversed to 'Fumé Blanc' by at least several respected wineries, but I have never been able to understand the reason for this. The vogue for wines made solely from this grape has resulted in its being cultivated by itself in many regions of France, the resulting wine satisfying the demand for dry, moderately fruity and agreeably forceful whites, although the Sauvignons of northern regions tend to have far more crispness than those made in the south: the gorgeous 'green' fragrance of a good Sancerre is especially appealing and the firm flavour makes the wine a possible partner to many foods that might otherwise seem to require something red.

Sémillon: This is a grape especially suited to the making of wines from grapes attacked by 'noble rot', and it is one of those producing the great Sauternes. As a straightforward table wine, however, it also has considerable appeal, possessing a lightly honeyed bouquet and softness on the palate. It is cultivated all over the world, being quite successful in California, it is the 'Hunter River Riesling' of Australia, and it is also planted in central Europe. It does, sometimes, seem to lack definition and backbone when it is used by itself, unless it is very well made. Another name sometimes found for the Sémillon is Malaga.

Chardonnay: It has now been established that this is not a relation of the Pinot family, although the name Pinot Chardonnay is still misleadingly found on labels. It is so highly regarded that sometimes wines are made simply from this one grape variety, labelled 'Blanc de Chardonnay'. In the Chablis region its local name is Beaunois. The Chardonnay is cultivated throughout the world, and it seems particularly successful in making the dry, graceful but moderately firm and full white wines that are today so popular; it is definitely a fashionable grape at the time of writing. There are, however, enormous variations in both quality and style: at one California wine tasting I was amazed to find in the Chardonnays from many excellent wineries a sweetness, spread, lack of definition and crispness that would have been a fault in any wine made from this grape in Europe. Since then I have discovered some exceptions, such as the fine examples made by Trefethen – but only a few. The high alcohol content of many wines from this area not only seems to coarsen such white wines but inhibits the delicate, rapier-like piercing attributes of Chardonnay wines from various other regions. Some Australian Chardonnays have also seemed to me to have a peachy, melony, fruity style that initially appears strange although not unpleasant. Such other wines from this grape as I have been able to taste seem usually to be at their best when they are *not* trying to imitate any white Burgundy; the 'family resemblance' usually appears with wines of top quality, but the peculiar 'buttery' smell and taste I so often receive from Côte de Beaune whites, also the very odd minerally dryness of Chablis, is something that seems to be peculiar and restricted to such classics. Recently I was shown on several occasions a New Zealand Chardonnay that was a fine wine by any standards, but it was not 'like' either a white Burgundy or a Chablis – although admittedly I would have preferred to drink it rather than the too numerous poorer commercial examples of these inevitably costly wines!

The Chardonnay is one of the few white wines that today seem to me to be able to benefit by at least some maturation in wood, without losing their freshness, but this is something to be dealt with in a later section. What is important, I think, is that the forcefulness of the wines this grape can make should not be forgotten: if the Chardonnay has its delicate but definite and aristocratic bouquet masked by a maker who has allowed the wine to be high in alcohol or who allows the 'wooding' to be obvious, then it is easy to overlook its rôle in the context of a meal. At its finest it is possibly the only white wine that, if required, will stand up without any loss of delicacy to a rich meat or poultry dish and even to certain types of game; years ago the makers of a first-rate VDQS Chardonnay and a similar Sauvignon (at the Haut Poiton Co-operative) warned me that, although the Chardonnay appeared to be a more delicate wine, it must never be served before the Sauvignon because it would overwhelm it, and I have found this to be true, although, from tasting, one does not easily discover this unless a side by side comparison is made. It is like comparing the action of a dagger and a rapier.

Chenin Blanc: This is another grape planted all over the wine world. It originated in Anjou around the ninth century and, often referred to as the Pineau de la Loire, it still makes all the quality white wines of the central part of the Loire and its tributaries. These include the Vouvrays, from dry to very sweet, still to *pétillant* to fully sparkling, also the other wines made with the action of the noble rot, such as those of the Quart de Chaume and Bonnezeaux, and also the dry whites of Anjou and Touraine in general. Its name apparently comes from Mont-Chenin.

Plantations of Chenin Blanc exist in many countries, although its delicate 'honey and flowers' fragrance does not always emerge strongly unless a late-vintaged wine is made or a wine with the noble rot on the grapes. In South Africa it has now been established that the Steen or Stein grape, once supposed to be either a local variety, or else the Sauvignon, is in fact the Chenin, and some very pleasant late-pickings are made there. Some people find it lacking in subtlety, but, when well made, it can provide great pleasure. If made by certain firms or growers, it is capable of a long life in bottle, although these days this is seldom economically possible; however, a Vouvray in the *demi-sec* or *moelleux* category made by certain establishments – such as that of A. Foreau – will last remarkably well for forty or fifty years!

Interestingly, I think that I am beginning to notice a slight but definite difference between Cape wines called 'Steen' and those labelled 'Chenin Blanc', the former being somewhat more compact and trim, the latter open in texture and, perhaps, slightly lacking in definition as regards bouquet. But this, it must be admitted, could be a personal illusion and noticing the label!

Aligoté: This makes the 'everyday' wine of southern Burgundy and is the foundation for *vin blanc cassis* or 'Kir' (Aligoté and cassis liqueur). It is a firm, moderately full, very dry even hard wine, without much bouquet, but it appears that it yields more quality in California, although I have not been able to sample any made there.

Columbard: This grape originates in the Charente region and is one of those used for distillation – Cognac. It is also planted in some areas of the Bordeaux vineyard, but in general its wines do not seem ever to have attracted much notice in Europe. In South Africa, however, it can make a full, moderately fruity dry white wine with some grace, and it would seem likely that in the California vineyards it might have a part to play, where it seems to make satisfactory sparkling wine.

Muscadet: This is the grape that gives its name to the wine made at the sea end of the Loire. It is said to have originated in Burgundy and its other name, Melon, or Melon de Bourgogne, may indicate this, although not many Melon vines are now planted there. The wine is direct, very dry and fresh; in recent years the vogue for Muscadet has caused many producers to soften its basically rather hard style. There do not appear to be plantings elsewhere.

Gros Plant: This grape makes the second wine of the Muscadet region – hard, high in acidity and thin in body. It will go with an eggy dish or mayonnaise, but in general lacks charm as such. However, as the Folle Blanche it is one of the grapes cultivated for distillation in the Cognac and Armagnac regions. When I have tasted it in wine form in these areas, I admit that it seems to me as acidic and dull as in the Loire – but that may be because of my rheumatism!

Meunier/Pinot Meunier: This is one of the Champagne grapes and gets its name because of the powdery white appearance of the underside of the vine's leaves – floury, like the coat of a miller (*meunier*). Experiments seem to have been made with it elsewhere, but, as far as I know, no wine is produced from it alone.

Muscadelle: This should not be confused with the vines of the Muscat family, to which it does not belong. It is one of the grapes of the Sauternes region and, in the southern hemisphere, is sometimes used for the intricate and rich dessert wines that are so beautiful but so seldom exported – for economic reasons. It has a pronounced bouquet and slightly raisiny back-taste.

Savagnin: This is a very odd grape, possibly of Hungarian origin. It makes the *'vins jaunes'* of the Jura and, according to Lucie Morton, is the Traminer of Alsace. If, as the same authority asserts, it is also the Fromenté and Fromantin of Hungary, then it is also the Furmint of the latter country, foundation grape of Tokay. But the Furmint appears to have been brought to Hungary in the thirteenth century by Walloon wine growers, invited by King Bela IV to settle in the areas ravaged by the Tartar invasion; the grape cuttings they brought with them made a yellow wine, which was, therefore, called after the ripe wheat (*froment*) it resembled in colour. Other southern and eastern European countries grow it, also Italy, its name supposedly from Tramyn in the Alto Adige. Many New World vineyards grow Traminer, notably Australia.

Ugni Blanc: This is an oddly-named grape that turns up, under totally different names, in various places. It originated in Italy, where in fact it is the Trebbiano Toscano, and where it makes a wide range of white wines. Here, to me, there is a characteristic smell, which I often describe as 'Everton toffee' – in case this old-fashioned sweet is unknown to readers today, it may be associated with butter, sugar and vanilla. These wines in Italy all tend to possess this fullish, slightly fat bouquet, which can be very attractive, even when they are quite dry. The Ugni Blanc makes a number of the light white wines of the south of France – it never seems to achieve fine quality, although it is usually agreeable. In the Cognac area it is known as the St Émilion as well as the Ugni Blanc, and here it is one of the main grapes used for distilling; on the few occasions when I have tried it as a local wine it seems thin and high in acidity – ideal for making into brandy and, except for the odd whiff of the bouquet, apparently unlike the Italian Trebbiano wines. Another name noted by Lucie Morton is Roussan and I think this must be the Roussanne, used in Rhône Valley wines, although the alternative spelling of this is usually given as Roussette; the Roussanne is used in many combinations of other grapes in the Rhône and, because of its acidity, is useful in the St Péray sparkling wines. Some small experimental plantings of the Ugni Blanc appear in certain southern hemisphere vineyards but as yet it does not make many wines outside Europe, although it may be used more widely for blending than I have been able to discover.

Marsanne: This is another Rhône Valley grape, used in this region in conjunction with others, and it is apparently planted in Algeria. It is cultivated in Australia, where by itself it makes a very good wine at Château Tahbilk, straightforward, very dry, slightly 'piney'. It is included here, in case other instances of its being used on its own are found.

Clairette: This is apparently an old Mediterranean grape, but there is also a Clairette Rousse, which, in Provence and parts of the Rhône, is also known as Bourboulenc and which is a black grape. It seems to make quantities of pleasant if not highly distinguished wine and, in the south of France, is used together with other grapes to make various wines, of which the most important is the Clairette de Die, which is sparkling and highly individual – although, as a Muscat grape is also used for this, it may be difficult to distinguish the particular Clairette character.

Chasselas: This is grown in many parts of the world and apparently is also cultivated as a table grape. There are a number of different types, the original Chasselas apparently being brought to France by the Romans. In France it makes the more ordinary wines of Pouilly-sur-Loire, and, sometimes called Knipperlé, is grown in Alsace also for rather ordinary wines. Its German name is Gutedel, in Switzerland it is the Fendant, which gives its name to agreeable, lightly scented white wines, notably those from the Valais, which

117

have seemed to me to achieve higher quality than Chasselas wines made in France. The name used in the US is Chasselas Doré.

Gewurztraminer: This is another of the great wine grapes of the world. The name is spelled Gewürztraminer in German, but in Alsace there is no *umlaut* as there is no contraction of an 'e' in French spelling. It is often shortened in speech here to 'Gewurz'. The grape came from the Palatinate region of Germany which, if you look at the map, you will see is virtually a continuation of the Alsace vineyard. Until comparatively recently there were both the Traminer and Gewurztraminer cultivated in Alsace, the latter being known as the 'spicey' Traminer, on account of its pronounced, complex bouquet. Now only the Gewurztraminer is grown there, although the Traminer, in which the bouquet is less obvious, is still grown in many other vineyards (see p. 116). Other names for it are Traminer Musqué, Gentil Rosé Aromatique and, in California, Red Traminer – the grapes do acquire a rosy tinge just before the vintage. The wines made from this grape are generally able to be picked out, wherever they are grown, on account of the distinctive bouquet, which is usually much liked. Although large amounts of medium quality Gewurztraminer wines are made the grape is not, as far as I know, used in blends of grapes, but stands on its own; the finer wines are very firm, complex and capable of great finesse and charm, also, as they are fairly weighty, they can be served with a wide range of foods as well as drunk on their own.

Müller-Thurgau: This is a highly successful grape, evolved just a century ago by the man whose name it bears, a Herr Müller, from the canton of Thurgau in Switzerland. He crossed the Riesling and Sylvaner vines, and on some wine labels (such as those in New Zealand) the name is given as 'Riesling Sylvaner', or Rivaner. It produces well, even in otherwise difficult years, which has resulted in huge plantings in Germany from around the 1920s. The Müller-Thurgau vines can always be picked out in a vineyard, because, from a distance, they have a very tufty, slightly irregular appearance, whereas the Riesling and other classic vines are much neater in their rows. The wines have a rather obvious, musky but fresh smell, the flavour being fruity, somewhat herby and fairly crisp. They are usually popular, but it is fair to say that this grape would

118

not seem capable of making the very finest wines within the German style, even though Müller-Thurgau wines give much pleasure and are very versatile drinks. The grape is grown in other parts of the world, but the big plantings, second only to those of Germany, are in New Zealand.

Muscat: This name is borne by a huge family of grapes, grown in many parts of the world. It seems to have originated in Greece and may have been brought to France by the Romans. Some Muscats are well known as table grapes and most wine made from any variety of Muscat can usually be picked out because – unlike other wines – it truly does smell 'grapey'. To put your nose into a glass of, say, Alsace Muscat, is rather like pushing your face into a bunch of ripe grapes.

In France the variety most planted is Muscat Blanc à Petits Grains, which is also referred to there as Muscat de Frontignan – a wide range of *vins doux naturels* (see p. 218) are made in the region around Frontignan and sometimes the grape is also referred to simply as Frontignac or, in other parts of the world, as 'Fronti'. Frontignac is a name that often appears in old wine lists because it was popular with our ancestors. The White Frontignan, which is the same as the Muscat Blanc à Petits Grains, is used to make some English wines. Other names for it include Moscato, Moscata Bianca (in Italy, where the grape is the foundation of sparkling Asti), Weisse Muskateller (Germany), Moskuti (Greece), Muscatel Branco (Portugal). The Muscat d'Ottonel, much cultivated in central and south-eastern Europe and Russia, is somewhat hardier and makes many of the sweet wines so popular in this part of the world, although in Alsace it is refined into a very elegant dry, weighty wine, often replacing the Muscat Blanc à Petits Grains. As 'Frontignan' the Muscat appears in many southern hemisphere vineyards, making some excellent sweet wines as well as crisper dry ones in Australia, but, even in the driest examples, the grapey fragrance is pronounced. The Muscat d'Alexandrie is another variety often found, although it does not seem to be very satisfactory in California, where a type called Orange Muscat, deriving from the Moscato Fior d'Arancio of Italy, seems to have been more useful in some plantations. A fairly recently evolved vine in

Germany is the Morio-Muskat, very pronounced in bouquet and flavour but useful in blending with other grapes.

Do not confuse any Muscat with Muscatelle or Muscadelle (see p. 116). But it is a useful grape to register in any 'blind' tasting, because of the bouquet – if you can pick this out, then you have at least made a start. However, there are those who say 'Muscat –musk rat', being quite unable to enjoy any wines from this grape, whether these are opulent and sweetish or truly dry and, as the character of the grape and the wine are so individual, it is useless trying to like either if you cannot at once take to the smell and taste.

Pinot Blanc: This is a grape that seems to be increasing in popularity, but it appears to be mainly grown in Alsace, where it produces four-square, fairly robust dry white wines that can be very useful commercially and, from certain makers in good years, may achieve an agreeable, mouth-filling style. It is much used for good Crémant d'Alsace. At one time it seems to have been confused in the Burgundy region with the Chardonnay, but it is quite different and, although it can be used for some of the lesser white Burgundies, such as Bourgogne Ordinaire or Grand Ordinaire, it does not appear to be much grown otherwise; Anthony Hanson reports that it is used in the production of the rather odd wine, white Morey, where it is supposed to have an 'eglantine' bouquet. In other countries it can do well, although I admit to finding the table wines it makes to be rather dull.

Pinot Gris: This is a far more interesting grape. Until recently, it was the Tokay d'Alsace, but now this name is soft-pedalled in the EEC because of possible confusion with the place name, Tokay, in Hungary. In Italy, however, the use of the word 'Tocai' to indicate this grape is still allowed. In Germany the Pinot Gris is known as the Ruländer, because it was a German merchant called Ruländ who first planted it in 1711. It is also called Chauché Gris and sold as such in New Zealand. It is the Szürkebarát ('Grey Friar') of Hungary. Other names include Pinot Beurot, Fromentot, Gris Cordelier, Auvernat Gris and – definitely confusing – Malvoisie; this last name, however, indicates the antiquity of the variety, because it originated in the Mediterranean, where its Greek name is Monemvasia. This became Malvoisie and then Malmsey, which is one of the grapes making a style of Madeira. The Malvasia grape is found in many different vineyards and, although as Malmsey it is generally associated with rather full, rich wines, both useful for blending and in the making of dessert wines, it is also very fragrant and quite zippy, so that, when it is used to make a dry white wine, it can have considerable charm; it suffers somewhat from comparison with the Riesling when it is used in Germany, but it is generally useful. I have recently sampled a good one, slightly *pétillant*, from Emilia-Romagna.

Palomino: This is the grape that makes the finest dry sherries and it is widely cultivated, sometimes blended with other grapes, sometimes also making a dry table wine, for which it is also used in the Jerez area. It gives the wines it makes great freshness and nervosity and, in California, it is used to make table wines as well as those of sherry type. It is in this region often referred to as the Golden Chasselas, but it is no relation to the Chasselas grape.

Viognier: This is one of the Rhône grapes which is sometimes used on its own to make the white wines of Château Grillet and Condrieu, also in conjuction with other grapes to make some of the red wines, such as those of the Côte Rôtie. It has a strange bouquet, slightly aromatic and herby, and a very dry, almost astringent style, but this can be very pleasant and lingering. It does not seem to be grown elsewhere.

Among other white wine grapes are Sercial, Verdelho, Boal (Madeira); Grecanico, Cataratto and Inzolia (Sicily); Vernaccia (Italy and Sardinia); Terlaner (Italy), Xynisteri (Cyprus); Hárslevelü, Szlankamenka, Kéknyelü, Mézesfehér, Budai (Hungary); Neuburger, Nussberger, Grinzinger, Sieveringer, Grüner Veltliner, Zierfandler, Rotgipfler, Bouvier (Austria); Zilavka, Yellow Muskatteler, Posip, Grk, Vagava, Marastina (Yugoslavia); Kerner, Scheurebe, Sigerrebe (Germany); Bukettraube, Schanderl (South Africa); Reichensteiner, Madeleine Angevine (England), and many others, of which only main growing regions are here indicated. Some or many of these, of course, are also used to a greater or lesser extent in other vineyards. Their names are given because they may be seen on labels – at least, if the language of the country can be read! – but, to the best of my knowledge, links between any of these and the better-known classics do not exist or, if they do, they must be remote.

[FOUR]

VINIFICATION

This, the process whereby grape juice becomes wine, is complex and fascinating. (If any reader has some knowledge of science, this wholly unscientific personal account of what happens may be skipped.) It took me a long time before I understood something of what occurs in fermentation, and, therefore, I never cease to marvel at the wonder that is wine in its finished state. As the stages of the process are not only interesting but quite exciting, I have thought fit to include a brief, simplified account of it, although there are volumes devoted to the subject if the technically-inclined wish to consult them.

YEASTS — WHAT THEY DO

Wine is made by means of the action of yeasts, which Alexis Lichine, the great US authority, pertinently calls 'the work horses of wine'. Yeasts are involved with various things as well as wine, the most familiar being brewing and baking. Anyone who makes 'home-made wine', or bakes using yeast, or even concocts alcoholic beverages with the aid of 'wine-making' kits, will be able to understand something of the working of yeasts, but although yeasts used in baking can sometimes be used for 'home-made' wines, this type of yeast cannot be utilized satisfactorily for brewing; these days what goes into bread is both controlled and subject to the established tastes of the buying public.

There are a huge number of different 'families' of yeasts and at least one of the giant liquor concerns has an enormous 'yeast bank' in which yeasts are stored, for experimenting and possible use in various ways. Most big wine concerns will have their own versions of this. The relevant point is that any old yeast won't do for wine, which requires a particular strain of yeast to work for a particular kind of wine.

Further, any yeast must have the appropriate conditions in which it can work so as to produce the desired results. It is no reflection on home wine-making kits to say that, although the use of a 'Burgundy yeast' will produce a different result from the use of a 'Champagne yeast', the ultimate beverage will not really be more than very, very vaguely similar in any way to whichever of the classic wines from which the yeasts in the kit derive. (There may be no perceptible similarity at all.)

Yeasts make wine, but certain yeasts are particularly successful in making certain wines. A strain that makes one type of wine in one vineyard region may not thrive similarly elsewhere, even in making the same sort of wine. One brilliant young Australian, whose careful explanations were a revelation to me, was always stressing that, in his homeland, the difficult conditions existing in many vineyard areas had stimulated a high standard of technology and research into yeasts which, he emphasized, cannot make a good wine better, but may make what would otherwise be an indifferent wine at least very much better than it would otherwise have been.

In a virgin vineyard remote from others under vines there are no wine yeasts. This affects those who are planting in previously uncultivated areas, but, even after a fairly short time, the wine yeasts do appear. In a mature vineyard there they are, already in existence. In case it seems incredible that something invisible to the eye, floating in the air, can arrive from hundreds, even thousands of miles away, it should be remembered that, as sufferers from certain forms of hay fever well know, it takes only seconds for spores likely to irritate their eyes and nose to travel to them from a very long way away. In fact, insects, such as the fruit fly, can carry yeasts enormous distances. In the US, it was discovered that each grape arriving at a winery had, on its single skin, 100,000 wine yeasts and more than *10 million* other yeasts, the 'wild yeasts' of any vineyard. It is no illusion that, at vintage time, the air around a winery is charged with excitement – and, I think, these yeasts abounding in the atmosphere 'charge' human beings, for it is certain that people manage to work all night or, as privileged visitors, attend parties all night and yet feel particularly well throughout the day. It is as if life is lived in a more intense, aware way.

In any place where wild vines grow there are wild yeasts, the main variety being called *Kloeckera apiculatus*. But these, like the wild vines themselves, are somewhat feeble. They can start making a wine but are unlikely to be strong enough to finish the task and, therefore – because nobody wants dead yeasts in finished wine – their presence is not sought after in a winery. They neither can complete the wine nor are strong enough to protect it.

The yeasts that make wine – and beer and bread – are all part of the family *Saccharomyces.* This word derives from the Greek *sakchar* (sugar) and *mykes* (fungus). According to Cedric Austin, *The Science of Wine* (University of London, 1968), there are thirty different species of this, the wine yeasts belonging to the group *S. cerevisae*; because the cells of these are more 'ellipsoid', a term explained by various reference works as 'oval and thin' or 'long oval' in Mr Austin's phrase, their name is *ellipsoideus.* (Anyone wishing to pursue knowledge of yeasts should consult Mr Austin's book, as it gives the history of the discovery of what fermentation really is in terms that even I can understand.)

The wine yeasts secrete substances called enzymes and these – which are catalysts, not being exhausted in the reactions that they promote – allow the yeasts to break down any substances to provide energy. The yeasts seek food and, therefore, consume the sugar in the grape juice, and as a result, they excrete alcohol, CO_2 (carbon dioxide) and several metabolics.

The *Saccharomyces ellipsoideus* therefore start or assist the initial stages of fermentation, along with any wild yeasts that may be present, and then they carry on when the wild yeasts die, which they usually do when the alcohol content of the fermentation vat reaches about 4%. The wine yeasts can go on after this, but the degree of alcohol to which they raise the must depends on the amount of sugar in the grapes: in rather cool vineyards the sugar content of grapes is usually lower than in hot ones, which explains the reason for many wines from southern European vineyards being slightly higher in alcohol than those in the north. A southern wine may go on to achieve 14° or even higher in terms of alcohol (expressed in the terminology of percentage of alcohol by volume), and a fine Mosel has been known to be a mere 7° (although this last is unusual).

STRENGTH IN TERMS OF ALCOHOL

There are several reasons why alcoholic strength is not invariably required: first, wine is intended to be drunk for the pleasure it provides; unless you want merely to drink for the sake of 'feeling' the strength, too high a strength can mask the emergence of the bouquet and even the flavour and, of course, for social purposes, most people simply cannot drink as much. In more aesthetic terms, it is fair to say that a table wine that is too high in alcohol will seem unbalanced. True, in some regions where a peasant or someone working hard out of doors is recommending a wine, he will probably opt for one that is higher rather than lower in alcohol – but that's because, among the cheaper wines anyway, it will usually provide the 'lift' that such a person needs rather than subtlety of drinking experience, and he will anyway be better able to tolerate the higher strength beverage. Most people reading this book will probably take a spirit if this is the sort of tonic or restorative effect they want from a drink. Wines that nudge the limit – 15° – at which they become 'heavy wines' according to HM Customs and Excise, pay heavy wine duty instead of the duty exacted on 'light' or table wines; this puts them at a disadvantage as regards price for the ordinary consumer, who will be used to paying heavy wine duty on a bottle of port or sherry, which is above the 15° limit, but who will be disinclined to do so for a possibly unknown wine that he wants to drink with food.

It has been significantly commented by a greatly respected American wine writer that too many California wines are, deliberately, made to 'win competitions' – in the upper levels of table wine strength, they stand out in appraisals of numerous wines and make an impression on the judges on such occasions. But, remarks the writer, can you *drink* them? Do you enjoy them with a meal? (And wine is intended for drinking.)

Alcoholic strength is in another way strength, because a wine needs it constitutionally; regulations for fine wines generally state the minimum degree of alcohol required in these wines. This is because such 'strength' protects the wines against various hazards and infections; the slight increase of strength in, for example, a *fino* sherry, often given prior to shipment, is to provide the delicate wine with some extra resilience prior to its travels.

PROBLEMS IN WINE MAKING

What the wine maker wants the wine yeasts to do is to start and maintain the fermentation, proceeding steadily without stopping, until all the sugar in the grapes has been converted into alcohol. This results in a completely dry wine (the sweeter wines will be considered later). But if the temperature suddenly drops or rises sharply, this alteration will inhibit the yeasts from working, as anyone using yeast in baking will know. This ceasing to work can cause trouble, because if it is necessary to start the fermentation up again a perfect wine seldom results. The same problem arises if, because of torrential rain, picking actually comes to a halt; then, too, the bloom tends to be washed off the grapes, which also means that the yeasts cannot take hold on the fruit.

So knowledge of the way the wine yeasts work – and there are a number of strains – and how they can be assisted to do their work well is of the greatest importance. It seems remarkable that it was as recently as 1860 that Louis Pasteur published 'Note on Alcoholic Fermentation', and in 1897 that Edouard and Hans Büchner were able to affirm that 'The production of alcoholic fermentation does not require so complicated an apparatus as the yeast cell' and were able to follow the part played by enzymes. Mr Austin gives this as a remarkable example of the unifying of both chemistry and biology and says it is possible to modify Pasteur's statement 'No fermentation without life' to 'No fermentation without enzymes; no enzymes without life.' These inert elements are, nevertheless, involved with life. It is, to me, equally remarkable that, had Pasteur not been a native of the Jura region of France, where the strange local wines – still little known outside the area – grow a 'veil' on the surface of the liquid while in cask or vat, it might have taken him far longer to discover the action of bacteria; this 'veil' is a true film of yeast analagous with the *flor* of sherry, benevolently affecting the wine, just as *flor* does on the surface of sherry; yet Pasteur had not, at that time, ever been to Spain.*

If the wine yeasts are unable for any reason to proceed with their task of converting the must or grape juice into wine, then the wine maker can help them; gone, fortunately, are the days when a sudden hot spell might cause the temperature in the fermentation vat to rise sharply and high, stopping the work of the yeasts and, in some instances, literally pasteurizing the wine or, at least, making it far less good than it should otherwise have been. But even in 1959 I can remember seeing blocks of ice being shovelled into some vats in the Médoc, and the tale is told of an estate in the Graves where the owner had an Australian visitor that year; he, seeing the worry caused by the soaring temperature and the furiously fermenting musts, suggested a few procedures he had found helpful in the baking vineyards of his home ... that property ultimately made a very fine wine. Already, the installation of vats with cooling devices had then begun – this was already fairly standard in many really hot wine areas, such as North Africa – but the traditionalists shook their heads and prophesied 'the end of claret as we know it'. But everyone who can afford the outlay fits a cooling 'jacket' around his fermentation vats today, so that, as the temperature inside rises dangerously high, a device switches on streams of water that flow down the sides of the vat and reduce the heat within; or he may have installed other means whereby 'controlled fermentation' is possible – enabling fine wines to be made in the very hot regions of the southern hemisphere. In some

* An examination of the properties of such surface growths on wine led Pasteur to discover the activity of the acetic acid bacteria: the *mycodermia aceti*. Would he have done so if he had not been familiar with one of the very few wines of the world that displays a surface growth?

installations I have seen in Tunisia a worm or coiled pipe carrying cold water circulates this inside the fermentation vat, to keep the liquid cooler. Controlled fermentation revolutionized wine making.

Even if the vat is a huge wooden structure of the traditional type – wood at least does keep the temperature slightly down as compared with stainless steel – the thermometer on the side is now carefully and regularly inspected. In the sherry region the *bodegas* are closed, with blinds drawn over the windows that are high in the walls, during the main heat of the day. Of course modern installations employ many different devices to keep the overall atmosphere fresh, the must coolish – and the wine maker calm. The result of the introduction of controlled fermentation cannot be over-emphasized: good and fine wines can be made in vineyards that previously could usually have made merely peasant-style beverages, acceptable only to the locals.

If the temperature drops, however, this is equally awkward. Below 10°C (50°F) the fermentation slows, may stop and, even if it naturally starts again, there can be problems for the maker. This is why, in the Chianti district, for example, where the early autumn can be bitterly cold, the cellar of an estate can be the warmest place in what are often solid stone medieval *castelli* having only the most basic forms of heating. The fan heaters go on in many chilly Burgundy cellars, too. Some strains of wine yeasts are able to work at low temperatures and makers prize them for this, but a sudden fall in the temperature in a region where vintage time is usually fairly mild can be a source of worry.

What, in general, the wine maker wants the yeasts to do is threefold: to start the fermentation quite briskly, continue it steadily without flagging and, finally, to produce the required alcoholic strength and stop. So, as will be realized, it may be necessary to have, as it were, a work force of several sorts of wine yeasts that will each play a relevant part in the whole process.

Although it might seem ideal to let the grapes alone, if they seem in prime condition, they may not remain in prime condition for long, due to outside circumstances – temperature, bacterial infections and so on. The delicacy of certain white wines puts them especially at risk, and the maker may choose to 'inoculate' the grape juice with suitable yeast strains so that these can go to work with more power than might already exist in the yeasts brought in with the vintage. The grapes, bear in mind, will have, in the bloom on their skins, all sorts of mould and fungus, some of it potentially harmful. If the weather is unpropitious at vintage time these moulds can be real enemies to wine. Sometimes, inadvertently, infection attacks the winery itself – although this would be unusual in a modern installation, but think of the more historic establishments, with much wood around, possibly stone and dirt floors, and much of the equipment difficult to disinfect as thoroughly as might be wished – you will then appreciate why insistence on cleanliness and the copious use of sulphur is and must be routine (see p. 145). If wine is left about, it may turn to vinegar – and then it may affect all the wine around it. In the great sherry *bodegas* the vinegar, much prized (for century-old sherry vinegar is superlative), must be kept in a completely separate building. In most wineries any spirit that is made will also be kept quite apart.

AIDS TO YEASTS

Suppose that the grapes simply do not contain sufficient sugar for the wine yeasts to get their food and do their work? This can occur if the climate of the particular vineyard does not bring the fruit to a sufficient degree of ripeness, either habitually or in a particularly unfortunate season. If wine is then made, the yeasts will stop working at an earlier stage than usual and the alcoholic content will be lower than is desirable. Great care may still enable a good wine to be made – but it may be a fragile one, unable to withstand the hazards inevitable if it is exported and, sometimes, liable to succumb to odd 'illnesses'.

This is when wine makers in chilly vineyard areas are allowed to give the yeasts a boost by providing them with extra rations – in other words, by adding sugar for them to feed on in the must. This process is known as chaptalization, after Jean Chaptal, who was Napoleon I's Minister of Agriculture and who gave his name to the process whereby, in the first decree permitting the addition of sugar to the musts of certain wines, it became possible to make at least acceptable wines even in somewhat adverse conditions. Today this 'sugaring' is strictly controlled and, in Europe, is best known for having been used for many years in Burgundy, although now Bordeaux chaptalizes as well, albeit usually to a lesser extent. Beet sugar is used for this in Europe, and of course whether the whole quantity permitted or only a little goes into the vat is up to the wine maker; it is, obviously, easy to make a wine of superficially assertive strength if the alcoholic degree is raised – the circumstance of some of the delicacy and balance of the wine being affected is often set aside by purely commercial considerations. Wines have to be sold and therefore must be made so that they sell. But insistence on quality versus commerce, as well as the wines' character in general, explains why certain Burgundies, from certain shippers and certain growers, are more highly regarded – and more expensive – than others bearing almost the same names from other sources.

In the New World, cane sugar is used for chaptalizing, and although I cannot pretend to detect the difference in the flavour of a wine made by quite discreet chaptalizing with beet from one with cane, I have known a New Zealander do so!

'SÜSSRESERVE'

In Germany and certain New World vineyards as well, the process known as *'Süssreserve'* or, as it is called in the southern hemisphere, 'back blending' is followed. Mr Simpson comments pertinently that

the addition of *'Süssreserve'* is essentially a finishing operation, which is undertaken with the finished wine before bottling. It thus, strictly speaking, does not have any immediate relationship with the use of sugar at the vintage, where the purpose is to enrich the alcoholic strength. You could, however, make the point that enrichment is not always undertaken with sugar. Where such enrichment in alcoholic strength is not systematically needed, the regulations tend to prohibit the use of pure sugar and, for example, in the southern French regions and in Italy enrichment is only allowed with concentrated grape juice. The quality of such enrichment is, therefore, very much dependent on the quality of the grape concentrate, which, if it is badly made or is caramelized, can have an undesirable influence on the quality of the resulting wine.

I have chosen to retain the reference and basic explanation of *Süssreserve* at this point in describing wine making, because I think that many people may, as I once did myself, confuse the processes, supposing 'enrichment' to include both chaptalization and back blending or *Süssreserve*; by explaining *Süssreserve* in the same section as chaptalization, the difference between the two processes may be easier to understand. They are different, they are used for different reasons, at different stages in making wine and, if you could compare exactly the same wine when this had been chaptalized alongside its fellow which had been composed with the addition of *Süssreserve* you would be more easily able to register the difference. Unfortunately, there would be no commercial purpose served in doing this, so very few people will ever be able to make this comparison.

Süssreserve involves incorporating a proportion of must that is concentrated into the finished wine, thereby providing enrichment. The subject is somewhat complex and the legal controls vary greatly from region to region in Germany as well as elsewhere, but it will be understood that the procedure does enable wine to be made of an attractive style that would otherwise simply not be possible. The finest wines of Germany and, as far as I know, elsewhere, are not, however, made with the assistance of this process. What must be accepted is that the *Süssreserve* addition exemplifies how 'blending up' can enormously improve even quite modest wines of a certain type; like the squeeze of lemon or pinch of spice in a sauce, its presence may not be perceived – but the difference it can make, especially when a popular wine of medium or low price is required to maintain its style and quality, is considerable. It cannot be sufficiently stressed that most forms of blending in wine making are done to *improve* both quality and acceptability, not to degrade, debase or vulgarize the ultimate product.

Of course, wines made in hot vineyards need no assistance by way of sweetening at all. It should, however, be clearly realized that none of these or similar processes that provide the yeasts with the sugar they need to do their job, nor any additional sugar added at the stage when the must is about to become wine, are the same as actually adding sugar to the finished wine. Neither chaptalization nor back blending, adroitly done, necessarily 'sweeten' a wine – although, naturally, the wine maker may be intent on making a wine that is acceptably 'soft' and therefore slightly sweet for the everyday ranges. But this is a different thing. If a red Burgundy is well made, it will in no way seem obviously 'sweet'. If it has not been well made, then – as with certain cheap and rather clumsily made German wines – the drinker may detect the maladroitness of the sweetening or enrichment as I do, by feeling a curious coating form on the teeth, sliding on to the gums, while the actual flavour of the wine seems clumsy, blurred, and the mouth is not freshened by the experience of drinking.

WHAT THE SPECTATOR SEES

The process of fermentation is fascinating to watch, although, if anyone is able to see it, they are generally advised not to breathe in while looking into a vat that is 'working'; the carbon dioxide (CO_2) that is given off during this process can, at best, make one feel ill if it is inhaled and, if anybody breathes it in deeply and constantly, can be dangerous. There are many frightening tales of how workers, going in to clean an empty vat after fermentation has finished and the wine been drawn off, have collapsed, overcome by the remaining fumes. It is now standard practice that no one should ever go into a vat alone, and that all workers descending into such redolent depths should wear some form of mask and be attached by ropes to the outside so that, if they lose consciousness, they can be hauled out to safety.

As the yeasts go to work, the grape juice stirs and begins to bubble. If you watch the start of fermentation, the must – which looks rather like runny jam, full of bits – begins, at first rather languorously, to move and swirl, and bubbles surface and break. This action becomes more violent and the bubbles get larger and larger, forming a foamy 'head' on the surface of the sticky liquid. If you hold your hand over this or dip it in, the warmth is immediately apparent and sometimes the temperature of a vat in full fermentation is really hot. Of course, it is not possible to see this going on in all wineries at vintage time but, if you get the chance to do so, it vividly illustrates the process I have tried to describe. There may even be a slight noise as the yeasts work; in the sherry region, where they are particularly vigorous (see p. 194), the clucking, plopping noise of the bubbles forming and breaking in the must sounds like a crowd of giants chuckling. This description, though, refers to the sound made by the sherry fermenting in cask, or, rather, butt; it is, however, only one version of the astonishing occurrence. Everywhere that wine is made the same stirring, churning, exciting bubbling up will take place.

As the more violent phase of fermentation dies down, a single bubble will go on rising here and there, or small patches of bubbles break over days or weeks. Wine in a vat can be more easily contained than in casks, which is why, when wine is put into casks to ferment, there must be an airhole through which the carbon dioxide can escape. This is the bunghole. When the wine is first put into the cask, the bung may either be left out or, if it is put in to keep insects from settling on the wine, then it is only loosely inserted, for the wine will bubble up and ooze out, pouring down the sides of the cask. This is why, in some red wine regions, the central section of a cask is always red, stained from the fermenting must. Although new casks are, ideally, used for the finest wines, they too soon become coloured. Some of the bungs used at this stage are simply fat round glass wedges, easy to insert lightly and simple to keep perfectly clean. If a wooden bung is used, then it is often wrapped in rough cloth; both the bung and this bungcloth have to be meticulously cleaned so that no infection is imparted to the wine. Eventually, of course, this wooden bung and its cloth wrapping or a new wooden bung replaces the glass bung; the bung is driven home tight when the cask has been finally topped up and it is turned so that the bung is on the side, to be left for a further period of maturation (see pp. 142–5).

Because this section deals in some detail with the work of wine yeasts, it is relevant to include here a note about how, in regions that make sherry, the film yeast that may form on the surface of this wine while it is in wood can be observed. Indeed, this is something that is so strange and impressive that anyone trying to understand wine should attempt to see it. Frequently, a sherry *bodega* or winery where sherry-style wine is made will have arranged for the phenomenon to be viewed, either by lowering a light bulb on a cord into the cask through the bunghole, or, ideally, by having one cask only half filled and with a glass 'head' or end, so that the formation of the *flor* on the surface of the wine can be watched. To say it is an uncanny sight is an inadequate comment. Sometimes the surface of the wine appears clear – then, maybe, a tiny patch of something like a bit of fluff or cottonwool will be noticed somewhere. Sometimes the entire surface will be covered with a palpitating fuzzy layer of creamy-coloured woolly stuff, which, as you watch, continually moves, linking up with adjacent bits of itself, breaking away, quivering, rising and falling. Sometimes only part of the surface is covered with this 'veil' or fuzzy layer, sometimes there are islands of it, some thick, some only transparent. This curious 'thing' is yeast in action. It is alive. I do not think that I have ever known someone viewing this for the first time not to fall silent – it is awe-inspiring.

MALO-LACTIC FERMENTATION AND FINAL STAGES OF FERMENTATION

When the fermentation has died down with the approach of the cold weather, it is usually important that the new wine should go into some container or containers to protect it during the next phases of its evolution. People like to picture wine being run from the fermentation vat to a series of casks and this does still occur with certain fine wines. But wood – casks – cost money and, for many of the more everyday wines and, even, some of the medium to fine whites, putting them into wooden containers of this sort would not improve their quality and might actually put them at risk. So it is probably possible to generalize that the majority of ordinary wines today – certainly most of the whites – never see any wood at all and, after the first period of their fermentation has finished, they are simply moved from the fermentation vat into another vat, tank or similar large container.

It is important that the new wine should be removed from any debris remaining in the fermentation vat, because there will be all sorts of 'bits' left there. The vat must be thoroughly cleaned before being used again. The debris, with the odd pips, skins, stems and general solids, also includes the dead yeasts, which should now have finished their main work. If this debris is left in contact with the new wine, all sorts of disorders may be communicated, not least the vinegar bacteria, *acetobacter*.

The wine is not 'finished', however. It is worth indicating that there are, in the world of wine instruction, two schools of thought: there are those who say that the fermentation process has two stages, whereas others aver that it has only one – although this one is interrupted by a winter pause, while the fermentation dies down in the cold weather. In addition to these two stages, or single interrupted process, whichever you prefer, there is another process – the malo-lactic fermentation. This involves the acidity in the grapes and, subsequently, in the wine.

Acidity has not featured large in the previous explanations of fermentation, but it is essential, both to grapes and to wine. Too much acid, of course, makes a wine tart and sharp – unacceptable even to those who really do like very dry wines. Too little, however, can result in a flabby wine, such as may be found in certain very hot vineyards, where the sugar in the grapes is high but the acidity low. It has been pertinently said that a well-constituted wine demonstrates the balance of the acidity and the fruit: the acidity to provide the zip and crispness (which should be present, even in sweet wines, to a certain extent), the fruit to provide the flavour and succulence. In one of my writings I stated that, if one thinks of wine in terms of human physiology, the alcohol may represent the skeleton (of scant interest, superficially, to anyone except a doctor or sculptor, but essential for construction and endurance); then the fruit may represent the flesh (differing in texture and affording much pleasure, both immediate and long-lasting), whereas the acidity represents the nervous system. The nervous system, it seems to me, accounts for individuality, personality – the element that makes a human being sensitive, charming, inspired, elegant. I still think this is, for the layman, an adequate interpretation of the three components of wine but the reader may prefer to make his or her own.

In newly made wine or alcoholic beverages, including apples as well as grapes, coming from cool climates, there is a particular acid that is known as 'malic' – from its association with apples, as might be supposed from the Latin name for an apple, *malum*. There are in fact three major acids in wine – citric, malic and tartaric. Pasteur observed that, in the progress of wine, the malic acid underwent a change; chains of formulae and complex scientific phrases supposedly explain the process known as malo-lactic fermentation, but essentially what happens is that the malic acid is converted into both lactic acid and carbon dioxide (CO_2). During this process the new wine has an odd, flattish smell that has a vague resemblance to milk and, certainly, to the sort of slightly sour but fat smell that one can sometimes notice when leaning over a mother who is breast-feeding her baby. If the malic acid is not thus changed, then the resulting wine retaining it is very crisp, zippy and fresh – in certain southern vineyards, such as those of South Africa, the malo-lactic fermentation is often deliberately prevented from taking place, because the wine makers want to preserve the crisp, dancing style of the wine they have made, which, in their hot regions, might become fat and soggy. In Alsace, similarly, there are some firms who regard the arrival of the 'malo' as something tiresome, although they will not suppress it if it has started; others simply let it run its course. In general, what is desirable is that this type of fermentation should take place before the wine is bottled – otherwise, if it occurs in bottle, corks may start being forced out and the wine will be slightly fizzy and not agreeable. In some regions the malo-lactic fermentation can take place almost at the same time as the first fermentation; in others, it may occur afterwards or, at least, during the early spring. There are more complexities of fermentation, but these few basics are what the ordinary wine lover will wish to grasp.

The wine, having been quiet during the cold weather after its vintage, will meanwhile have been carefully watched. If it is in casks, then these will be individually tasted and continually topped up – exposure to air is exposure to infection. Also, if it is in cask, it will have been run off the lees – the deposit settling in the bottom of the cask – at certain intervals; this is to ensure that any yeasts that may be still alive and in the debris in the bottom of the cask will not start working again and stirring up the wine. The process is known as racking – moving off the lees into another cask.

Here it is pertinent to mention that Muscadet *'sur lie'*, bottled off the lees in the cask from which it has not been racked off, is usually a wine with a little bit of 'life', or 'working' noticeable in it, in the form of a 'prickle' on the palate or a very slight fizz; this is much liked, but it would not be acceptable in, say, a great claret or red Burgundy. With wines such as the latter, which lie for up to two years in cask (the exceptions are dealt with later on), the process of racking or drawing the wine off the lees into fresh casks is done at certain periods. With wines in large containers, such as vats or tanks, the lees fall to the bottom and the wine can be pumped off.

The secondary fermentation or, as some prefer to call it, the second part of the fermentation process, takes place in the spring after the vintage. In a few instances, such as when making *'nouveau'* wines, of which Beaujolais is the best known (although not the only one), this part of the fermentation is either hurried on, so as to follow the initial stages, so that the wine, once bottled, is at least moderately 'finished'; or else this stage of fermentation is suppressed by various means. The problems about doing this suppressing is the possibility that a wine treated in this way may later start up fermenting once it is in bottle; this can cause a great deal of trouble, because, although the slight prickle of fermentation in a wine that is finishing its transformation from must to wine is not necessarily disagreeable and can be a sign of outstanding quality (as with certain of the great German wines), it is wholly undesirable that a merchant or his customers should find corks being blown out of bottles and the wine being in a very 'lively' state, unpleasant to drink. This is one of the reasons why *'nouveau'* and similar wines should usually be consumed while they still *are* 'new' and delicious. With time behind them, few good examples retain their initially pleasant character.

As the warmer weather comes, the wine yeasts start working again and the fermentation proceeds. It is not usually as bubbly and vigorous as the first stage, but the degree at which it proceeds depends on the type of wine and the weather – a sudden warm spell will hurry it along. As it goes on, the strength rises as any of the remaining sugar is converted into alcohol; with ordinary table wines, when most of the sugar in the original grape juice or must has been so converted, the rise in alcohol stops the yeasts working and they die. It is now important that they should not be allowed to remain for long in the finished wine, as, together with them, there are various other forms of bacteria and the dead yeasts can impart a peculiar and not pleasant flavour to the wine. Mr Simpson's comment here is to the effect that 'A modern wine maker would not wish to see any substantial quantities of sugar remaining unfermented over the winter, to be converted in an uncontrolled way by a resurgence of fermentation in the spring. I am sure that this does frequently happen, and certainly so with the malo-lactic fermentation, but, as a matter of good vinification practice, it is desirable to have both the primary and malo-lactic fermentations completed as expeditiously as possible.' Here is an example of exactly why it is unwise to rely too much on authorities – whether these are books still in print or lecture notes – that are even a few years out of date: before improved methods of communications made it possible for those making wine to keep in touch with discoveries made every week and research reported every month, there must indeed have been many wines suffering from what is known as the problem of residual sugar. The minute by minute control exerted on wines made today alerts the person in control as to potential dangers – preventive medicine rather than anything curative in a condition that need not nowadays arise. When I submitted my draft to Mr Simpson it was, as far as I could then be sure, in accordance with what I had been taught and read not very long ago.

If wine has been moved from vat to cask, so as to be 'finished' by having some contact with wood, then it will again be racked off its lees and, depending on how long it is to be left before bottling, it may be put into another cask; this will be topped up and the bung driven home tight, the cask then being stored so that the bung is at the side, held tight by the pressure of the wine which continues to mature until a sample, taken from a hole or spigot in the head of the cask, informs the oenologist that bottling can be done. The way in which this is done often fascinates visitors to a winery. The spigot is inserted in the head of the cask and then, with the claw end of a hammer, the person drawing the sample will insert this between the piece of wood braced across the cask head and the stave underneath it; he – I have seen women do it, but it requires some strength – will then lever the claw against the head stave so that the slight increase of pressure on the filled cask forces out the wine through the spigot or piece of piping inserted in the cask head. People cannot understand why, when the tap or pipe is first inserted in the cask head, the wine doesn't immediately surge out and I once had a long argument with an editor who simply could not understand that I wasn't playing a joke on her. But of course the terrific pressure of the wine against the cask head prevents any rush of wine through a tiny hole: a little dribble there may be, but nothing more until the pressure on the cask shoves out the wine into the glass or tasting cup (*tastevin*) that may be ready to receive it.

Similarly, when a sample is drawn through the bunghole, an instrument variously known as a *velenche*, *pipette*, 'thief' (in Cognac), or the supple-handled *venencia* of the sherry regions is used: this goes into the wine through the bunghole. The *velenche* – which looks rather like a big squirt or basting device with a loop for a finger – gradually fills up with the wine. The person pulling the sample then puts his thumb over the top of the *velenche* (which may be glass or metal) and lifts the instrument away from the cask; while the thumb stoppers the one end, the wine won't trickle out from the other. A judicious regulation of pressure by the lifted thumb enables the wine to be directed into glass, *tastevin* or whatever without spilling any. It is astonishingly easy to do – it must be, because it was the first task I learned in a cellar!

The *'preuve'* or 'thief' used in Cognac is a metal cup on a wire, which hauls up the brandy through the bunghole. The *'lopa'* used in Hungary has a rotund vessel at the top, holding a litre; the operator props it on his shoulder.

The *venencia*, used for sherry, is usually made of whalebone – for whippy suppleness – with a deep metal cup at the end and a hook, rather like that on a large coathanger, at the other end. The metal cup penetrates any covering of *flor* in the sherry butt or cask, without disturbing it; the coathanger loop will catch on the side of the bunghole if the person drawing the wine lets the *venencia* fall. The wine is drawn from under the surface of the *flor*. The whalebone handle enables the *venenciador*, or person drawing the samples, to swing the metal cup around (displays of this sometimes involve the *venencia* being swung, while full, over the head and in whirling circles and twirls) and direct the wine exactly into the glasses held in the other hand; one champion performer can hold thirteen glasses and, from high above his head, pour arcs of sherry into them, never spilling a drop. The *venencia* used at San Lucar de Barrameda (see p. 198) is made of bamboo, a chunk of the hollow stem being used instead of the metal cup.

If the wine has remained in a vat or tank, then it may also be drawn off any lees that have sunk to the bottom of this and be transferred to another container. The modern pump is, as may be imagined, essential to the smooth working of any modern winery! Moving wine from cask to cask by hand, before the days of easily disinfected pipes, was a hazard.

BOTTLING

Some wines, especially cheap ones and those that are considered most enjoyable when they still possess their youthful crisp, zippy style, will be bottled soon after their fermentation is finished. Bottling depends on the wine, the desired result and the views of the wine maker. But, even among the finest wines, it is unusual for any to remain in cask or vat for much longer than two years prior to bottling, with only a few exceptions, which certainly do not come into the category of 'everyday' drinks.

Wine that is to be bottled in the spring after its vintage will also be subject to various processes intended to clarify and render it free from any possible infection. Certain elements, such as proteins, which may become active within it can do great damage. This is why some of the special technology that makes the laboratory an indispensable adjunct to any winery these days must be involved.

Wine that remains in cask or vat for some time must also be clarified – this process is known as 'fining' and, when I was beginning to learn about wine, it was difficult to differentiate it from filtering, because our instructors would inform us (remember, this was thirty years ago, although that is not really a long time in the world of wine) that fining agents 'dragged down with them' to the bottom of the cask all the odd particles still at large in suspension. In fact, as is now known, fining doesn't work like that: if egg whites are beaten up and then poured into a cask (as is done in Bordeaux, where the wine order takes its name – 'Bontemps' – from the wooden bowl in which the whites used to be beaten), the spreading web of the egg whites catches and attracts the particles to itself, like a magnet. There are many other forms of fining, including some chemical ones that are now strictly prohibited; it is apparently possible to fine with blood (animals' blood), with fish (for many years one great Bordeaux property used this and I always smelled glue when I tasted their wines), and even with water, as I have seen demonstrated in the Beaujolais, also with albumen, isinglass and gelatine. Casein, which is found in milk, is another fining agent. The most usual type of mineral fining is a substance called bentonite and there is also kaolin. Correctly used, a fining agent can clarify and stabilize the wine, but excess of fining may make the wine taste and smell of the fining or, with certain mineral finings, it can taste vaguely earthy. But it is possibly sufficient to say that such particles as may be in suspension are removed before the wine – at least, any fine wine – finishes its sojourn in cask or vat.

How long a wine remains, as it were, at large, is up to the decision of the wine maker and, of course, the regulations governing production in any area. There is no point in keeping a wine around if it is not going to get any better – and, even if it is perhaps going to yield something special if it does remain in wood for longer than the usual time, these days it has to be calculated as to whether this additional 'something' will truly repay, in hard cash, the additional time that the wine isn't in bottle, being offered for sale, and thereby paying back at least some of the production and keeping costs.

WOOD

The contribution of the cask, whether this receptacle is large or small, to the ultimate wine can be important, although it tends to be more so with the making of red wines than whites. These days, virtually none of the white wines sold in the medium and cheap price ranges will ever have seen the inside of a wooden cask or vat, but will have spent the time before bottling in large containers, either stainless steel, glass or vitreous enamel lined tanks. They are not at risk from any infection in the atmosphere because the tanks are not open and the samples the technician requires can be easily drawn off from one huge quantity at a time, whereas it is obviously more difficult to go round sampling the contents of possibly hundreds of casks. Once an installation has bought a huge tank or vat of this type, it does not require much maintenance and can easily be disinfected, whereas wood is far more awkward, costing a fair amount in the first place – a great deal if a cask is purchased from a famous cooper and made of high-class specially suitable wood – and requiring care in handling and great skill if any repairs are necessary. If you visit an installation where there are many casks, often piled high in rows upon each other, it can well be imagined how much labour is necessary to move such things around or withdraw from use one found to have a 'weeping stave' or similar defect, which may not be easy to spot until damage has been done to the wine.

What wood does for wine is subject to much discussion. Many wine makers of the New World countries, especially those of the US and Australia, are often surprised at the lack of emphasis on the type of wood used for casks (a special oak is ideal but expensive), the maker, and the exact time a wine is 'wooded'. John Avery MW tells of the astonishment expressed by the head of a Burgundy establishment being questioned by a visitor: 'Where does my wood come from? The forest! Which? I suppose I can find out.' It inclines me to wonder whether the part played by the cask in a clean, dry

142

atmosphere, such as that enjoyed by many New World wine makers, is not different from that of a cask in use in a colder, damper, possibly thicker atmosphere? Humidity swells wood and slows the rate of evaporation of the wine; dryness does the opposite. Until a New World wine maker tries his hand in an Old World vineyard and records his impressions it is difficult to say. One British merchant reports on the 'California obsession with maturation in oak' and notes the 'different forests and different methods of maturation (kiln-dried or seasoned); of cutting (split or sawn); of bending (fire or steam) and of internal char (rare, medium or well-done)' (Simon Loftus in *Wine and Spirit*, September 1982).

The overall style of some wines is and has been changing, simply because the taste of the much wider buying public has changed too: people no longer want heavy, fat wines, high in strength, often less than 'star bright', smelling and, often, tasting of the wood in which they have spent several years and in which they may have acquired various flavours and smells that today are no longer much liked. It must also not be forgotten that the locals in a wine area may keep on liking a particular style that an export market does not care for. But the local wine makers need to make their profit, and, if possible export their wines.

As far as white wines are concerned, the demand is for crisp, light, dry or at least dryish pale-toned drinks for all but the most special occasions; with reds, people want wines that don't take many years' maturation to be enjoyable, without too much deposit that requires the wine to be decanted off, a fruity character, without much astringency. Many wines such as these can be made without long periods of maturation in wood. It is still possible for a wine maker to put a particular white wine into wood for a few weeks or several months, however, allowing it to acquire a particular additional character from this stage of maturation, and then perhaps letting it finish in a vat. Red wines can similarly be given a brief period of wood maturation. But good examples of both, right up to the very finest wines (and even including some of these), can be made without any recourse to maturation in wood at all. Anyone reading this book has certainly enjoyed a number of wines made in this way.

If you want to register what long-term maturation in cask does to a wine, try sampling certain white and red Riojas, made in the traditional way – a specialist in Spanish wines should be able to indicate these. You will certainly find them unlike most other white wines, and the reds may also demonstrate both their regional character and the wood in which they have spent more of their lives than most other wines in the 'table wine' category. The whites will be somewhat dark in colour, very aromatic, with a pronounced back taste; the reds will possess a soft, spread character, also being very aromatic, with a back taste that can be somewhat astringent and tannic. This is a very rough generalization, but an appraisal made even with such wines in the medium price range should show the added 'something' that maturation in cask for what, these days, may be longer than usual, can bestow on table wines.

There are many respected wine makers who do not think that wood can add anything to the attributes that make white wines attractive. If they do make an exception, it is usually for the Chardonnay; certainly some of the finest examples of wines made from this grape are still in the traditional manner, matured at least partly in cask. But it must also be said that some wines both smell and taste as if they had been 'wooded' when they have never been anywhere except in a stainless steel vat! (And although there is a business in 'wood essences', I do believe various world-famous makers who have assured me that certain of their wines, albeit both smelling and tasting of what I have always thought was wood, have never been near a cask, only a vat.)

With red wines, the length of time these are left in cask, if they do go into wood, is entirely the decision of the wine maker. In some installations, two years – going by Bordeaux practices – is routine; in others the period may be shortened to fourteen months or slightly less, with the wines passing some time in a vat anyway. In the past, many reds were left three years or even more in cask, but, it should be borne in mind, they might also have been fermented with the hat on the must in the fermentation vat for far longer than is usual today.

As far as the great sweet wines are concerned, they are also made subject to the theories of the wine maker. Some Sauternes remain in cask – often they are put straight into cask to ferment instead of into a vat – for three years or even more; this depends on the year. Wines such as many Sauternes and Barsac, however, are fairly high in alcohol and not as vulnerable as, for example, the lighter German and similar wines. Hungarian Tokay, in its small casks in the mould-tapestried cellars of the region, remains almost indefinitely in cask, one theory being that it never quite stops undergoing some form of fermentation. The true 'black wine' of Cahors, in the south-west of France, can remain in cask for fifty years and not taste in any way 'casky' or tired. The odd Jura wines, such as the *vin jaune*, remain in cask, without being topped up, for at least six years. These, of course, are very special wines.

In general, the use of wood is up to the wine maker and, in some instances, it may simply not be possible for him to make use of small casks for economic reasons. The larger casks, such as may be seen in wineries either in Germany or with Germanic traditions (often with finely carved heads, commemorating various events), are used less and less today, although they do play a part if, for example, a grower chooses to finish off a particular wine in wood prior to bottling, as may happen in Alsace; here, though, the use of small casks as well is still usual for maturation. With fortified wines, such as port and sherry, the use of wood is still prevalent – but it is perhaps worth noting that, in the regions where these are made, wood is still adequately available (albeit at a price) and coopers are still in business. In areas where this is not so, alternatives must be considered, though I do not know that any other equivalents to casks have as yet been introduced on a large scale.

SULPHUR AND NITROGEN

Sulphur is a word that recurs in any conversation about wine with those who make it and, therefore, I have asked Mr A. C. Simpson to contribute a note on both this and nitrogen in terms that lay persons, who did not do chemistry at school, can easily understand.

By 'sulphur' is signified sulphur dioxide (SO_2), a substance that is a gas at normal temperatures and pressures and is used in wine as a preservative and anti-oxidizing agent. Confusion with the solid 'parent substance' sulphur may well arise because of the practice of burning a sulphur wick or candle in empty casks to preserve them and, in this traditional way, so to add the product of that combustion, sulphur dioxide, to wine. Thus, sulphur dioxide has effectively been an agent of preservation and anti-oxidation in wine for centuries. (If, when visiting a winery, you find yourself clearing your throat or coughing, this is because of the sulphur that may be being used somewhere.)

In modern wine-making practice, sulphur dioxide is added in a convenient solid form as a salt which dissolves in water and in wine and releases sulphur dioxide in contact with the acidity of wine. Alternatively, it may be metered in as a liquid, in which form it can be obtained under pressure in cylinders (those elongated sausage-shaped containers that can remind visitors of the cylinders used for oxygen in hospitals).

Sulphur dioxide is first added to the grapes as they are crushed. This is very important in wine-making, because, as soon as the berry structure is disrupted, oxidase enzymes are released which begin to attack the oxidizable substances in the juice, particularly the tannins. Sulphur dioxide added at this stage and well mixed with the crust inhibits this oxidation process.

Whenever during its subsequent life wine comes into contact with the air – and this contact, of course, has to be strictly controlled anyway – some sulphur dioxide is needed to counteract the effects of the entry of oxygen and the potential for oxidation to occur. In the case of racking into cask, this is achieved by the freshly-sulphured cask, but small quantities of sulphur dioxide always have to be maintained in wine to offset the threat of potential oxidation.

The second property of sulphur dioxide is as a preservative or antiseptic. In this respect its power to suppress different micro-organisms differs: it is, for example, very effective against wild yeast, less so against the major wine yeasts (as a group), while some of the more persistent spoilage yeasts are extremely tolerant of sulphur dioxide. Thus, the preserve of some sulphur dioxide at the outset is useful in creating the environment for a clean and healthy fermentation, and, subsequently, for discouraging the growth of yeast and bacteria in the finished wine.

Sulphur is generally very effective in controlling the growth of bacteria in wine – and wine is not a very favourable medium for bacteria anyway. This is why it is important to delay the addition of sulphur dioxide to the new red wine until after the malo-lactic fermentation has been completed (pp. 134–6).

There is another important point about sulphur dioxide. When it is added to wine, it reacts and combines with some of the constituents of the wine, in particular the aldehydes. In this combined form the sulphur dioxide is inactive as an anti-oxidant and a preserving agent: it is effectively locked up. As aldehydes tend to increase slowly in the wine with age, more and more sulphur dioxide becomes combined and therefore it has to be renewed by successive additions.

While, therefore, sulphur dioxide is of critical importance to the wine maker, its use must in no circumstances be abused. A wine which has been badly handled and oxidized or infected with spoilage yeast needs larger quantities of sulphur dioxide; while, in these circumstances, the sulphur dioxide will provide some correction, the quality of the wine will inevitably suffer. Sulphur dioxide must be properly and sparingly used and, in these conditions, will contribute to the excellence of the wine.

Nitrogen's rôle has assumed importance in the techniques involved with making the styles of wine particularly liked today. Until fairly recently, I don't think that the word would easily have occurred in wine talk, at least not outside the laboratory and serious technical discussions.

Air contains approximately 20% oxygen and 80% nitrogen. In contact with a material such as wine, the oxygen of the air will first dissolve and then combine progressively with substances present in wine. Sulphur dioxide has some delaying effect on the progress of oxidation, but excessive contact with the air and the oxygen will irreversibly alter and destroy a wine.

Some wines demand or are capable of absorbing more oxygen than others: wood-aged port and *oloroso* sherry, for example. *Fino* sherry, however, is much more susceptible and the *flor* is an effective insulation against the penetration of oxygen. With the increase in popularity of fruity young red wines and aromatic white wines which carry over into the glass the characteristics of the grape, it is important to curtail and, in some cases, eliminate as far as possible any contact with the air. As a result of this technique, pleasant aromatic wines can be made in warm climates where, without the prevention of contact with oxygen, such wines would not be possible.

Several techniques are used, many of them being just common sense: keeping tanks and containers full, avoiding the entry of air in transferring from tank to tank, storing in metal – preferably stainless steel – rather than wood, careful attention to the condition of the wine and to standards of hygiene in general.

One helpful technique is to use nitrogen or, in some cases, carbon dioxide as a means of replacing or excluding air from contact with the wine. For example, if a vat or tank has to remain partly empty, the headspace can be filled with nitrogen gas to replace the air and avoid contact with oxygen. Another method is to inject a nitrogen gas under pressure into wine as it is being moved from container to container, or to the bottling line. The injected nitrogen has the effect of sweeping out any oxygen which is dissolved in the wine and which would otherwise be available for oxidation.

These techniques involving nitrogen gas are used by many wine makers in the New World, where the aromatic substances and the general excellent flavour qualities of young white and, in some instances, red wines are particularly susceptible to oxidation. While it is imperative to avoid undue oxygen contact for all wines at all times, some of the traditional aromatic wines of Europe would seem to be more hardy (for example, those of France and Germany) and, perhaps, this explains why such wines were, even many years ago, able to be produced without the knowledge and support of modern wine-making technology.

[FIVE]

BASIC WINE TYPES

The foregoing has described how grape juice becomes wine. In making the various main types of wines, however, different procedures are followed. The resulting wine may often be within a long tradition of wine making, updating some of it so as to accord with the requirements and resources of today; or, sometimes, wines of a virtually new style are created to cater for contemporary demand.

People who are fortunate enough to drink fine wines frequently, and who have detailed knowledge and appreciation of these, sometimes overlook the circumstance of wine being a highly important commodity in which to trade. If it cannot be sold, there is no point making it – however technically or traditionally interesting it may be; if only a minority buy it, then it is, in every sense, made at a loss. If it is not what a particular market requires, even huge expenditure on promotion and advertising won't – thank goodness! – compel that market to drink it regularly or, at least, to drink it more than once. If it is not the style to suit the drinker it may have to be 'adjusted'. (For example, one of the best-selling white wines in the world is made slightly sweeter for the US market, as compared with the European version. The extremely low temperature at which white wines are served in many parts of North America, dominated as I believe it to be by the insistence on ice-cold drinks, stress on cocktails, central heating and air conditioning, through which conditions any light-bodied wine has to fight its way, makes this extra sweetening sensible marketing.)

Price is another factor that the fortunate drinker who is able to follow his fancy may not always bear in mind. It is, obviously, better business for a firm to attract the sort of customer who buys a bottle of wine a week rather than the one who splurges once a month when giving a dinner party. But it is also important to consider the appeal of a wine to a public that is beginning to enjoy wine as against the public that does already enjoy it – but has had to cut down on what it may consider to be 'luxuries' – i.e. wine. The novel wine may appeal to the former, the 'known name' to the latter; the first may – at its introduction – be cheap, the second, sustaining the change and chances of the world, may also be cheap – and of mediocre quality.

It should also be remembered that the speed with which contemporary economic events affect what money can buy will react on wine prices. If, say, the foreign currency of one wine country declines against the purchasing power of that of the export market, then a 'bargain' – at least for a time – may be achieved. But when things change, the price of the wine changes as well. Price can indicate the possible quality standing of established wine, especially of a classic wine. It need not *guarantee* anybody an enjoyable drink.

There are, in history, various examples of fashions in wines, most interestingly linked with the changing social patterns, variations in international trade and so on. We tend to 'drink dry' these days, for example, because we all consume more sugar (cheap nowadays) than our ancestors, and we don't therefore prize sweetness in many wines; also, as we can usually keep warmer in the winter with greater ease than was possible fifty or a hundred years ago, the 'warming' type of wine is not in such demand; Málaga and Tarragona ('poor man's port') are seldom seen at smart parties today.

The way in which the main or classic wines of the world are made is still important, however, because knowledge of procedures involved with them affects the drinker's views as regards standards of quality. For example, if you discovered a white table wine that was brownish in colour, you would at least suppose something was wrong with it – white table wines are not the colour of, say, a sweet sherry. If a 'Chablis' tasted almost sweet, you would, likewise, be hesitant, because true Chablis is and should be very dry indeed

– far too dry for most people if they are truthful. There was once a wine journalist who indignantly commented that certain Hungarian Tokays were 'maderized, oxidized', in other words, smelling as if they had been exposed to the air – but of course they *were* like this because the wine spends years in cask and develops its curious individual character precisely by being exposed to the atmosphere.

In this section the different styles of wine are considered, so that the reader may know how they are made special, according to the type of each.

It should be understood that, in many wineries or large properties making one basic type of wine, there may well still be several grades of quality made, either because only grapes from the finest sections of the vineyard are used and these are processed separately from others; or the new wines themselves are graded and sorted out according to quality; or certain wines are thought worthy of receiving additional maturation in vat or cask prior to bottling; or a high proportion of free-run juice or the yield of the first pressing or pressings will be kept apart. Sometimes, in properties where the estate-bottled wines have numbers on their labels, people can even find a difference between two bottles that have been numbered several hundreds or thousands apart – and it is up to the individual drinker to decide whether the wine bottled earlier (by days, weeks or even months) is better than that bottled late.

But anyway, there are sometimes wines that the makers consider are a cut above even the best of the routine production, for various reasons. These may be denoted by various terms, including 'Special reserve', *'Tête de cuvée'*, 'Personal selection of . . .', *'Kabinett'* and so on, or the particular way in which the wine in the bottle is 'special' may be indicated, perhaps by a mention of the age and quality of the vines or the additional maturation. All this depends on the regulations governing the wine and region concerned, but it is a general category of wine that should be registered by an intelligent drinker; experience may or may not enable the drinker to judge in the case of, for example, a Burgundy labelled *'Ancienne méthode'* (made in the traditional way), a German *'Kabinett'* wine (something above average, subject to all the German Wine Law requirements), an Australian wine labelled 'hand picked' (as compared with machine harvested), or a California wine adorned with a strip label stating that it has been the particular wine selected by a well-known wine writer or merchant. Does any or all of this make the wine truly superior in quality or more enjoyable? The decision must be individually made, by the person who buys the wine.

In some of the very finest German wine estates, for example, certain of the wines are still matured in 'small wood' – medium to small casks. These will be numbered and, when a buyer goes round inspecting and sampling, he will buy, literally, the contents of one cask rather than that of its neighbour, the cask's number being put on the label. In Burgundy, casks are not numbered – but, as one eminent British merchant used to say, when a particular cask was purchased in the cellar of a small grower, it was prudent for it to be moved by the buyer's agent or broker *immediately* afterwards to the security of his own cellars: the maker, impressed by the choice having been made for an export market, might, if given time, 'arrange' the wine in this selected cask, sharing it between other casks. Many wine makers, in fact, sort out the wines they mature or make in cask and can direct the potential and regular buyers to those casks that will appeal most to them – the wines may vary infinitesimally slightly, but they can definitely vary.

The same applies to wines in vat, but here, with the larger quantities involved, the variations are obviously either very great indeed or not so subtle; there have, however, been serious discussions between owners of wine estates and directors of great wineries when, on tasting the different vattings of the new wines, they found this sort of variation occurring at the higher levels of quality. Should, at these levels, vattings give way to smaller containers? It takes both power and considerable security to downgrade a wine that is, as it were, born to a great name – and will probably fetch a high price, even if those most closely involved with it find one particular vatting less good than others. To 'declassify' a certain proportion of the wine of an estate means not merely a loss in terms of finance but a possible shrinking of the market. because of less than the expected amount of the wine of a 'known name' being available. It is not always possible to sustain demand until the next vintage – and that next vintage may not be sufficiently good or prolific to satisfy created demand.

As has previously been mentioned, it is essential to distinguish between wines that are sweet, either because of the higher proportion of sugar in the grapes – whether this is routine or the result of special vintaging, such as late picking – and those that are in various ways 'sweetened'. It would not be satisfactory, even if regulations permitted (which they usually do not), to stir a sugar syrup into a finished wine and sell it as 'sweet'; try, if you wish, to do this with a wine you may find over-acid for your taste. The result is unlikely to please. But the straightforward addition of sugar is also unlikely to be an improvement – you will merely be aware of drinking something that is, to you, sour, into which sugar has been added; it will not become a part of the wine. One does not want a clash of character of this sort.

Chaptalization, the adding of sugar to the must, has already been described. Its purpose is not primarily to sweeten, but to provide food for the yeasts, so that they work adequately. Over-chaptalized wines do have a sticky flavour and texture, however, although it would require a *large* quantity of additional sugar to transform an essentially dry wine to a sweet one, and regulations control the amount that may be incorporated.

Wines may, however, be at least softened and sometimes definitely sweetened by the use of a proportion of very sweet wine in the ultimate blend. This is what may be done with cheap wines, slightly sweetened so as to appeal to a mass market, in which drinkers find it easier immediately to enjoy a wine that is not palate-scrapingly dry. The use of blending in this way can also be helpful in years when bad weather has made it difficult for grapes to ripen properly, and therefore even a small amount of sweeter wine can make a surprising difference and, when carefully chosen and incorporated, need not unbalance or distort the essential character of the basic wine. Champagne is an outstanding example.

There are still many members of the UK wine trade who are sufficiently adept at blending in their own cellars, who deplore some of the rigidity with which many of the controls on some classic wines are now applied. In the Beaujolais region, for example, the weather can, quite often, permit only the making of rather thin wines, lacking the delectable fruit and lip-smacking 'moreishness' that is the supreme attraction of the wine of the Clochemerle country. In the past, the Swiss market was only one of its export customers requiring such Beaujolais as they bought to be full, rounded, warm-bodied, a charmer by the side of their own some-what austere – and never cheap – reds. Many British, too, will have had their first experience of Beaujolais by drinking a wine that, in former days, might often have had 10% or less added of something produced in a southern, warm vineyard, where the full, softish style was less likely to be affected by lack of sun. This type of addition, when done by someone of discrimination, no more 'changed' the essential style of the wine than the addition of a pinch of some herb or a few drops of lemon juice or similar fla-vouring will change the entire character of a dish, and it should be noted (see p. 183) that in the Champagne vineyard, the addition of a certain small amount (up to 20%) of the wine of another vintage can quite legally be done so as to improve the wine of one year that may need just a little assistance to be at its best. Of course, the type of fat, sloppy, thick 'Beaujolais', so dosed with North African or inferior Midi wine that no one of experience would find it typical, was never conducive to the interests of the wine makers of this smiling region. But the problem remains, even with present re-strictions.

Consider – would you rather that a wine is made solely according to the available local produce – the grapes – and put up with a possible lack of charm and no satisfying rotundity for the year in which this type of wine happened to be the *only* one available? Or would you accept the ever so slight 'extra' that makes the wine of an otherwise rather dull and possibly unattractive year into something still typical of its region but very pleasant to drink? In fact, people who inveigh against any use of a wine from outside a particular demarcated area for blending, or, indeed, the use of any method whereby the wine may be made more acceptable, are forgetting that, until Jean Chaptal authorized sugaring the must at the beginning of the nineteenth century, many vintages of Bur-gundy must have been verging on vinegar and that, until well into the nineteenth century, red Bordeaux, even the wine of great estates, was sold – at the request of the merchants in response to the demands of the consumers – 'cut' or blended with many more robust wines of the south, much Rioja going up to Bordeaux for the purpose, or even from the Rhône, making certain wines that fetched higher prices when they were 'Hermitagé' than when they were 'natural'! In many archives old lists offer both.

Today, the use of means whereby a wine is rendered pleasant and appealing to a wide market – and need not be expensive because of these means – is something to think about. A quarter of a century ago Muscadet was, as many books will tell you it still is, a very dry wine indeed, the sort of wine that would cut through the most unctuous mayonnaise or egg-enriched sauce on a fat fish. Today, most Muscadet isn't truly as dry as that, for the very good reason that more customers prefer it to be slightly less acidic; there is no reason why they should not prefer a wine that, to them, is more agreeable to drink and easier to enjoy. Other wines have also been adapted to contemporary drinking. It is true that, for various reasons, the experienced drinker tends to 'drink dry', simply because by the time he *is* experienced he has not so much reason to seek sweetness to please and warm him (he probably is aware of his weight anyway); if he wants to drink a variety of wines, it will usually prove pleasing to drink more of those that are dryish, at least before meals and with food. We do not, these days, always lead active outdoor lives. Even those who do are conscious that some of their hardy ancestors may have shortened their lives by imprudent eating and drinking.

The sensible drinker of wine will sort out the place of wines that are dry and those that are sweet and, once the step up from the very cheapest everyday wines has been made, it is not difficult also to sort out the wines that are softer and easier to drink *because* they have had their natural regional and traditional styles adapted to current requirements from those that are simply yuk-sweet, in a wholly commercial attempt to present something that may appeal to public taste and, possibly, sell and make a profit from an otherwise unsaleable type of wine.

It has already been explained how red wines acquire their colour

– from the skins of the black grapes. White wines, these days, tend to be much paler than in former times, especially if they are being sold as 'dry'; this is because people associate a deep golden colour with a rich, sweet wine. In fact, white wines not matured in wood do remain pale in tone for quite a while, whereas in former times they would take on colour from the cask in which they were kept. Many of the very finest sweet and late-vintaged wines, which are kept usually for some time in wood, will be deeper in colour. But it is also worth noting that, with white wines, the colour varies (and the depth also) according to both the grapes making the wine and, to a certain extent, the warmth of the vineyard. (And colour can be lightened as well as deepened.)

For example, the white grapes making the white Rhône wines impart a straw-like tone, even though this may be quite pale; the Sémillon grape usually seems to make rather more yellow wines, the Chardonnay those that are lemon-yellow. The Riesling is pale but a pale gold, deepening somewhat as it ages. The Gewurztraminer seems to start by being a more definite gold, but does not darken much, the Sylvaner tends to be pale lemon. One of the most curious of all is the colour of Chablis – the 'real thing' has never, in my experience, been satisfactorily imitated, because the colour of a young Chablis is a pale but definite lime-lemon, an odd glint of green – the green of a clear sea near the shore – being noticed at the point where the wine makes contact with the glass; although, with many years' ageing, Chablis darkens in colour like other white wines, it does not usually darken to anything like the same extent, so that a wine of a big year will not *look* as old as, say, a neighbouring white Burgundy, because this greenish tinge appears to retain and hold the youthful colour. It is an easy way of detecting a false Chablis – or one that is in fact a blend of some Chablis and ordinary white Burgundy – simply by examining the colour; I have seen writers praise the 'deep golden hue' of a 'Chablis', but it is unlikely that true Chablis is ever a really golden wine.

Pink or *rosé* wines get their colour either from a short period of skin contact of black grapes, or from some red wine being blended in. In the past the former method was rated best, but nowadays it does not seem to have been established that, if the pink wine is blended from red and white, this may be inevitably inferior. The type made by allowing skin contact is sometimes labelled *'vin d'une nuit'* to signify the brief period of the skin contact.

The classic pink wines are all controlled as to how they may be made. The colour varies enormously, from a pale, almost lilac-bluish-pink in certain northern vineyards, such as the *vins gris* or 'grey wines' of Lorraine, to the deep red, verging on tawny, of some Mediterranean *rosés*, which are almost claret-coloured. In very general terms, I think that pink wines made from certain grapes are more pinky-red – these include those made from the Pinot Noir or with a high proportion of this grape in the blend – than those of warm vineyards, including those made from the Cabernet Sauvignon and certain of the Rhône grapes; the famous pink wines of Tavel, for example, are, when mature, a beautiful tawny-pink, reminiscent of the colour of an azalea. Many Spanish *rosés* are slightly orange in tone, those of Portugal more plum-pink. A brilliant pink, a true rose, almost blue, is typical of certain South African *rosés*. Sometimes Burgundy *rosés* and certain pink wines from the south of France are described as *'oeil de perdrix'* (partridge eye) in colour, but, as has been crisply commented, how many people have been eyeball to eyeball with this bird? The colour is a pinky-red.

The warmth of the sun releases the skin pigments to tint the must, so that wines made from northern, chilly vineyards tend to be paler in tone than those made in southern ones. With age, the beautiful colour, which is such a charm in a good pink wine, does tend to fade and lose its brilliance, but few *rosé* wines are made for long keeping.

TABLE WINES

Many white wines are made from one white grape variety or from a blend of white grapes; many red wines are made from one black grape variety or a blend of several black grapes. This is easy to remember. But some wines are made from several grape varieties, both white and black. This includes many fine Rhône wines and certain Italian wines. (Champagne and port are other classic wines made from a mixture of black and white grapes, but they are discussed later. As most grape juice is greenish-yellow, rather like grapefruit juice in colour, it will be understood that it is perfectly possible to make white wine from black grapes if you remove the skins prior to the juice undergoing fermentation. It is odd tasting wines like this: the eye has registered 'a white wine', but on the nose and palate the smells and flavours usually anticipated do not materialize – the wine is 'different' and unexpected. It is even odder, however, when you know what the wines have been made from, because if the grape name Pinot Noir or Cabernet Sauvignon is mentioned the senses definitely prepare to register impressions associated with these grapes – and then both the mind and the palate receive a jolt, because, although one can understand the contribution of the grapes, they are, when they make white wines, not the same as when they make red; even if you taste in a 'black glass' so that the colour is not registered by the eye, the contribution that would have been made to the flavour by the skin contact is missing – and one reacts to this. I was first able to sample some white wines made from black grapes at Mission, the oldest winery still in production in New Zealand and, subsequently, to taste the red wines made in the usual way plus the surplus skins removed from the must of the white wines – this additional skin contact resulted in a magnificent colour! There are some grape varieties that have pinkish juice but these are not numerous and they are seldom used for fine wines.

Mention has already been made of the way in which some makers, for good reasons, hope either that the malo-lactic fermentation will not take place or else actually suppress it, so as to conserve the 'apply' freshness of the ultimate wine. This is sometimes done in hot vineyards, where the wine needs as much verve and briskness as it can get or be given and, also, when it is likely to be drunk while fairly young, when the youthful crispness is particularly appealing in both red and white wines. Makers of the *vinhos verdes* or 'green wines' of north Portugal want this acidity, which is why their vines are trained high, so as to stress the tart, almost shrill style and, also, why *vinhos verdes* do not bear vintage dates – they are ready to drink as soon as they are sold. (More about them in the section on sparkling wines, pp. 181–2.)

FACTORS GENERALLY AFFECTING STYLE

It is important to know the source of the wine you buy. This means both the grower and the shipper; the latter may either buy the wine already made or buy just the grapes and then process these in his installations. With wines not bottled where they are made, when they will bear the name of the winery and, usually, the statement where the bottling has been done, it is also important to know who actually bottled the wine and where. It would be pleasant to think of grapes being grown in a single defined plot, adjacent to a winery where the wine is made, matured and finally bottled but, although this does happen with some of the world's finest wines, it is the exception rather than the rule. The way in which different people and different organizations are involved along the way the grape juice travels before it goes into bottle as wine can radically affect both its style and its quality. There may be a weak link in the whole chain of production, there may be a change of ownership of vineyard or winery, or a change of top management involving more or less expenditure on equipment . . . The possibilities are considerable.

In some wine regions, the man who arranges to buy either grapes or wine from the farmers may know both them and the quality of their crop very well; but his requirements as to the quality of the grapes and wine may be too high for those who currently budget for the winery – so he may be directed to make a profit quickly because of other considerations in the firm. One grower or one winery may hold big stocks of fine wines almost as a type of insurance against a bad year; but suppose the economic situation means that these wines must be unloaded on to the market so as to enable the individual or the firm to keep in business? Where those wines have come from in detail and exactly how they have been kept is of great importance if re-sale is contemplated.

There is also the possibility that, in a particular year, one section of the production of an estate or a winery is not up to the usual quality standards, although some is fine. Does the owner (or the board of directors) reject or downgrade anything inferior – using another label – to enable them to dispose of the wine, or do they actually sell it to someone else? Or do they, needing wine to sell at the best prices they can get, label all the wine – good and medium good – as the same, or perhaps actually blend the less good with the better wine prior to bottling? (You blend up, not down, so this can be a great advantage to the drinker.) It is easy to say that profit should not be more important than quality with a commodity such as wine – but even the millionaire proprietor of a world-renowned estate, or the chairman of a huge public company dominating the drinks world, even they, like the peasant farmer, must make *some* profit, both for themselves, their colleagues, their shareholders and for putting back into the vineyard and wine installations.

This is why, with the truly expensive wines of the world, every detail of their production, from grape to bottle, is of importance and may or may not account for some of the great variations in price between wines that bear similar names or at least seem to be generally similar. One member of the wine trade remarked that, with German wines, it is more important, with the finest, to see the name of the grower and the shipper, even more so than the name of the site or the date of the vintage. In Burgundy, the wine made by a grower need not necessarily be better than the wine made or handled by a shipper, who will control larger quantities at a time and, probably, a wider range than the individual with the equivalent of an allotment-sized patch, but it is likely to be *different* in possibly a more individual way – sometimes for good, sometimes for a more 'popular' quality. In the Burgundy vineyard area, vineyards are greatly subdivided; for example, one well-known single vineyard, Clos de Vougeot, which, with its clearly marked boundaries, is one of the more obvious self-contained 'names', has as many as 66 different owners, so it will be understood that there will be around 66 different Clos de Vougeot wines made in the one year: picking will be differently timed, possibly differently tackled; the wine-making likewise may be varied as much as it is possible to imagine, even though the basic procedures are, like the vineyard, subject to established controls.

The name of the winery can also be influential in the style as well as the quality of the wine. Some firms enjoy much respect, others rise and fall, misfortunes affecting some gradually, changes such as the death of an owner, departure of the chief wine maker, lack of reinvestment and adequate maintenance altering the wine within a fairly short time. Sometimes a firm will be bought and the change of ownership will cause quality as well as quantity to soar. Big is not necessarily the same thing as 'bad'. More money may mean higher quality! Some firms are aiming purely at a mass market for cheap wines, others try to have some top quality wines even though they make their profits from the 'bread and butter' inexpensive ranges.

The ordinary customer, possibly unaware of so many caveats and variations until at the point of sale, can, in the end, only buy the bottle, draw the cork and see if the wine is enjoyable. But, if it isn't, then it is worth noting the wine's pedigree and, if possible, seeking some information as to whether the source of supply is reputable.

Bottling at the vineyard or winery should be some form of reassurance, simply because, when the wine does not have to travel far before it goes into bottle, it runs fewer risks of infection and deterioration. But this is not always a reliable guide with many very cheap wines: if they are transported in bulk, then they can at least resist various perils that can attack smallish quantities of delicate fine wines. The containers in which wines are moved around today are far more secure and impervious to the dangers incurred by old-style casks. Sometimes the entire hold of a ship will be one giant 'container'! Also, there are not always the ideal technical resources close at hand where a wine has been made, but these may be immediately available to firms who receive it in an export market; sometimes even wine makers refuse to adopt certain precautionary measures, notably certain forms of stabilization, before they ship their precious wines – which may therefore arrive in less than perfect condition and need instant remedies. It is, after all, in the export market that those wines which have been moved far away from their origins have to be sold and make their favourable impressions.

All this indicates why wine can vary so much, within all the degrees of being 'good'. A cheap, branded, blended non-vintage wine may, for some years, be bought from a particular region or country and then, either because better value is offered from another source, or something actually cheaper or very slightly more attractive is produced, the wine's origin will be altered. This is why, even with wines that will not vary greatly from bottle to bottle, there can be variations as a result of alterations in the source of supply – yet one more reason for not sticking to the same brand, however good you find it at one time. Wines that may have seemed rather indifferent, dull or even actually unattractive from one source may suddenly change – new plant may have improved them; a different wine maker or a fresh, up-to-date scientist in charge of quality control may lift the status of a winery and its wines: this is only one reason why facile and thoughtless criticism such as 'All the wines from Country A or B are awful' is pointless and limits many possibilities of pleasure. The same applies in the finest wines, too: suddenly a son will take over from a too-conservative father, a partner or colleague with fresh ideas will install new equipment, the retirement of the vineyard manager or the grasped opportunity of someone longing to transform a laboratory, alter a bottling line, re-design the layout of the fermentation area – all these will propel a sound but previously unexciting estate into becoming noticed, appreciated and, if luck and funds last, prices will rise along with the quality of the wine. Of course, misfortunes can also arrive as the result of too many and too futile innovations, and quality and reputation will decline, although it is surprising how – I suppose to the 'drinkers of the labels' – wines that have won great names tend to keep their prices up even when their wines are not invariably what they used to be.

One thing that has also greatly influenced wine production is the co-operative concept. A winery is only working all out for a few weeks each year, when the wine is being made. For the rest of the time machinery lies idle, though it must be maintained; space is not occupied, unless wines in bottles are stored in quantity, although they should ideally be, if not below ground, at least somewhere cooler and quieter than the main work area and away from the site of the bottling line and packing department.

Many co-ops, therefore, receive the grapes of small-scale growers and make the wine for them. Sometimes this is done almost between groups of friends; sometimes several hundred farmers will be members of a co-operative. The big co-ops are frequently extremely up to date, some with many additional attractions, such as facilities for showing visitors round, selling wines and providing refreshments. Nor need the wines only be of moderate or meek quality; there is one Burgundy co-op which draws customers from the cream of the U K wine trade and many other important overseas buyers; relations between this establishment and the individual shippers and merchants are cordial. This co-op knows the sort of wine Shipper A usually buys, which is different from that preferred by Shipper B, whereas Merchant X can afford more than Merchant Y and, although Merchant Z can only buy in small quantities, he always goes for top quality and his firm's prestige, and the publicity he attracts, are such that it is worth satisfying him as well as Shipper C, who regularly keeps huge amounts of wine for a giant chain of retail outlets . . . The wines are individual, prepared to suit the needs of the different customers – they do not, as I have heard someone suspiciously inquire, all 'come out of the same tank'. Most co-ops' standards are high and, after doing business with certain customers over some years, these installations can cater for divers requirements.

All these variables indicate the way in which table wines of all types can be individual. This is why, when somebody makes a statement such as 'I like Nuits Saint Georges' it is virtually meaningless, unless they specify whose Nuits Saint Georges they have found pleases them. It would be more intelligent to say 'I like Burgundy' – at least such a big generalization can comprehend all the wines made! It is equally foolish to condemn the wines of a particular country or region unless you have gained considerable experience of the majority of them, because there are probably some that you would like, or at least admire, although you may have been unfortunate in those you have tried.

Among other statements often heard but indicative of ignorance or prejudice are remarks which reveal that the speaker thinks age is in itself 'good', so that a very old wine is certain to be somehow 'better' than a younger one. It is for the benefit of people such as this that unscrupulous firms have been known to print labels bearing old vintage dates and, in a slightly less dishonest but still somewhat misleading way, for quite ordinary wines to be put up in bottles with dust blown on and stuck there, sealed with lumps of wax and labelled with pseudo-parchment paper in olde worlde type or script. As will have been understood by the account of how wine is made, age is not necessarily an advantage, however wonderful it can be to taste an old wine still showing its quality and providing great pleasure; some old wines are, merely, old wines – many of them tired, thin, fading and at least some half-way to the vinegar crock. Somebody who would prefer to drink a weary, flabby beverage that is partly distintegrating but bears an historic vintage date in preference to a young wine at the top of its form is merely, 'drinking the label', without truly tasting. Some people, indeed still insist on 'a vintage wine' even when the wine they are ordering – and the price they are prepared to pay – both mean that what they require and would like is a non-vintage. This is another silly type of snobbery. With some wines the date goes on to make sure that the bottle is drunk soon, before the wine can age too much; with many wines intended for current drinking it is assumed that they are ready to enjoy when they are offered for sale. This type of wine can not only be enjoyable, it may be *far more* enjoyable than something on which the bottlers have slapped a vintage date so as to cater for the wine snob drinker, but which is at least rather a dreary example of that vintage anyway and would have done better service to wine by being incorporated in a non-vintage blend, where its deficiencies might be remedied in conjunction with more vigorous and healthy wines. It is astonishing how, rather like the squeeze of lemon in certain recipes, even a very small amount of a good wine can 'lift' the quality of a large quantity to something more than satisfactory.

It has been understood how some wines can be made agreeable; how, for red wines, colour can be deepened by additional contact with the black grape skins (and it is possible to bleach wines, though this is not usually a desirable thing to do); how wines can be prevented from suffering from the types of infection and deterioration that, in the past, could ruin or at least damage them. The following gives some specific variations. In referring to some of the famous but not necessarily plentiful wines of various European vineyards, I am only citing examples known to me from some personal experience and it should be accepted that similar practices may be in use in many other vineyards of which I have only limited knowledge.

MACÉRATION CARBONIQUE

A method that is of fair importance today in the making of red wines is called carbonic maceration, though the French term *'macération carbonique'* is also widely used. The process is one evolved in the Rhône Valley within the last fifty years, although there are some authorities who claim that at least some stages of this method have been used in various vineyards for longer than that. There are also some wine makers who consider that this is only a part of the ordinary procedure of fermentation and nothing new. But many good wines, especially in the medium and low price ranges, are today made with at least a proportion of the ultimate blend having been produced by the carbonic maceration method, so it is worth noting.

Essentially, the aim of a maker of wine is to produce a beverage that is pleasant and, if possible, commercially successful. Nowadays, apart from the really small-scale grower, who probably has another business or way of earning his livelihood anyway and can look on his vineyard as something of a hobby, disposing of his crop or his wine locally, possibly even among family and friends, all those growing vines for wine must be aware of at least the possibilities of making a profit by exporting some of the crop or the wine, even if to a fairly nearby region. The wine must be able to compete in export markets and also to achieve the sort of style that can be maintained from year to year.

Many casually produced old-style wines were locally consumed, mainly because the locals had nothing else. Today, the smallest village often has the type of miniature supermarket where at least several wines from other regions will generally be available, so local taste can be fairly widely indulged too. Now it is certain that many of the very 'regional' wines of the past were not only those getting names for themselves as 'bad travellers' (no properly made wine should be incapable of reaching its destination in good condition, unless subjected to definite disaster en route), but they might not have been very good anyway: some, such as those made from unsuitable grapes that just happened to be planted in a particular place, might be far too acid, or tannic, or simply require too long a period of maturation – in wood – during which time they could be attacked by various ailments as well. Anyone who has sampled a recently made red wine conventionally produced from grapes such as the Cabernet Sauvignon, Grenache, Nebbiolo, will seldom feel drawn to drink this immediately, as the hardness and astringency, the very elements that are going to make a good wine given time, are stridently unattractive before they have mellowed with maturation. But even if time were able to be bestowed on many such local wines, they still wouldn't – couldn't – compete with the big classics; one patch of earth isn't able to make the sort of wine that may be produced a few miles away and create a world-famous name. So, although wines intended for agreeable and short-term drinking, at viable economic prices, could and can be softened, lightened and adjusted to an extent our ancestors would have found remarkable (wines can be lightened as well as given additional colour, all in a reputable way, these days), basic difficulties remained in many regions. The presence of tannin and a general stalkiness were possibly the two main drawbacks in little local wines, especially the reds.

It was then discovered that if, instead of being destalked and pressed immediately on arrival at the winery, the grapes were left piled up, a type of fermentation would start within each berry and, at the same time, juice would be running from the pile simply because of the pressure of the fruit. The first and 'free run' juice from any grapes is always highly regarded, as are the first runnings from the press. If a pile of grapes is allowed to remain, in wholly clean surroundings, for a certain time before being pressed in the usual way, then, if rot can be prevented by careful and informed supervision, the resulting wine when these grapes are pressed is both similar to what it might otherwise have been but also different. The basic character, of the region and of the grapes, will be retained, but the wine will be fragrant, fruity and soft – it can almost be drunk at once; it is certainly ready to be bottled and therefore enjoyed at a much earlier date than if made in the usual way. It won't keep for very long – but then, it wouldn't improve by keeping. The saving of time spent otherwise in cask or vat is enormous. The wine can be put on the market within a few months or even weeks of having been made – an obvious saving in labour and money.

There are some wines made wholly by this method and it is also surprising how the use of even a small proportion can render a local wine highly enjoyable. It is fair to say that very many of the French *vins de pays* could never have found buyers outside their localities had not this method influenced the way they are made now; the ease with which they can be sold at moderate prices in important export markets speaks for them. It is necessary for makers to have some technical skill in wine, and it is essential to maintain standards of cleanliness that would have seemed fussy to many wine makers at the beginning of the century, but the wines' success has confounded the suspicious and conservative. It would be unlikely that today's drinker would enjoy an old-style red wine made from, perhaps, the Carignan grape, so widely sown in many warm vineyards; today, even a 25% amount of *macération carbonique* in a blend of Carignan can make a delicious wine, often at its best when served lightly chilled, like a young Beaujolais.

WINES THAT ARE NOT VINTAGED IN THE USUAL WAY

In this section the main categories of wines are mentioned which are 'different' mainly because of the way in which they are harvested. There may of course be additional reasons for their being different, but traditionally it is the vintaging that has, originally, created the style.

Drying of Grapes Prior to Pressing

The length of time a grape is left on the vine is of great importance in the making of the great sweet white wines. But because there is obviously some risk in letting the grapes remain there after the main vintage period, some regions pick at the usual harvest time and then dry the grapes slightly on straw mats or else hang them in special racks, where they can concentrate their flavour while some of the juice in each grape evaporates. Some of the sweet Italian wines are made in this way, including those that may be labelled *'amabile'*; so are the 'straw wines' (*vins de paille*) of the Jura. The slight drying of the grapes prior to their being pressed gives a touch of raisiny sweetness to the juice, which will be richer than the ordinary type; the alcoholic strength will usually be higher, too, because of the sugar, and the fermentation tends to go on for a much longer period than for ordinary table wines. The wines, being of this slightly higher strength, are therefore less vulnerable to infections while they are in cask and some of them remain in wood for far longer than would otherwise be practical or desirable. All the main types I know are white, although, with such exposure to air as they get, they acquire golden, straw, or even almost caramel tones.

Late Picking

There are then a vast number of wines that are made with grapes which are generally described as 'late picked' – left on the vines until they are actually over-ripe. This time may be a few days after the main vintage, it may be several weeks. The effect of leaving grapes on the vine is to make them more luscious, more, even, like table grapes, although even at this stage few wine grapes are very pleasant to eat. In many instances, of course, the grapes left in this way are running the risk of developing grey rot, which makes them unsuitable for use if it takes hold. Or they may be virtually destroyed if there is a cold snap after the vintage that will shrivel and blacken them, or they may simply be prevented from getting any riper by heavy rain. In vineyards with more constant climates and not much risk of rain or frost immediately after the vintage these dangers are slight, but it is not always easy to make late picked wines and, when only wines that are to be in the medium and low price ranges are concerned, it is not really worth while trying to do so if much risk is involved.

All the wines that have come my way in this category are also white. In theory there might not seem to be any reason why black grapes should not also be left on the vines and picked late, but, if you think about their rôle in wine making, especially in the context of food, it is easy to understand that there is no point in making them luscious or sweet, when, at their best, they are already fruity – adequate accompaniments to a meal because of this, simply agreeably fruity for anytime drinking, or delectably extra-fruity in certain years.

Late picked wines, then, are not necessarily or obviously sweet. It is relevant here to stress that they are not and cannot be 'sweetened'. They are made from the grapes in the natural state in which they were picked. In some areas, such as Germany, the controls are very strict about this; no sugar may be added to the must, nor may the process of fermentation be halted in any way so that these wines – table wines, remember – contain only the natural sugar in the grapes when these grapes were picked. But it should be realized that such wine may contain a higher than usual proportion of sugar, simply because, in certain conditions, the grapes may be almost over-ripe anyway; the wine yeasts work, but cannot convert all the sugar in the must into alcohol. It is this sugar which is left that is termed 'residual sugar' and, although its presence can be attractive in a well-made wine, it can cause lack of overall balance and, sometimes, its presence can disturb the wine (p. 276).

What the late picked grapes give to a wine is a certain intensity and amiability and, just as in some vintages a proportion of slightly under-ripe grapes may go in to the vat, so as to provide zip and a higher fresh acidity to the ultimate whole, so the late picked grapes can contribute a full fruity rounded style and, usually, a particularly agreeable fragrance and lingering bouquet. It is easy to say that such wines are also sweeter, but they do not always appear so, or, indeed, register additional sweetness when analysed, which is why a generalization of this kind can be misleading; I have certainly never had a late picked wine (note – *only* 'late picked', not those in the following categories) that could not, if required, have been drunk with food or as an apéritif.

Selected Clusters of Grapes

Late picked grapes are usually harvested in bunches, like ordinary ones. But a further stage in making wines of this special type is when the grapes are picked only in small clusters at a time, the vintagers waiting until they can select the little bunches that have attained the requisite degree of over-ripeness. This results in the wine that the Germans call *'Auslese'* (specially selected). Generalizations about these are risky because, as has been rightly remarked, one maker's *'Auslese'* is another's *'Spätlese'*, meaning that, although in Germany the controls require certain conditions to exist in order to call a wine either *Spätlese* (late gathered) or *Auslese*, these controls cannot, for obvious reasons, lay down hard and fast rules about the *exact* degree of ripeness; therefore individuality remains and variations occur within the categories.

In countries that do not use German nomenclature, the term 'special selection' is sometimes seen; the wines in this category will all be of particular quality and should exemplify, in an immediately perceivable way, the character of a fine wine of the particular region and grape or grapes. An interesting example occurs with certain Italian wines, including some red ones, where the bunches of grapes are vaguely triangular in shape, the clusters that form the outer and broadest span of the whole being as it were the 'ears' (*'orrechi'* in Italian) to the bunch. These 'ears' are the ripest part of the bunch, because they are more exposed to the sun – so they are often picked separately and the fact is mentioned on the wine's label.

Selected Single Grapes

Above the category of grapes picked cluster by ripe cluster, comes that of those picked literally grape by overripe grape – the *Beerenauslesen* wines. These are definitely sweet, because of the delicate intensity of the concentrated juice; *'grains nobles'* is the term used in Alsace and it seems accurate – the grapes are individually selected for their 'nobility' and it is the power they contribute to the wine, in terms of huge, wafting bouquet, length and lingering flavour, that makes them so special. They are just that bit more 'special' than wines made from grapes picked in clusters, although (which should never be forgotten) the wines made in this way will vary enormously from maker to maker – sometimes, simply because it takes so much more time, labour and, therefore, money to make a *Beerenauslese* wine, a grower will simply pick cluster by cluster and even grapes affected by 'noble rot' (see below) will go into the vat; they will, of course, make their contribution there and a wine that has a fairly high proportion of such specially ripe grapes will be slightly but perceptibly more 'important', displaying more shades of quality than a wine with the same categorization, complying with the same regulations, where the grower has not yet been obliged – or been practically able – to go round the vineyard late, in a favourable year, so as to make a *Beerenauslese* or, even, a *Trockenbeerenauslese* (see pp. 171-5).

Noble Rot

Finally, there are the wines that are made from grapes which have been attacked by a particular form of fungus, *Botrytis cinerea*, *'pourriture noble'* in French, *'Edelfäule'* in German, *'muffa nobile'* in Italian. There are other national versions of the name, but 'noble rot' is the English one and the phenomenon – for it is truly that – is best known for its action on certain German and French wines, even though it can occur in other regions. The term differentiates it from the ordinary type of rot (grey rot), which merely destroys the grapes; noble rot is something that acts upon them, so that the resulting wine is quite unlike that made from grapes unaffected by it – indeed, in some of the vineyards of the Sauternais completely dry wines can be and are made, the grapes being picked all at one time and the wine made in the usual way. One can sniff a bouquet associated with the grapes making this wine, both from the Sauternais and the great German vineyards, also those of Tokay, but this will be, in the wines made from 'nobly rotten' grapes, magnified to an opulence and allure that the ordinary wines, however good, do not possess. Immediately the wine makes contact with the palate the difference is at once registered.

The fungus that forms on certain white grapes at a certain time and has been termed noble rot is a capricious infection; it will only do its work in certain conditions. Although experiments in some New World vineyards have actually involved spraying the *botrytis* on to the over-ripe grapes, I have not been able to sample the resulting wine, so cannot report on its quality. It seems, at the time of writing, to be something of a wine maker's *'gage d'or'* or challenge: 'If I can make such a wine,' says the wine maker or estate owner, 'I will have achieved the heights of . . .' Well, what *will* he have achieved? For the problem about these wines is that, simply because of what is involved with making them, they must not only be expensive but *very* expensive and, perhaps even more important, they do not fit easily into the pattern of drinking in the latter part of the twentieth century. They are the survivals of a time when the banquets went on for hours and the high price of sugar meant that anything sweet was a prized but occasional luxury. (The black teeth of Queen Elizabeth I were virtually a status symbol – she could eat sweetmeats whenever she wished.)

These wines are also survivals of a time when the preprandial drink was not usual as it is now. Even today, there are many French households where one sits around making polite conversation before being invited to sit down to the table – and of course, then or afterwards, a glass of something luscious may seem delicious. But if, after a working day, ending with a reviving cocktail or a couple of glasses of sherry or Champagne or simply some dry white wine, these drinks are then followed by wine with the meal, 'a big sticky' (as the Australians term the sweet table wines) is not always what diners require: a fortified wine, such as port, or, with coffee, a liqueur, is an acceptable extra for special occasions, but many people simply do not feel inclined to drink a table wine at the end of a meal, especially if they subsequently have to drive home. In the days when some of these other drinks would not have been offered, the big sweet wines were highly acceptable; indeed, I have

172

a menu of a dinner at the White House during the visit of King George VI and Queen Elizabeth (now the Queen Mother) as recently as before the Second World War, when the formerly usual custom of serving a big Sauternes with the oysters at the start of the meal was followed. But ... *autres temps, autres plats,* and, certainly, *autres vins.*

What the *botrytis cinerea* requires in order to work well is a vineyard where the grapes are perfectly healthy and ripe to over-ripe; all of these, by the way, are white grapes, with fairly thin skins. Then, during the period after the ordinary vintage, there should be warm, sunny days, with cool nights and the sort of mist in the early morning that makes autumn in many wine regions so beautiful. The proximity of water is somewhat conducive to this – all the great *Trockenbeerenauslesen*, Tokay and most of the Sauternes are fairly near to rivers, from which the mists can rise. Frost and extreme heat are not good – nothing too extreme is favourable. There should be warmth at this stage rather than heat, coolness rather than cold at night and certainly no frost, no rain, although the moistness of a morning mist will encourage the fungus.

There are various suggestions as to who made the first wine with 'nobly rotten' grapes: the first records allocate 1845 to Sauternes; around the beginning of the eighteenth century for Germany (where Schloss Johannisberg was then owned by the Bishop of Fulda), in both instances the wine being the result of an owner not being present or able to send a messenger to give permission for the vintage to begin, so that, when it was eventually started, the grapes were afflicted by the *botrytis*. But as early as 1650 the Tokay vineyards of Mount Oremus were unable to be vintaged on time because of war and it seems that their first great sweet wines were made then. However, I think myself that they may have been deliberately made even earlier. A writer cited by the late H. Warner Allen, a noted historian of wine, mentions a Chian wine praised in 400 BC, which, in the way this 'mellow wine' is described, echoes the phrases of my colleague Hugh Johnson when he writes on *Trockenbeerenauslesen* wines as regards its extraordinary fragrance – so it is just possible that, given the appropriate grapes and the right weather conditions, the cherished late pickings of Chios might have also been the result of at least some action by a fungus or noble rot.

What the fungus does is to penetrate the skins of the grapes which, anyway, are thinner at this stage of their fruiting than earlier in the year. The presence of what is one of the 'cryptogamic' diseases would in the ordinary way alarm the grower, but here, when the pinkish tinge begins to be visible on the grapes, it is – if the owner wishes to make this kind of wine – a hopeful sign. The grape's skin begins to wrinkle and, gradually, acquires a fluffy coating as it does so. This fluff looks exactly like the least desirable sort of mould, but in fact gives and yields and falls away if touched – and, merely by the action of a breeze, will be spread to other grapes, carrying the spores of the fungus around. My colleagues Jeffrey Benson and Alastair Mackenzie, in their study *Sauternes* (Sotheby Parke Bernet, 1979), say: 'The fungus digests the skin of the grape by a process of enzyme action' (it will be remembered that an enzyme acts as a catalyst) 'so that when a very ripe grape is attacked by humid and sunny conditions it soon dies and becomes dehydrated. The grape wrinkles and shrivels up more and more while its juices undergo a pronounced natural concentration. Alongside this physical change the physiological action of the *botrytis* plays an important part in changing the balance of the normal composition of the grape juice. The fungus grows at the expense of the grape tissue, but the metabolism of organic acids is proportionally greater than that of sugars. *Botrytis* thus produces a must that is considerably enriched in sugar without a significant change in acidity.'

This explains why *Trockenbeeren* wines are not necessarily obviously sweet; the great Sauternes are more so, but even they, if correctly balanced, should rather be luscious in the way that a white peach, grown against an outside wall, or that rarity, the greengage plum, ripened in a walled garden, are luscious, implicitly sweet maybe – but never cloyingly so. It must also be remembered that wines such as those of Sauternes may be far higher in alcohol – even nudging the limits of table wine – than those of Germany, so that the 'push' behind the impression they make is more evident, not merely their sweetness.

It will be seen that this type of sweet wine is definitely in the 'special' category, often to be enjoyed on its own.

Eiswein

At the pinnacle of this it is probably correct to place *Eiswein*. This is a great rarity – although, alas, some are now made to cater for the craving for novelty and the ability, on the part of the buyer, to boast of the price paid. This would not have been practised in former times, or at least I am sufficiently idealistic to think so.

Eiswein is made only in Germany as far as commerce is concerned, although I have known the owner of an English vineyard make one – a few bottles for fun – and to see whether he could! In fact, in this instance it was a *faute de mieux* exercise, because these wines are usually only made in years when the vintage is not such as to send growers home happy and make their bankers sigh with content.

To make an *Eiswein*, the grapes, which will have been left on the vine even after all hope of making other wines has been abandoned, should nevertheless be ripe or, if possible, over-ripe; in a rather poor year they may, with luck, achieve this state but be simply hanging on the vines long after pickers have stopped working and the presses have become idle. If there hasn't been a lot of rain but a long, warmish autumn, and the sort of early winter weather that can sometimes follow a dreary, washed-out summer then brings on such grapes to ripeness, and then there happens to be a really severe frost at night, these grapes will actually be frozen. Then they should be picked as fast as may be, rushed to the winery, and put into the press while the coating of ice still surrounds them. The juice that flows from them is, naturally, somewhat concentrated and the fermentation process is very slow – often presenting problems to the presiding oenologist. But the result can be interesting. (It can also be advantageous to such growers as have earlier made only mediocre wines and, fairly enough, want something with which to recoup their depressed fortunes.)

Eiswein is odd, in every way. The wines are delicate, very expensive and, I must admit, to me they do not justify their prices, although it is good that some wine is made in certain otherwise dreary years. They can present problems as regards regulations because, in certain unusual years, they are made from grapes left on the vines until the turn of the year – so what vintage can be put on their labels?

These wines are not sweet. Nor are they very fruity. I find them 'shadow wines', the *Doppelgängers* of what might have been. But they are a very special category and anyone able to try an *Eiswein* is privileged. It would certainly be wrong to sample such a thing except quite by itself.

[SIX]

WINES THAT ARE MADE
SPARKLING

It will be noticed that people writing and talking about wine seldom use the terms 'light' or 'heavy'; these words imply in the first instance table wines, in the second those that are fortified or 'stronger' – and, therefore, being higher in alcohol, pay higher Customs duty. The words 'lively', 'vivacious', are primarily associated with wines that are sparkling, and seldom used except in relation to them.

When a wine is undergoing some stage of fermentation, it is said to be 'working', but sometimes this little prickle of liveliness continues for years – even with some of the great *Trockenbeerenauslesen* – and this slight stirring of activity in the wine is considered a mark of quality: the wine is alive, the seasons outside, especially at the flowering of the vine and the vintage, stir up the bottled liquid, and, with certain wines, the recurrent capriciousness of a simulated awakening to 'work' again is a great charm. Of course, the residual sugar (see p. 276) in some wines means that there could, just, still be something for the wine yeasts to work on, but in general, wine makers today know enough to control and quiet too aggressive stirrings.

The various processes whereby sparkling wines are made, however, are one of the most intricate and marvellous achievements in wine making. Since the seventeenth century we have enjoyed wines that are stranger in even more ways than other fine wines – for all good wine is mysterious. Today, there are so many sparkling wines available that some understanding of the different methods the different methods whereby they arrive as a pleasure to the palate are well worth understanding, even though the complexities cannot be explained in a short space.

Sparkling wines, in general, are either very fizzy – fully sparkling – or they are slightly sparkling. In this latter category they can be so mini-sparkling as to show no bubbles rising in the glass, but register only a slight vivacity within the mouth of the drinker. The sparkle is, basically, carbon dioxide (CO_2), which is given off during the process of fermentation when ordinary table wines are made, but which, with sparkling wines, is either retained by or added to them in various ways.

This carbon dioxide is a gas and measured in terms of atmospheres. One atmosphere is the equivalent of a pressure of 15 lb per square inch, or 1.05 kg per square centimetre. This sort of measure may mean nothing to you – until you think of it in terms of the way you blow up a balloon for a party, putting pressure into the puff. The atmospheric pressure behind the cork of a fully sparkling wine, 5.6 atmospheres, will be roughly the same as that in the tyre of a double-decker London bus: would you like to be on the receiving end of that, if it blew out in your face? (This is why people can lose their eyes and much damage can be done, because the force of the pressure inside the bottle of a sparkling wine is essentially a force to be reckoned with. It should always be handled with care and the bottle must never be pointed at anyone.)

This terrific force, however, only exists in wines that have been specially made so that the carbon dioxide gas is retained within them. In many other wines the little 'whoosh' after the ordinary cork comes out need only indicate an agreeable liveliness in the wine, a myriad of tiny bubbles clinging to the side of the glass and an impression of zip and tingling vivacity on the palate.

The requisite for an acceptable slightly or fully sparkling wine must start with the wine itself, just as good wine starts with good grapes. In his great book *Champagne* (Gollancz), Patrick Forbes has said that nothing reveals the deficiency in a wine like the ordeal of being subjected to the Champagne process – an ordinary wine will be made more ordinary, a pleasant but 'little' wine will be . . . well, nothing much. But I think that, even with all the resources of contemporary technology, the base wine must anyway be of a certain standard, whether or not the Champagne process is to make it sparkling. The way in which the drinker considers what the sparkling or semi-sparkling wine is going to be affects the procedure: is it going to be a dancing, light-hearted drink, toning up the palate for a meal to come? Is it going to be a full-bodied but frivolous enchanter, accompanying delicate dishes or partnering rather succulent recipes? Is it simply a drink to toss back at a party?

If you reflect on what all these types of drink have in common, it is easy to see that a certain refinement or, at least, a direct, almost piercing and moderately delicate quality is what is likely to make them appealing. Therefore, the conclusions must be that this type of wine should, ideally, be basically crisp, with a certain pleasing fruit acidity, dry or dryish, moderately assertive but not aggressive.

The wine is, therefore, usually white. There are some fully sparkling red wines, but they tend – as with sparkling red Burgundy – to be drunk mainly by people who do not often drink other table wines; the fruity style and slight softness appeals, no more is required. The zip and acidity of many white wines makes them obvious choices for making into sparklers. In addition, some at least of those that are used for this purpose would be very big, hard, somewhat dull wines if drunk in still form. The little fizz that is evident within such specialized red wines as Lambrusco is rather different – such wines have a crispness in addition to their vivacity and, as with certain other slightly sparkling wines, I think of them as providing the sort of fruity freshness agreeable with some rather fatty foods, just as the British serve redcurrant jelly with mutton or lamb, apple sauce with pork, the French have the bitter orange (*bigarade*) sauce with duck, the Americans cranberry jelly with turkey.

The wine, ideally, should be fairly high in acidity and have some weight and 'push'. If it lacks sufficient acidity, it will be flabby and soggy when made sparkling in any way, also, if it is not moderately firm, it will lack definition; it is simply not worth while subjecting a lightweight wine of only very modest quality to any process making it sparkling, because all these procedures involve more time and money, in terms of labour, than making such wines as still wines; if the result is poor and doesn't sell, everything will have been a loss. This is why a sparkling wine will always be more expensive than its exact equivalent in still wine.

GASIFICATION

A wine can be given a slight fizz or at least a prickle by deliberately giving it a shot of carbon dioxide. Until only a few years ago this was regarded as something used only for the most common and cheap wines – 'the sort of sparkling wine you might win at a fair in the provinces' was how it was once described to me. Students of wine were told to experiment by passing an adequate but fairly ordinary wine through the sort of siphon that makes soda water, gasifying the liquid. The bubbles, one was taught, would be large, rise sluggishly, cease to rise within seconds, the wine would be flat, dull, dreary. It was true then.

Today, it has been found that, with certain, light-bodied wines, a minute judicious addition of carbon dioxide will not only provide the wine with a pleasant crispness – even a very slight vivacity – but also retard any tendency to maderization. This seems admirable to me. Many white wines in the cheap and even moderate price ranges suffer extreme hazards from climatic changes and possibly appalling keeping – what sort of wine can remain in even vaguely adequate drinking condition if left in a shed or outside under the sun and in a temperature that goes up to 40°C for days at a time? No time in the refrigerator will restore it to health. Some stabilization is nowadays likely but, with wines of slightly superior quality, the additional stamina provided by the CO_2 is valuable.

There are also wines that please a wide market because they have a very slight sparkle – and are cheap. These are definitely those that, until recently, came into the 'fairground sparklers' category. No longer do they deserve this condemnation. If the basic wine is sound, then some gasification – pumping in carbon dioxide – can make a pleasant, slightly lively drink from what would otherwise have been an agreeable but possibly rather simple still wine. I have now tasted a number of wines made by this method from a wide range of countries and all those that have been basically well made have given pleasure. They are not – they are not intended to be – fine wines. They are fun wines and the little extra that the slight fizziness provides is rather like the ribbon bow on a prettily packaged gift – an enhancement.

It is fair to say that I still think that, within limits of moderate fizziness and with a well-constituted base wine, this type of wine can be good in the medium and cheap ranges. But a *fully* sparkling wine made simply by pumping in CO_2 is unlikely to be more than the sort of drink you take for politeness. After all, if the base wine is all that good, why do the makers pump the gas in?

PÉTILLANCE

There are, as most people will know, wines that are possessed of a mini-sparkle, for which the term *'pétillance'* is usually employed. These include the range of *vinhos verdes*, the 'green wines' of Portugal – in which, traditionally, the malic acid is high, the vines being trained high to achieve this, and therefore there is a very slight prickle on the palate and indication of tiny bubbles in the glass. These bubbles tend to be more easily seen as they cling to the sides of the glass rather than actually rising in the wine, and they should be slightly different in the way they make themselves evident by the minute foam around the edge of the wine in an opened bottle which signifies it is still a fraction 'lively'. If you shake a bottle up vigorously, there will of course be bubbles, but these will break and the wine resume its still appearance almost at once. With any trace of continuing fermentation, however, the tiny beaded border of the wine will show what is going on.

With the white and red *vinhos verdes*, however, the phenomenon of *pétillance* is too important to be left wholly to chance. Some *pétillance* will usually appear naturally but customers like continuity of style and, therefore, the amount of this fizz is nowadays regulated so that it will not vary from year to year. If you are able to compare several *vinhos verdes* from different makers, you will see how they differ in the amount of gas they contain, some hardly showing any traces of this, others being definitely fizzy. It is often not realized that there is more red *vinho verde* made than white – it is a curious drink, very good with some of the rich dishes of *bacalhau* (dried codfish) – also that the world-famous Mateus Rosé is not a *vinho verde* at all, but a pink wine encouraged to be *pétillant*.

In other regions, a slight *pétillance* can appear in certain wines traditionally known for their crisp, vivacious style. These include certain white wines from the Loire, including Vouvray – which can be *pétillant*, fully sparkling or still – and also a number of Italian wines.

THE CHAMPAGNE METHOD

Although this is the most complex of the methods whereby a wine is made sparkling, it is important both because the finest sparkling wines of the world are made according to this process, and because some of the ways in which others are made certainly derive from their producers first knowing in detail about it.

In the first place the wines are made as still wines are made. The basic wine must be of high quality – the Champagne process involves so much time and skill that dud results would be disastrous. There are even some firms who still pick over and sort grapes in the vineyard, so that only selected prime quality fruit goes to the winery.

The traditional press used in Champagne is a *maie*, circular or rectangular, made of wooden slats, in which the grapes are piled and on which a lid comes down or the receptacle is raised to squeeze them. The juice resulting from the various squeezings is kept in separate containers, the first to run usually being the best. Nowadays the horizontal press containing a bag that inflates to squeeze the grapes against the sides is also in use; it always has been utilized in regions where the Champagne method is followed but the *maie* – which is difficult to work – has not been elsewhere introduced. The horizontal press is of course much easier to keep clean.

The wine then proceeds like a still wine, although it tends today to be kept in vats rather than casks; if, in cold, wet weather, the fermentation cannot proceed as it should, then it may be necessary to help it on by adding some yeast strains or, sometimes, some wine that has already begun to ferment vigorously. During the winter, when the cold weather causes the fermentation to die down, the wine maker will plan and sort out the various vattings and eventually, with much care, arrange how he will blend the wines of the different grapes, the wines from a variety of sites, work out how to balance the lack of fruit in one lot of wine with the fruitiness of another and so on. Then, before the wine can start working again as the warmer spring weather arrives, the various completed blends are bottled, plus, usually, a little dose of what is known in Champagne as *'liqueur de tirage'*. This is sugar dissolved in a still wine of the region and it peps up the dormant yeasts in the newly-made wine, starting up the second process of fermentation – only, by this time, the wine will be in bottle, sealed down with the first cork inserted. So the carbon dioxide gas cannot be given off as it would be in an open vat, but it is retained in the bottle where it becomes part of the wine. This is the sparkle.

The *liqueur de tirage* also dictates the amount of bubbliness that is to be produced. Approximately 4 grammes of sugar will produce one atmosphere of pressure, so, depending on the amount of sugar that may already be in the wine, which has to be verified by the laboratory, the additional sugar will be calculated so as to achieve the atmospheric pressure desired: sometimes, too, it may be considered necessary to add some more yeast to complete the fermentation process satisfactorily.

The wine in bottle, on its first cork, now undergoes the stage known as the *'prise de mousse'*, the taking on of the sparkle. If you opened a bottle at this point in the wine's life, there would be about 6 atmospheres pressure behind the cork, but, for a fully sparkling wine, about 5.6 atmospheres are eventually the norm. During this *prise de mousse* the bottles are stored on their sides for varying periods: in Champagne there is a minimum requirement of one year's maturation for non-vintage, three years for vintage, but many reputable establishments will give their wines longer than this. At the end of maturation, the bottles must have the sludge or deposit that will have settled in the wine removed – they cannot be filtered, as this would take out the sparkle. The process called *remuage* is therefore followed; the bottles are put, necks down, into frames in which, at regular intervals, often daily, skilled workers agitate them from side to side and shake them, so as to fling the wine right round in the bottle as well as up and down, finishing each 'riddling' by turning the bottle slightly to one side and increasing the angle at which it is upended in the frame; this can take six to twelve weeks, during which time both the fine and the sticky sediment in the bottle will be gradually flung down so that, eventually, it rests on the cork of the almost upside-down bottle. It is very hard to do this, as the action means turning the bottle, shaking it and circulating the wine. In many regions making sparkling wine, therefore, various other methods have been tried so as to bypass the work of the *remueur*: in the Penedés region of north-east Spain, for example, huge 'sunflowers' or bottle frames are rotated on octagonal bases, easily operated by a couple of comparatively unskilled workers. This seems to work there, but the deposit in Champagne tends to be heavier and stickier. Some Champagne and Loire firms now use electrically powered frames, which turn at intervals without any attention.

After the deposit has slipped down on to the first cork, the bottles are binned upside down, the neck of one resting in the hollow punt of the one below. They look very strange but can remain many years like this – remember, the wine ages slowly while on its first cork and in the cellar of its homeland, often actually underneath a vineyard where the grapes may have been grown.

When the bottles are required, the first cork is removed, any wine spurting out is replaced and, in most instances, a *dosage* of slight sweetening is added; this is because a wine without any *dosage* at all in Champagne is very dry indeed and, although there are fashions for *brut* and *brut zéro* wines, the market generally prefers the wine to be rounded out by the very slight sweetening. It may be as little as 1.5 or 2 per cent for a *brut* and, in outstanding years, non-existent, but this is the exception in this northern vineyard. Following the *dosage*, the second cork is inserted, the metal plaque added to prevent the wire muzzle biting into the cork, the long foil capsule put over the cork and wire, the label attached and the wine is, technically, ready to be drunk, although ideally it should get a further period of maturation to allow it to settle down after the disgorging and second cork being inserted.

Not only does all this take time, but the cellar workers have to be highly skilled – and therefore highly paid. There is then the fact that huge stocks must be held, so as to maintain the great blends – one year there may be a lot of wine made but it may lack acidity, whereas in another the crop may be smallish but of a quality to improve any blend to which it is added. Even with vintage Champagne, a small proportion of another vintage wine – up to 20 per cent – may be added to the wine of one year, so as to correct any deficiencies. This has never created any complaints about Champagne and, of course, every stage is completely controlled by regulations.

CRÉMANT WINES

There are also some wines that are not 'fully *mousseux*' or sparkling. These are categorized as *'crémant'*, which is possibly best translated as 'foaming'. They usually have 3.5–4.5 atmospheres behind their corks, but in fact you might not notice the difference between a *crémant* and an ordinary Champagne unless you compared two glasses side by side. These *crémant* wines are now made in a number of other regions, including the Loire, and other countries. They should not, however, be confused with the fairly recently introduced 'Crémants d'Alsace'; these are *fully* sparkling wines of Alsace, made by the Champagne method and, in certain details of their production, even more stringently controlled.

Wherever a Champagne method wine is made, however, time, skill and capital must be involved. In EEC countries and Spain the name of Champagne is strictly limited only to the wines of that region, made sparkling by the Champagne method. Even sparkling Blanquette de Limoux, which prides itself on having been sparkling before the sparkle was harnessed in Champagne, cannot use this term, except as regards the method. In the EEC the term 'Champagne' is both esteemed and respected – it is the only French wine that need not say *'Appellation contrôlée'* or state any other category on its label, the simple *'Vin de Champagne'* being enough. Elsewhere, especially in the New World, a number of wines made by the same process are called 'Champagne', legally, but not, in my opinion, rightly; using names of classic wines casually is both inaccurate and misleading – and can be unfair to the wine wrongly labelled with the name of the classic. Anyway, since 1973 even the Spaniards must not use the term 'Champagne' for any of their wines and it seems foolish that often they, producers of excellent sparkling wines, together with many others in the world, do not appreciate the reasons for precision in nomenclature.

In many EEC regions, however, the description *'Méthode Champenoise'* is cited with pride for the quality sparklers. With these and other top quality sparkling wines, the criterion is the same as for Champagne: the wine should, basically, be good – if you want to study how good, let a glass go flat and then taste the wine again. There should be a freshness and generally pleasing appearance and smell, and the *'mousse'* or bubbles should be minute, rise fast and remain rising for some time. It is extraordinary how, even when a glass of Champagne has apparently gone still, a tiny bubble may suddenly hurtle to the surface. Large bubbles, sluggish action, cessation of sparkle in a short time are all indications of an indifferent and badly made wine.

'CUVE CLOSE' OR SEALED VAT WINES, TRANSFER METHOD WINES

This method was perfected and developed commercially at the beginning of the century by a Monsieur Charmat, whose name is often used for it. Essentially, the wine goes into a large vat, sealed at the top, instead of being bottled during the fermentation period; the carbon dioxide is therefore retained in the wine while it is in the vat. The deposit drops to the bottom and, when the wine is to go into bottle, the bottling is done under pressure so that the gas does not escape.

Monsieur Charmat's original wine was Veuve du Vernay and no wine drinker needs telling how world-famous this is; the majority of inexpensive sparkling wines enjoyed today – with demand continually increasing – are made according to variations of *cuve close* method. (Do not, however, confuse the use of *'cuve close'* (sealed vat) with the word *'cuvée'* or blend of wines that is made up by the wine maker and, in Champagne, is the triumph of his art. The *cuvée* or contents of the vat is, of course, made in a *cuve* or vat.)

The advantage is that the *cuve close* method can be used to make good sparkling wines that would not benefit by the Champagne process to any extent anyway: these do not require long maturation and, by saving on the time and the skills required in the handling of the individual bottles, a great price advantage is obtained. This is the way that most non-vintage sparkling wines of more modest price than those made by the Champagne method are produced: they will not benefit by being kept, either in vat or bottle.

Most wine of this kind is in fact never given a vintage date, because it is immediately enjoyable and, indeed, will deteriorate if allowed to lose its freshness. This applies to most Asti, one of Italy's best-known sparkling wines. Asti originally presented many problems to the first makers because the high proportion of sugar in the Moscato or Muscat grape from which Asti is made, and which gives it a particularly delicious grapey smell and taste, caused fermentation to be more violent than usual; it was impossible to keep the wine in bottle because the bottles were always exploding and the loss of wine was naturally serious. Eventually, the Gancia firm, one of whose ancestors had studied in Reims and tried to make a Champagne method wine without success with the Moscato, discovered, a century after the first attempts, that it was possible to stop the fermentation in its early stages – when the alcoholic degree was only about one-third that of the eventual wine; this was done by refrigeration, the cooling of the vat causing the yeasts to stop working. The wine remains in this state until it is required, when it is allowed to begin fermenting again, completes the process, is bottled under pressure and, when about to be sold, is disgorged into a tank, from which it is rebottled, the deposit remaining behind. This version of what is elsewhere known as the 'transfer method', because of the way the wine is transferred from bottle to bottle, is used, with certain variations, for a number of wines; indeed, in the United States, a wine that is sparkling and that is labelled 'Fermented in bottle' will have been subjected to the transfer method. If it is made according to the Champagne process, the label will probably say 'Fermented in *this* bottle'.

From the foregoing, it will be seen how the natural liveliness and vivacity of certain wines, especially some of those produced in regions where the cool temperate climate provides a fair amount of natural acidity and in vineyards where the soil is light, both in colour and texture, has been cultivated and this liveliness both accentuated and harnessed within the wine. A good sparkling wine is thus a true work of art – man and nature combining to make it.

[SEVEN]

FORTIFIED WINES

The term 'fortified' requires some explanation. It means 'made stronger' and, in this context, the 'strength' is the additional alcoholic degree, which has been raised by the spirit added to the wine. In French, however, the term 'fortified' in translation is not quite the same thing; the term *'viné'*, which does mean the addition of extra alcohol, is used in a derogatory sense, to imply a wine that has been pepped up by extra alcohol. The French – one has to stress their singularity here, but they do sometimes tend to suppose that, if something doesn't exist in France, then it doesn't exist at all – use the term *'vin muté'*, which means a 'stopped' wine, the fermentation having been arrested by the introduction of spirit, or even a *'mout muté'*, a stopped must, to signify certain wines, such as the *vins doux naturels* (see p. 218), though these are not really the same as the great classic fortified wines – port, sherry, Madeira, Marsala. In this section, therefore, the classic fortified wines will be described and the less usual 'stopped wines' and others, including vermouth, treated separately.

It is relevant to mention that a fierce discussion broke out in the EEC as to the term that should be used for wines such as port and sherry, the French wishing to refer to them as *'vins de liqueur'*. The confusion in the mind of the English-speaking public throughout the world if this had been made law is fearful to contemplate! However – and it should be remembered that wines of this type are not made in France at all – the description 'fortified' is easily understood by all except the most chauvinistic Frenchman.

Yeasts cannot work if, as it were, hit on the head by alcohol. But some yeasts are stronger than others: Lionel Frumkin (*The Science and Technique of Wine*) says:

... while some yeasts may be paralysed by 5° alcohol, others may function up to 16° alcohol. For a long time ... it has been thought that natural fermentation can continue up to a maximum of 16° GL (Gay Lussac) at which strength the alcohol stops further fermentation, but recent tests have shown that some yeasts can withstand up to 18° or 19° alcohol ... The action of alcohol also depends upon the degree of evolution of the yeasts. For example, young yeasts are less resistant to alcohol than those in full activity. 15% of alcohol (added) to an actively fermenting must will prevent any start of fermentation, but if one adds 7% alcohol to an actively fermenting must containing 8% alcohol, the fermentation will not be completely stopped. It will probably continue to form another 1–1.5% alcohol.

This sums up the situation admirably. It indicates how the wines may be made. It is also worth noting why they came to be made in this way.

Alcohol provides strength – the skeleton supporting the body that is the wine. It was the little addition of brandy prior to sending out the wine of that obscure Portuguese abbey in the upper Douro, at Lamego, that made the resulting drink so delicious that some others of those in the wine trade began to adopt the same practice. They then found that even a little brandy enabled the wine to seem very much 'better' in its export markets. But the Jerezanos had known about this a long time before the Portuguese: Chaucer, in 'The Pardoner's Tale', refers to the 'white wine of Lepe' of which

> ... there ryseth suich fumositee
> That when a man hath dronken draughtes three,
> And weneth that he be at hoom in Chepe,
> He is in Spayne, right at the toune of Lepe,
> Not at the Rochell, ne at Bordeaux toun.

Chaucer, son of a vintner, was one of the first of those who have written about wine in English, and Julian Jeffs, the great authority on sherry, comments that 'it appears that wines from southern Spain were already fortified when he wrote his "Tales", and this is borne out by the knowledge that the Moors distilled alcohol and used it for medicinal purposes. Elizabethan "sack" was certainly fortified.' Arnaud de Villanova, a Catalan, who wrote the *Liber de Vinis* in about 1310, knew at least something about what he called '*aqua vine* . . . but some name it *aqua vitae*' (water of wine . . . water of life), and he may have been the first physician to note the use of alcohol as an antiseptic. So the pepping up of a wine before it underwent a journey – in cask – to some market either overseas or far overland, with all kinds of changes in climate on the way and the absence of any form of treatment on arrival (when the wine would be drawn and drunk from the cask, any bottle or carafe being merely used to bring it to table) is established quite early in the history of wine.

The production of 'port' and 'sherry' type wines in other countries today shows clearly the variations that are possible when subjecting certain wines to the 'fortifying' method. Either the wine can be allowed to ferment 'right out', all the sugar in it being converted to alcohol, any sweetening thought to be necessary being added by subsequently blending in sweet wines; or the fermentation process can be stopped at a stage decided by the wine maker, so that a certain amount of sugar remains in the wine, unconverted by the wine yeasts. Neither process, it should be noted, means that the wine is completely arrested in its development: all sorts of changes can continue to take place. These changes depend, first, on what the wine was when it started to undergo fermentation, or at least what it was intended to be: this means that the type of grapes used and, to a lesser extent, the sort of spirit, are or can be influential. A wine made from, say, Cabernet Sauvignon grapes will not be similar to a wine made from some or several of the family of 'Tintas' grapes used in port, or to one from a mixture of classic table wine grapes some used for the classic fortified wines.

Then, the method of making and, more important, of maturation, are influential. In what, how and with what additions is this stage of its progress likely to take place? A wine matured in wood and drawn off, in carefully-portioned measures, from the series of casks in *bodega* or lodge or the equivalent cannot be the same as a wine blended from the vattings (in stainless steel or concrete) of various other wines from various sources that the maker thinks might, with the added alcohol, make an acceptable fortified wine.

Nor can a wine that is simply a pepped-up must be directly compared with wines that have been carefully blended and assembled from matured wines – all these are different. It should also be remembered that, in various parts of the world, a wine made by methods that would have produced only a vaguely palatable beverage in one region can make a quality drink in another. This is all relevant to the casual use of names such as 'port' and 'sherry' for wines that, to those who know the originals, bear no resemblance to these, except in their being 'made stronger' – i.e. containing more alcohol. It is, to me, a pity that some of the great wines of the world have been so liked that those who have used the methods whereby they are made to produce wines that are good – even potentially great – have chosen and still choose to call them by the names that established the original great wines. To say 'port-style', 'sherry-type' is, I accept, an indication of the sort of wine that the drinker may expect, in that it is possible for one commodity to be similar to but not the same as another, but nowadays it is not expecting too much for the customer to differentiate between wines that are intended to be drunk as apéritifs and those that are drunk as the accompaniments to dessert or (as this term means 'the sweet course' in American English) with the fruit – dessert – for which they were traditionally intended, rather than with the pudding or ice or whatever the word tends to mean on menus today. It is significant that many of my friends in various countries where these wines have, by reason of their quality, made an impression on export as well as domestic markets do not always now make use of the old terms to attract customers. It is fair that wines should be categorized, but not that they should be produced or passed off as imitations.

SHERRY

Although in the lists of traditional wine merchants port is usually given first place, sherry certainly has precedence historically. It has been made since very early times, and when Sir Francis Drake 'singed the King of Spain's beard' and sacked Cadiz in 1587 his fleet went off with 2,900 pipes of wine that were waiting to be shipped. Julian Jeffs, QC, has, in his great work on sherry, propounded the theory that 'sack' is derived from the Spanish word *'sacar'* – to take out, i.e. to export, so that 'sherris sack', eulogized by Shakespeare's Falstaff, was the wine of Jerez destined for export, which seems to me wholly believable.

The wine is made in a delimited area around the town of Jerez de la Frontera in the south-east of Spain. A peculiarity of the vineyards is the *albariza* soil where the finest wines are made, a shiny white, glistening surface that dazzles the eyes under the sun which favours the area for much of the year. Several grapes are involved, the most famous being the Palomino, of which there are, as Mr Jeffs points out, at least two types, Basto and Fino, the latter also having various other names, including Listan, Tempranilla, Ojo de Liebra (both the latter being used elsewhere in Spain) and others. The Pedro Ximinez or Ximenez is another grape famous for the sweet wines it makes, but this is apparently now more cultivated in the Montilla-Moriles region, where a slightly different type of wine is made (see p. 203). Moscatel is another fairly important variety. When, at vintage time, the grapes are picked, it is customary to leave them out on esparto grass mats for days or even weeks; this drying in the sun slightly brings down the quantity of juice, increases the proportion of sugar and reduces the malic acid and tannin.

In former times the sherry grapes were crushed by treading, the men doing this work wearing special boots, with inclined nails in the soles so that the pips would not be broken in the process. After being trodden, the broken grape pulp would be pressed by means of a screw exerting pressure on a grass-bound mass of the solids in the *lagar* or trough where the treaders had been working. Today, however, mechanical presses do the work, at least one type being a version of a mangle, through which the grapes pass to be crushed. Very ancient presses akin to this may be seen in wine museums elsewhere. In both traditional and modern methods, the free run juice that first comes off is the most esteemed.

After the must has been pressed from the grapes, this is put into casks, ideally for most a special type of new oak, and fermentation begins within a few hours – 'tumultuous' is the description of this, because sherry yeasts are particularly vigorous. The must foams and bubbles out through the bungholes, the chuckling noise of the fermentation being surprisingly loud. In very modern installations, however, large vats are used to ferment the wine; these can, of course, be cooled by what is now the fairly usual method of having water run down the side of the vats when a thermostat releases it, should the temperature rise to around 25–30°C. This is certainly easier to control than the temperature of a number of butts, also fewer workers are required. But the ultimate destination of the wooden cask as used for making sherry is important too – for it can be prized as a container in which Scotch or Irish matures.

The young wine that is going to be sherry then undergoes a type of maturation that is somewhat complex, and those interested in following its progress in detail must be referred to Julian Jeffs's book. But, essentially and in very general terms, what happens is that the initial violent fermentation quietens down, after Christmas the wine 'falls bright', and by this time most if not all the sugar within the must will have been turned into alcohol by the action of the yeasts. By now the wine will be in the *bodega* or wine installation or store of a firm, the fermentation will slow down and, at around 12°, will almost cease to work, although it can continue until the must is around 16° but, as Julian Jeffs says, 'such strong musts tend to develop into coarse wines'. When the fermentation has completely died down, the wines receive their first fortification; this is usually after about two years.

What is important to realize is that all sherry – even the rich, dark, sweet versions of the wine that are widely promoted and enjoyed – begins by being a 'fully fermented wine', that is, a wine in which all the sugar in the must has been converted into alcohol by the process of fermentation. It is therefore *dry*, and anyone who visits a sherry *bodega* and is able to taste a minute quantity of wine from a butt that will form part of the most precious foundations of the whole establishment may find this wine, the colour of black treacle and almost of the same consistency, impossible to drink – it is dry, wholly dry, of a dryness that stuns the palate and rasps the tongue. A single such butt will be the basis of a great sherry in the *solera* system – which is why the owner of one *bodega* once told me that, should all his stocks go up in smoke (and the fire risk of a big *bodega* is something horrific to contemplate, both in terms of risk and insurance costs), it would still be possible to evolve a great sherry should one single butt of an 'undrinkable' reserve of this type be left to use.

The *solera* system, by which fine sherry is made, is definitely complex and space cannot permit an account of it in detail here. Essentially, the wines are admitted into a firm's *bodega*, where, as young wines, they will be sorted out and allocated to various maturation stations. The *solera* is at once both the specific part of the *bodega* in which wines are stored and the system by which a wine emerges as the result of blending from wine within that. There are 'straight *solera*' wines, which will come from the same vineyards and not go into any other part of the *bodega*, spending their lives contributing to a single great sherry, such as San Patricio, Tio Pepe, Tres Palmas and so on. They are, as it were, like pupils of a school, all dominated by the same educational system. Then there are the wines that do go into the *solera* of a firm, but which will be used in conjunction with the wines coming from other sources – as it were, the pupils of other masters, less regulated by the one single tradition. There are also the wines that are made up by blending from one *solera* and another – these may still be excellent.

A *solera* – the term is also used in association with the production of both Madeira and Marsala – is a collection of casks, stacked one upon another, in a cool section of a *bodega*. Not for nothing are such places referred to as 'cathedrals', because the columns that support the high roofs (for coolness) and the vistas of casks give the impression of aisles; the freshness of the atmosphere, which is carefully preserved by blinds over the windows high up in the walls, the quiet and the somewhat dim light, are both calming and vaguely religious.

In the *solera* there may be several tiers or rows of stacked casks, and one of the most usual misconceptions as regards the *solera* system is to suppose that, in making up a blend or 'mark' of sherry, the wines that have been put into the casks are drawn off from the top row or tier and, eventually, progress to the one underneath and eventually to the bottom. This is not so. The arrangement of the casks and the way in which the different butts are drawn on to provide the wines to compose a particular sherry is entirely up to the wine maker of the establishment. The casks from which wine is drawn are, of course, topped up – but the wines with which they are filled up may come from the more recent consignments or from other wines in the *solera*.

A 'straight *solera*' wine will come only from the one *solera* – the single system of casks. It will be made up from the contributions of various casks within that *solera* and continue the style of a particular 'mark' of whatever sherry is required. Some of the great sherries have made history – and delighted many generations of drinkers.

There are also the requirements of various merchants, who want a particular type of wine composed for them – and this, according to price and agreements between merchant and shipper, may be either a slightly varied version of a straight *solera* (which will naturally be an expensive wine) or a blend of wines from the others that the shipper holds in his *bodega*.

All sherry, it should be remembered, is a wine to which brandy is added – to 'make it strong'. The wine usually gets its first dose of brandy when it is about six months old and, when a delicate wine is about to be shipped, there may be another strengthening dose of spirit then. But it is a wine above the strength of table wine in terms of alcohol. If anyone visits the region, the half bottles of sherry that punctuate the table at lunch or dinner will be only very slightly upped in strength – which makes the term '*vino de pasto*' (table wine or wine with food) acceptable; it should, however, be noted that the visitor may arrive in the hot weather. The dry, warm climate may make it quite easy for the relaxed diner to take several glasses of *vino de pasto* during a meal – the 'Spanish strength' alcoholic content will be somewhat sweated out and the amount drunk by someone on holiday may not prevent them from being wholly alert, especially after the customary siesta.

What is curious and significant about sherry, however, is the way in which the different wines that arrive in the *bodegas* are sorted out, because of the way they develop. In certain wines –

remember, these are fully fermented and therefore dry – there may develop a curious film, called *'flor'*, on the surface. This odd thing, Julian Jeffs says, is 'a deadly enemy of the *mycodemia aceti* or vinegar *flor*, and if any particles of vinegar *flor* fall into the butt of sherry, the two yeasts fight for existence and the stronger wins'. *Flor*, which means flower or 'the veil', is what may develop on the top of a sherry in cask. (It may, incidentally, grow on the top of a wine left in bottle – not necessarily making this better to drink, but it can be interesting to view.)

Flor on a wine makes the wine underneath it different – this will become a *fino* sherry. If *flor* doesn't develop, then the wine will become an *oloroso* – not, it should be noted, necessarily a sweet wine. In recent times it appears that at least some forms of *flor* can be implanted, but I do not know whether these wines are wholly successful. *Amontillado* sherry is a matured *fino*.

These are the basics. The shades of flavour and style imparted by the drawing of wines from a *solera* and the subsequent blending are virtually infinite, and there are many sherries sold as *'amontillado'* or 'medium' that have been the produce of blending, rather than ageing. This of course enables even more variations to be made at slightly lower cost.

The sweeter sherries – which, it should be noted, were originally made to cater specifically for the taste of northern (chilly) export markets – are made by blending in sweeter wines after the basic wine is made. The sweet wines used are, according to Julian Jeffs, of five styles, each different; the two that may be known best are Pedro Ximenez and Moscatel. These are almost liquorous in texture and intensity. As well as the incorporation of sweetness by the blending in of these wines – none of which is cheap, all of which are subject to controls – certain sherries require *'vino de color'*, itself requiring careful production and use, so as to achieve the depth of tone and rich colour that can be so attractive.

These sweet sherries, because of their sugar content, are able to withstand ageing, so that as 'old bottled sherry' some of them can be most impressive when available; they are unlikely to be cheap if truly aged sweet wines of this sort, although a sweet sherry type of wine can of course be made by blending in sweet wines with others.

There are several other styles of sherry that should be mentioned. A *manzanilla* is a wine that comes from the seaside town of Sanlucar de Barrameda, and it is reputed to have a 'salty' smell and flavour; the name seems to derive from the Spanish word for 'camomile'. The description Julian Jeffs gives as 'the wine of joy' is apt – it is a very delicate, crisp wine, but, which is not often realized, it can change if it is moved to Jerez from Sanlucar, when it becomes a *fino*! It is also within the range of *manzanilla* to be not merely a *manzanilla fino*, but also an *amontillado* and *oloroso*. But it is perhaps essential for the taster to register this style of wine on the spot – because, as will be seen, it is not necessarily the same when drunk on export markets.

The various other names and styles of sherry are numerous – *amoroso*, milk, cream (the latter two being very sweet), and the wines for individual merchants being blended so as to meet the requirements of their particular customers. Customers sometimes have odd notions as to what a wine will taste like, forming opinions from its name and the colour or label, not honestly from the wine itself.

It is worth noting here that, on one special occasion when the wines served came from Avery's of Bristol, I found myself among several people, including various self-styled 'experts' and at least one wine writer, when a dinner was prefaced by a tasting of certain sherries. It so happens that I find sherry not to agree with me very much these days and therefore I was not drinking at this stage; the comments of those sipping the apéritif wines, however, were so astonishing that I had to listen. 'So sweet', 'So full', 'Not at all the dry type ...' They were talking about a set of wines offered before a dinner. I was interested, I sniffed – 'Do you *really* find this "sweet"?' and eventually I went up to the tasting table and sampled all the sherry presented. There was certainly nothing 'sweet' about the great dry *olorosos* that my neighbours had been trying. They were moderately dark in tone but not especially so. There was one that, as John Avery himself said, would have been a rare and prized find even in Jerez itself. The idiotic thing was that this was so very *dry* that the tasters simply didn't like it. Therefore they condemned it as 'sweet' merely because, supposing themselves to know so much that they expected a preprandial drink to be 'dry', they were totally misled by a deep-toned wine that was indeed *absolutely* dry, assertively so (unlike any other *oloroso* I have ever tried), but it was also so full, definite and generally – to them – unattractive that they couldn't begin to like it. None had either the sense, the humility or the knowledge to say that it was too obvious and too big a wine to enjoy *easily*, which was true – what they really would have liked was a medium to slightly sweet sherry, possibly with a pale colour and maybe a name incorporating the word 'dry'. The quality and power behind these wines was overwhelming. But, whether you like a wine or not, you should take care not to confuse fullness with sweetness.

Thus, whereas there are *finos* and *amontillados* in one branch of the sherry 'family' and *olorosos* (developing from the wines that do not grow *flor*) in another, there are truly only ramifications within these two main styles, plus the very sweet wines (used for sweetening purposes, which would rarely be enjoyed by themselves). There is, however, as will have been noted, a huge range of variations within these categories. For example, although a true *amontillado* is a matured *fino*, this type of wine, beautiful in its amber tones and with a wonderful fragrance and flavour, simply cannot be cheap; cheap *amontillados* therefore are made by blending. The wine that has progressed through one single *solera*, where its ancestors lived and to which only the produce of one set of vineyards has contributed, will also be somewhat expensive so, for cheaper versions from the particular establishment, blending will be done. As has been indicated, few people truly like the bone dry character of a *fino* – even in Jerez this is a wine that is not always the inevitable choice – and so some softening is usually added to these wines to meet popular taste; a well-known maxim of a highly successful sherry shipper used to be 'For the British market, call it dry and make it sweet.' A large number of the sherries categorized by their names involving the word 'dry', or sorted out in lists as 'dry', are actually sweetened up to the permitted limits. It should be noted that this process, like others, is subject to controls, but you have only to compare one well-known brand of 'dry' sherry with another within the same price range to see how different they can be.

With *olorosos* likewise the general assumption is that these – which will be deep in colour, something usually associated with sweetness – are 'medium' sherries, in other words, medium dry or medium sweet, although a real *oloroso* is a fully fermented and bone dry wine. The rich 'milk' and 'cream' wines are also sweetened and these, which are virtually unknown in Spain, have been specially created for export markets, where their silky style and warmth is much liked, especially in cold climates.

Palo Cortado, an unusual and rather special sherry, is a deep-toned wine, which in fact is very dry and has grown little or no *flor*.

Sherry changes somewhat in bottle. The most delicate wines slightly lose their crisp, fresh character; not only would the true sherry devotee prefer to sip *fino* or *manzanilla* from the butt if possible, but even the exposure to air of a wine left in opened bottle or decanter for a few hours will, to the sensitive nose, cause a decline in bouquet and taste. With the very sweet wines, the sugar preserves them, so that very old bottled sherries can be remarkable – concentrated, velvety and impressive.

There is no such thing as 'vintage' sherry, and the dates marked on some butts or in some *bodegas* will refer to the year in which the *solera* was laid down. The blend of wines, made up from a number, will be so as to 'follow a mark' for the customer, who will expect both colour and style to be similar to the previous consignment. Usually, shipments of sherry are made in bulk, then bottled wherever they are going to be sold, but nowadays some Spanish-bottled sherries are seen on export markets. In order to protect the wine against the hazards of travel, some slight extra fortification is given, which is why sherry bottled in an export market does not go cloudy or even throw a little deposit, which a Spanish-bottled wine may do – and which uninformed customers find cause for complaint. But it must be realized that all sherry is and must be fortified – the term *'vino de pasto'* (table wine) which many bear on their labels merely signifies that, in the Jerez region, this wine indeed will be drunk with food. According to the particular wine, the amount of fortification varies, just as it does when the wine is first fortified.

It will be understood that the 'sherry method' is potentially subject to far more variation than, for example, the Champagne method. Wines made to resemble sherry are, therefore, more varied too. Some are made in a *solera*, some simply blended. The grapes used may of course be very different and the effect of the different climates in which sherry-style wines are made is equally influential. In Cyprus the wineries making this type of wine store certain of their vast stocks in compounds out in the open – the aeration and proximity to the sea contribute to the wine, just as the sea air is said to do to the *bodegas* in Sanlucar de Barremeda, where *manzanilla* is produced. In South Africa, however, the butts of wine remain under cover – the heat would be too great for them to be exposed out of doors. But in Cyprus and at the Cape, the use of air conditioning in the *'bodegas'* where the most delicate wines, made with *flor* on them, are stored has made it possible to make quality sherry-style wines as never before.

The production of sherry-style wines in certain wineries in both California and Australia is often done in installations making a wide range of other sorts of wine as well – table and fortified – something that surprises anyone familiar with the Jerez region. Sometimes the wines are matured for a considerable time, sometimes not, although the presence of the strong sherry yeasts is often a feature: in a winery in Coonawarra, one of the strangest regions making fine table wines in Australia, I was recently shown a cask with a glass head, so that visitors can view the ebb and increase of the *flor* on the surface of the wine made there.

The tremendous progress achieved in the knowledge of what yeast is and the evolution of different strains has made it easier both to make even finer wines in the sherry region and for fine wines originally inspired by sherry to be made elsewhere. This can be illustrated from the time when I was comparing several 'sherries' from Cyprus and other regions and admitted some disappointment as to the bouquet and flavour of one I had previously regarded as extremely good. (In fact, a Cyprus *fino* from another source topped the tasting!) It so happened that, within a few weeks of mentioning this to the London source of supply, I visited Cyprus and talked with the head of the winery producing this example. I stressed that there was nothing bad about this particular sherry-style wine – it was just not as good as I had expected from knowing it quite well in the past. The wine maker looked up the records – and discovered that, for the particular consignment from which my sample had been taken, a different strain of yeast had been used, for various good reasons. But it had not, in my view, made as delightful a wine, though a perfectly adequate one. The winning Cyprus wine used an island *flor* – but, admittedly, it was an expensive bottle.

It will certainly be possible to note differences in flavour between 'sherry' made from grapes other than those used in the Jerez region and true sherry, because, in an odd way, the Palomino grape endows the wines it makes with a curious refinement and crispness that are frequently lacking in other sherry-style wines. The possible give-away, as far as I am concerned, is that even dry wines made in the sherry way but not coming from the sherry region tend sometimes to have a raisiny, fat, fruity character, unlike the very light, crisp, piercing dryness of a first-rate *fino*.

You may be able to distinguish 'the real thing' when comparing *fino* and *amontillado*-style wines, simply because the dryness means that the palate is not blurred by any sweetening and the grapes' character comes through more apparently. It is fair to say that, among the sweet wines, it is not always easy to note an appreciable difference between the sherry-style wines of some countries other than Spain if these are made utilizing the Palomino and other basic sherry grapes and are matured in the same way; many people might prefer a fine South African or Australian 'sherry' rather than an indifferent Spanish version when choosing in this category.

Nor should it be forgotten that some world-famous sherries are not or have not always been made in one single *bodega*: one great sherry establishment provided the wine that, years ago, made a best-selling and now world-renowned sweet sherry for another equally famous firm. In one comparative tasting that I have done of the sweet versions of this wine the quality was remarkable and evocative; but the establishment named on the label of this top brand now either buys elsewhere or makes its own 'X Cream'.

In this section the wines of Montilla or Montilla-Moriles must be included. This region, near to but separate from the sherry region, was, until 1933 when the sherry area was defined, producing wines either used in sherry or being sold as sherry. Today, this is changed. Montilla is Montilla. But it is somewhat hard on the makers that the term *'amontillado'* which first began to be used because it was the wines of Montilla that evoked the typical flavour of a matured *fino*, cannot now by law be applied to the wines at all!

The dominant grape of Montilla is the Pedro Ximenez, and in the vineyards there is plenty of the shiny white chalk soil, known here as *albera*. The wines are first made in huge Ali-Baba-like jars, called *'tinajas'*, just as they would have been in Roman times. Although in the more modern *bodegas* their place has been taken by vats, they are still very much in use, their loosely-fitting lids allowing the carbon dioxide gas to escape, after which the wines may either be matured in a *solera* system, or else sold to other *bodegas* for maturation. The important thing about Montilla wines is that they naturally achieve a higher degree of alcohol without any fortification or added spirit; this makes them very agreeable, easy drinks. *Flor* appears on the surface of the finer wines.

It is fair to say that any wine of quality, made even vaguely according to the system whereby sherry is produced, is at least an interesting drink and may be a worthwhile one. What is essential, for anybody fortunate enough to be able to compare true sherry with any of the other wines made according to at least some of the processes, because of sherry's original popularity, is for the drinker only to assess like against like – a cheap, blended, so-called 'dry' sherry cannot and should not be appraised by the side of the product of a single *solera*; apart from anything else, if you pay twice as much for a particular bottle, there is usually some reason why – if only the cost of the original wines or even the grapes making the ultimate product.

The comparison of the top 'sherry' wines from the various other vineyards of the world can be most interesting: if you can do this, put in an equal wine from Jerez as a 'marker', selecting according to category – *fino*, *amontillado*, *oloroso* and so on. The 'real thing' will not lose by the comparison, but the difference between wines from different countries made because of the classic wine's popularity and according to an approximately similar process can be helpfully registered.

It is also of great use to the student to compare brand against brand – both those made famous by advertising and those specially prepared for reputable wine merchants of all types. If you do this, try to buy all the wines, especially the *finos*, when they are as fresh as possible; of course, you are not to know when they may have arrived in the shop, but it is at least fairer to compare several purchased at one time and at least possibly having had approximately the same shelf life than it is to put in wines that you may have had in your home for many months. It is also wise never to base your like or dislike of one brand on just the single experience: sometimes, for various good reasons, the blend of a brand may be slightly altered and the result be more to your liking or less (see pp. 201–2).

The majority of the great Spanish *bodegas* contribute wines to certain special blends and brands and in, for example, any expensive sherry there will certainly be some very fine and maybe some very old wine. Trying several side by side can show you why one justifies a higher price than another. Trying wines made from totally different grapes but in rough accordance with the sherry procedure will show why some of them have achieved world popularity – and perhaps incline the taster to my opinion that the use of words in any way suggesting that 'sherry' itself is involved is a mistake. In Cyprus, for example, one of the very best wines, made from *flor* native to the island, is simply called 'KEO Fino', using the name of the winery and style of the wine. The same sort of thing happens in South Africa – brand names, without inclusion of the word 'sherry', are nowadays on many of the labels, although such wines do get listed in the 'sherry' section of most wine lists.

The law, however, requires that in the EEC any wine labelled 'sherry' must have the country of its origin clearly stated before the word, in the same sized type. So no one should be misled by any labelling – and it is silly to pour off a fortified wine made originally to provide the same pleasure as sherry but now meriting appraisal in its own right into a decanter and attempt to 'pass it off' as 'the real thing'. Any price advantage is far less these days than at one time and there are cheap and expensive sherries, cheap and expensive sherry-style wines. Try all!

PORT

Port is the other great fortified wine, which has held its popularity for several centuries with the northern European countries. It may astonish some to learn that this, 'the Englishman's wine' as it has been called, is drunk in larger quantities in France than in the UK; *'Un peu de porto'* is a frequent apéritif there!

Port is made in a defined region of the upper Douro Valley – the 'river of gold' – in north Portugal, very wild, savage country where one would have thought it almost impossible to grow anything on the granite chips that make up the vineyards. How our ancestors went there, arranged to make wine and continued to do so, often with a mere handshake between themselves and the peasant farmers providing a 'contract' lasting many generations until the present, is extraordinary – and port is an extraordinary wine.

A large number of different grapes can be used for making it, although today the finer ports are tending to utilize only a few of those that have proved to supply quality; fewer white grapes go into the finer red wines and although it is not necessary to believe, with one great shipper of former times, that 'the first duty of port wine is to be red', there is far more red than white wine made. Among the black grapes are several each having the prefix 'Tinta', and it is the Tinta Francisca that is thought to be the Pinot Noir, imported centuries ago to Portugal. The Roriz, Mourisco, Touriga, Bastardo, Sousão, Periquita, and, with the white grapes, various of the Moscatel, Malvasia families, plus the Donzelinho (used in a black form as well), Rabigato, Folgosão, Esgana-Cão, are only a few – most of them peculiar to port making and not often found anywhere else.

The traditional vineyards are terraced, but the maintenance of the earth-retaining walls (originally built in many instances by imported labourers from Galicia) is costly today and machines cannot easily work these vineyards. Sloping contours have been cultivated and today there are experiments with vineyards that can be worked almost wholly by machines which deal with each stage of the vine's progress up to and including picking.

Hand-picking, however, is still usual. Bands of workers arrive at each *quinta*, led by musicians – mostly including an accordionist, a drummer and some odd and primitive instruments (a *quinta* is Portuguese for a farm and here has the significance of an estate or single property). The musicians are important: the accordionist usually gets a higher rate, for he will keep playing during the treading, throughout the night. At the end of the vintage, the workers parade dancing up to the owner's or manager's house, bearing garlands; sweets, cigarettes and money are distributed, everyone rejoices and jokes and comments are exchanged, before the bands dance away – until next year.

The grapes, transferred from small baskets to huge ones, are loaded on lorries and taken to the winery. Nowadays the loads then go into the huge recipients so often seen just outside all wineries, usually across from the weighing machines where the loads of fruit are recorded, so that the farmers can be paid. Then the grapes proceed, by means of a continuous screw, into what is a series of platforms; the fruit is whirled round so that the grapes are broken up but the pips are not split. It is possible to regulate whether or not the stems go on with the grapes at this stage – in some years their tannin content would be too high and unbalance the ultimate wine, so they can be taken out.

Although some of the great port firms own vineyards, several of them now making wines from their own *quintas*, the bulk of port is made from either grapes or wine bought in from the Douro farmers. Traditionally, the grapes are put into a *'lagar'* or stone trough, which is then trodden by teams of men, working in shifts, to break down the hard-skinned grapes and render the pulp partly liquid; the thick layer of skins and pips makes a very firm 'hat' or *'manta'*. This, when the must begins to ferment, is pushed down by wooden paddles, the workers standing on planks bridging the *lagar*. Today, this circulation of the solids within the must is sometimes done by pumping, the individual maker deciding whether the pump should move the wine from below or by spraying it on the top and dunking the hat.

The modern method of making port, however, and one which takes fewer labourers and can continue, unsupervised if need be, through the night and until the fermentation is complete, is to circulate the must in a device called an autovinificator. This, by utilizing the gas given off as the fermentation proceeds, forces the must down and then up through a tube giving on to the top of the tanks; the tank 'blows' like a whale, the must whirls back into the autovinificator, deluging the *manta*, and then the whole thing begins again.

The above is a very general account of both the traditional and modern methods of first making the wine, but there are many variations from farm to farm and firm to firm. Some firms rake the must as it languidly circulates above the autovinificator, before falling back into the tank; others leave it alone. Some ports are made from 'trodden' wines as well as those made by autovinification, others only by one or other method. One eminent shipper related how he and his brother had gently to accustom their father to the possibilities of using the autovinificator – 'And how we were so nervous when the first tastings were held side by side with the traditionally made wines! But my father and his brothers and colleagues had to admit that the difference was not such as to affect the ultimate style and quality.' Another great buyer for a world-famous firm said that he wouldn't accept any wines except those traditionally made – trodden. 'But,' he added, 'old Farmer X, from whose family we've been buying for two hundred years, decided he wanted to get a small autovinificator a couple of years ago (rather a status symbol) and we couldn't stop buying from him, although, frankly, I don't think he uses it for all his wine and he supplies such a small amount anyway that we don't think it's made any change.'

At this stage, of course, the wine or, rather, the fermenting must, is much as ordinary table wine might be, although anyone used to looking at wines at this stage will note the depth of colour and, if sipping the must, its power and toughness. From the early stages of fermentation the wine maker will be watching the rate at which the alcoholic degree rises and the sugar declines. At a determined moment the must will be directed to flow from the fermentation vat, *lagar* or tank, into another vat where the *aguardente* or spirit – supplied by the Portuguese Government authorities – is then added. This arrests the work of the ferments and sugar not converted into alcohol remains in the wine. George Robertson, in his excellent book *Port* (Faber), expresses it as follows: 'If the original grape sugar is 14 per cent and the fermenting must is drawn off when it has reached 6 per cent, 8 per cent will be left in sugar. An easy formula to remember is "The earlier the fermentation is arrested, the sweeter the port".'

It is perhaps important to differentiate between *aguardente* (in Portuguese 'burning water') and another spirit, called Bagaçeira. The *aguardente* is distilled from wines that may be made in the Douro region or the south of Portugal, under Government control. This spirit – which I do not think anyone would like to drink – has caused some interesting events in the port trade from time to time. If, for various reasons, it has been in short supply in the past, other spirits have then had to be used to arrest the fermentation; the most famous instance of this occurred in 1904, when there was very little Portuguese spirit available at all and firms sent far and wide to obtain some. One used spirit from the Azores, another is reported to have rushed supplies down from Cognac, another even to have used Scotch! But the 1904 vintage was a great year and the varied spirits involved did not, apparently, affect the wine when it was matured. The subject cropped up again more recently, when, in Germany, an appliance used for dating archaeological items upset many purists when it revealed that apparently grape spirit (distilled from wine) had not been used for certain ports. As this device, which detects the ages of the findings of 'digs' by a process known as 'Carbon 14', first indicated that the ports submitted to testing were hundreds of years old, the situation had to be further investigated and then it was suggested that mere 'alcohol' had been used. However, with neither the 1904 or more recent ports have any of those qualified to pronounce admitted (even in confidence) that the use of this type of spirit was deleterious.

Bagaçeira, however, is the squeezing or final pressings of all the debris left after the wine has been made. It is, as George Robertson comments, 'a type of *marc*'; it can be matured in wood and be an acceptable postprandial drink.

Once the port has been made, it goes down to Vila Nova de Gaia, the *entreposto* opposite Oporto, where it is received into the lodges of the shippers. The few wines that remain up country, sometimes spending all their lives in casks, are, eventually, quite different from those finished down river: they display what Ben Howkins, in his book on port, *Rich, Rare and Red* (Heinemann), describes as the 'Douro bake, or "burn" ', a shade of difference that is nevertheless marked. The wine is delicious when you taste it on the spot and some of the finer examples can be enjoyed even further afield, but it isn't 'port port' as we usually know it. Indeed, the difference is worth knowing about, even if it is not possible often to try the wine, because this is exactly the sort of thing that can demonstrate how a different environment can change a wine during the process of maturation; this can happen with wines made with the same grapes and in the same way, but in a different vineyard and 'finished' in different circumstances. It can never be quite the same as certain of the classics – and may not be any the worse for that. But it will be *different*.

The various types of port are, of course, varied between shipper and shipper. The house style of each great establishment is distinctive. It is even possible to attempt – if one is a privileged visitor – to differentiate between a trodden port and an autovinificated port, both wines only just having been made. On the occasion when I did this the wines had come from adjacent plots on the same estate. (It was somewhat similar to another experience when I was given to compare a hand-picked and a machine-harvested table wine in Australia.) The trodden port, at this outset of its life, was deeper in tone, less aromatic, more reserved, less obviously attractive and promising – but with the implication of terrific 'push' and force behind it. The ultimate wine, or wines, however, need not have shown this obviously – the processes of maturation alter a wine's character, just as education and experience alter that of a person, but it is possible for two people brought up in different environments and in different ways to be, both of them, similar in character and qualities when they are mature.

All port, except for vintage port, spends its life in cask – the huge wooden pipes of the lodges. It is very bad manners for anyone walking through a lodge as a visitor to tap or bang on the head of a pipe – this can reveal, to the experienced ear, whether or not the cask is full and, therefore, give an idea as to the reserves of the establishment! (The note sounded is different according to whether the cask is full or empty.)

At the outset of its progress, port (except for white port) is dark red. It will become lighter with age. The pipes in a lodge contribute to the ultimate blend and the blends of the establishment and each type of port has a part to play to please the drinker. Ruby port, which is a young or youngish wine, is intended for anytime refreshment, though the finer examples can certainly be served for after-dinner drinking.

Tawny port, however, the wine that the shippers drink themselves and share with privileged visitors, is essentially matured ruby port – but it depends on the wines that make up the blend of this, even more than with the rubies, as to its ultimate quality. I have written elsewhere that a fine old tawny is the triumph of the port maker's art – the beautiful colour, glorious fragrance and delicate but fascinating set of flavours that delight the palate are entrancing. A 'fine old' tawny, costing a lot of money, with a famous name, is a remarkable wine; a good ordinary tawny, with some matured wines in it, with the label of a reputable firm on it, is capable of giving much pleasure; a cheap tawny, which may have been made by blending ruby and white port, or some tawnies rejected for the finer blends, is at best adequately enjoyable wine. You pays your money . . . In both these categories the price of the wines in the blend reflects the quality the drinker can expect. Many people suppose vintage port to be the supreme port wine – but, although this is the child both of nature and the wine makers and always of great interest, I will venture to say that it is the finest old tawnies that have probably given me more perfect pleasure than all but the most superb vintage ports of outstanding years.

Vintage port is the wine of a single year. It is up to the individual firm and wine maker whether a particular year's wines merit being 'declared' as a vintage; in some years the majority of shippers declare, in other years only a few will do so. It must, of course, depend on stocks and what the firm's policy is as regards exports. At the time of writing, one great establishment has not declared the 1980s, I suppose because they wish to put the finer wines of this year into the great blends with which they hope to extend the demand for these in markets such as those of the US, where vintage ports cannot rely on being kept and served with the care essential to their performance. In some years a firm may, because of the sources of supply from which their wines come, prefer not to declare a vintage but to consolidate their stocks, which must be maintained so that the more everyday wines can be sold to established customers and markets.

The declaration of a vintage comes after 'two winters and a summer'. The wine is put aside and, usually after two years, goes into bottle. This is quite different from the bottlings of the rubies and tawnies, which are done when the shipments are required, from wines matured in cask, bottled from the blends of various pipes. The vintage ports spend most of their life, therefore, in bottle rather than in wood and, in recent years, they are bottled in Gaia; formerly, they would be shipped in bulk to be bottled in export markets, either by the shipper at his headquarters there, or else by such wine merchants to whom a proportion of the shipment might be sold. It is still a matter of debate as to whether Portuguese bottlings are in any appreciable way 'different' from those done in, say, Britain (the chief export market) for vintage port, but it is certainly possible that a difference might be distinguished between a vintage port bottled by a shipper conversant with the wine and well equipped to handle it, or a merchant who might have received his consignment after some delay and had to hasten to bottle, or a firm famous for the quality of its bottlings and very experienced, or another trying out what might be a tricky wine at not exactly an ideal time . . . All these factors have made a difference, even to this fairly robust wine, and 'D & Co.'s bottling' might, in former times, have been esteemed above that of 'Y and Co.'. But, with a precious and perishable commodity such as vintage port, it is probably fair to say that today few ordinary firms have the resources to handle quantities of it or to put right anything that may seem amiss, so the saving by having it bottled at source does anyway ensure a continuity of basic style.

Because it spends its life in bottle, vintage port throws a 'crust', as the special type of deposit in this wine is called. If the bottle is allowed to lie quiet, in a suitable place – and Gaia, built on granite and certainly as cold and wet for part of the year as any place in Britain, is in many ways as suitable as a 'damp bond' or wet cellar elsewhere – then this crust will form firmly and, after three to five years (depending on the character of the vintage) the wine can be moved and the deposit even shaken up; it is likely to settle and reform again after a few days or weeks if the wine is carefully cellared. Disturbance in the early stages is, however, not good: the deposit never seems to settle properly again and the particles can remain in suspension in the wine, when not even the most careful handling can get them out, so that the beautiful colour of the wine is never able to delight the eye.

The length of time a vintage port should be left before drinking naturally depends on the particular vintage. Generally, it is said that no decent vintage is worth drinking before it is ten years old and, ideally, shouldn't be broached before it is at least twenty years from its vintage. 'Light' vintages do come on faster than more classic years, but the reason why port is the wine traditionally laid down for the newly-born is because twenty or twenty-one years are often the ideal time to broach this great wine. But ports can live for much longer so that, when buying, it is necessary to remember that a vintage older in date may nevertheless be younger in character and vice versa, so that you may drink a younger vintage port and keep an older one still in the cellar.

The wine 'feeds' on its crust and very old vintage ports may have eaten up most of their deposit. Also, in former times, bottles were 'shot' or pitted inside so that the deposit could cling to this, whereas now it slides about on the smoother interior. So too close comparisons between the great vintage ports praised by past writers and those available today cannot be quite fair: the wines may, however, be handled with the same respect.

Several other types of port are now being sold, of which perhaps the most significant is 'late bottled vintage' – LBV. This is port of a single year, but it will have remained in cask (wood) for between four and six years prior to being bottled. When the wine is drawn off to be bottled the lees will be left behind, therefore the port does not throw a deposit. This makes it suitable for anyone wanting to serve a fine port but not able, for reasons of time or simply lack of decanting skill, to decant it. This type of port can be very fine. Quinta do Noval, one of whose previous owners, Luis Porto, pioneered the style because he realized that people living in flats, with no staff, simply couldn't cope with serving vintage port on many occasions, have always made a very aristocratic version of this wine and there are now many others.

Sometimes people are surprised that port makes an impression of dryness rather than sweetness. It is probably general to say that, as one great port shipper informed me, the ports made today are 2°–3° less sweet than those made prior to 1939; this would be difficult to determine solely by tasting, but it is true that, these days, it is the delicacy, finesse and shades of flavour that appeal to drinkers of good port more than anything else, not just the force behind the wine. The consciousness of diet, the availability of central and other methods of house heating and the huge range of sweet foodstuffs have inclined drinkers to prefer drier ports. It is possible that ports made slightly drier than those of the beginning of the century will not have such long lives, because sugar acts as a preservative, but they may do so and, for those who drink them in their prime, they are certainly able to provide as much pleasure as any made in the past.

White Port

This wine, usually much enjoyed by visitors to Portugal and appreciated by many export markets except those dominated by sherry (such as the UK), is a wine varied by quality rather than method. It is made, as port is made, from the grapes grown within the Douro region and is subject to controls. It is made from white grapes but, according to the maker and the style of wine wished for, the fermentation is either arrested late or, even, the spirit is added after fermentation is complete so as to make the white ports of a certain type virtually 'fully fermented' wines – in other words, truly dry. Until fairly recently, white port was supposed to be somewhat sweet and some of the medium-priced wines of many establishments are at least medium-sweet. But some finer white ports are definitely dry, fresh, full – because of the grapes and the vineyards that make them – but hardly more than that. So, when buying, it is worth noting both the shipper and the price, because the drier wines will be more expensive and, for apéritifs, more suitable.

Wines made according to the port processes vary enormously. Essentially, it is the stopping of the fermentation that establishes the style of port. The other wines that port has inspired throughout the wine world – because it is something so outstanding in its quality and appeal – are not necessarily made in the same way, except in so far as the stopping of the fermentation is involved. Some certainly ferment right out, having their fortification afterwards, others are stopped before this stage; if some of the classic table wine grapes, such as the Cabernet Sauvignon, are involved, it seems to me that there could be a lack of balance if the fermentation were allowed to finish as usual and the spirit were then added.

There are most interesting wines made, especially in Australia, by leaving the 'port' in cask, as might happen in the Douro on a farm, only bottling it when it is required for sale. At least one excellent New Zealand 'port' came into being because the wine maker was experimenting with small quantities of wines, finishing them according to certain classic procedures; I remember this because, just after my New Zealand hosts had welcomed me there and I, on my return, had stated in print that I did not know whether a wine fortified in a way similar to port existed there – this one was produced! It was and is extremely good. It had been left to mature and been forgotten, until one day it was discovered. There are others.

In South Africa several port-style wines are made, and these probably benefit from the dry heat of the vineyards and the high quality of the spirit that is added. One famous estate, Allesverloren, uses one of the port grapes – Tinta Baroccas – to make a table wine as well, and a huge, husky red this is, but they also make a fine port-style wine, with a gentle, fiery, lingering character that is memorable. California also makes port-type wines, although as yet these tend to be somewhat indeterminate in style – the place of a port in the US social pattern is not yet settled. If I were to be asked to drink this style of wine in Australia, I think I might opt for the rich old Muscats, which are remarkable and seem particularly acceptable in the dry heat of many of the wine regions, but it will be understood that the maturing of true port in the wet, granite-founded lodges of Gaia or the humidity of a 'wet bond' in the UK must result in a wine that is different from one aged in even an air-conditioned winery or a below-ground 'cellar' in a region that is dry even when it is not very hot. The grapes, the spirit and the time of ageing in wood – and the wood itself – all affect the end product.

It seems a pity that there is no alternative to the word 'port' to describe this wonderful wine's progeny in the world's vineyards. But no one should pass by the chance to taste any relations of the wine of the Douro. These will usually reward the drinker.

MADEIRA

This wine, made solely on the island of Madeira, is produced by a method that incorporates certain stages of the *solera* system and, like sherry, very few Madeira wines are now sold bearing the date of a specific vintage, any date usually referring, these days, to when the *solera* was first laid down. The main grapes are Sercial, Verdelho, Bual or Boal, Malmsey, in ascending order of sweetness, and usually the wines are made from a single variety. The Malmsey vine is one of the oldest in the world, probably originating in Greece, and, as Monemvasia, still making wines in various Medi-terranean vineyards. The Verdelho grape is one that is occasionally used elsewhere too: I recently tasted a good table wine made from it, coming from Sicily; the odd 'maderized' bouquet, plus the curi-ous hazelnut fragrance associated with Madeiras made from the Verdelho, was quite evident in this 'Verdello'.

The fermentation is arrested by the addition of brandy, but this fortification varies according to the type of wine being made: with the drier wines, such as the first two named, it is slowed rather than stopped; with the sweeter wines the brandy arrests it and the wine is luscious as a result. Originally Madeira wines were exported without the addition of brandy, but its use was becoming usual by the middle of the eighteenth century. The circumstance of the casks of wine being used for ballast for ships making – by sail – the long voyages to and from the Far East revealed that wines subjected to this slow heating and slow cooling, as the ships passed through the tropics and later returned, were rendered very much more attractive than those simply put into the shippers' lodges on the island for maturing in cask there. So it began to be routine to subject the casks of new wine to a gradual heating and cooling, a process known as *'estufagem'* from the *'estufa'* in which it was done; sometimes the wines were exposed outdoors to the sun, but a controlled heating indoors began to be accepted as more satisfactory. This procedure gives to Madeira an odd, lingeringly warm undercurrent of flavour, quite different from that of port.

The Madeira vines are trained high, usually on trellises, with other market garden crops, such as vegetables, often grown underneath the vine canopies that are arranged on terraces. Space is short on the island – at least for growing things. Recently much attention has been paid to the selection of superior clones for the vineyards, and it is recognized that the style of the wines may need adaptation to contemporary tastes: some blends are made, so that the contribution of the different grapes can provide complexity to the wine.

Madeira has always been popular in the US, one reason being that it was a 'patriotic' drink in opposition to port during the period when the would-be independent inhabitants of the 'American colonies' were hoping for their independence; the 'establishment' in Britain drank port. There was another practical reason: wines from Europe might only be imported to North America in 'British bottoms' (ships), but as Madeira was, technically, accepted as being in Africa, any ship could bring in the wine to the 'colonists'. There are not, as far as I know, wines made in accordance with the Madeira method anywhere else, but Madeira probably did influence the creation of another important fortified wine – Marsala (see below). There is also a great tradition as to Madeira being the world's longest-lived wine, and it is still not unheard-of for an eighteenth-century Madeira to be offered to fortunate guests of the shippers. These, whose headquarters are in Funchal, are mainly members of the Madeira Wine Association, where their wines are made and stored, although individual styles of the different establishments are scrupulously followed; the same applies to firms who are not members of the M W A, many of these having been founded in the eighteenth century.

It is Madeira which has added the word 'maderization' to the wine-drinker's vocabulary: wines deepening in colour and having acquired a certain smell and taste because of having been exposed to the air are thought to be reminiscent of Madeira.

MARSALA

This is a wine that was created for the British market towards the end of the eighteenth century, when in 1773 John Woodhouse of Liverpool began exporting it from the vineyards around the town from which it took its name. Sir Benjamin Ingham, and Whitaker, a descendant of his, continued the trade, and it is significant that the British firms who built up this business had some connections in the port, sherry and Madeira wine trades. Today, Marsala produces a large amount of wine, but the former British firms are now all owned by the Florio establishment, itself founded in 1833, and belonging these days to Cinzano. There are many other Sicilian establishments, and the port of Marsala won world fame when Garibaldi landed there before his march on Rome in 1860 . . . and also because in 1800 Nelson ordered 500 pipes of Marsala for his fleet; the letter of contract about this with John Woodhouse, bearing Nelson's signature, scrawled awkwardly because he was having to start writing with his left hand, is still in existence.

Marsala is made from Sicilian wines, a variety of grapes being utilized; small amounts of sweet concentrated wine, a *'vino cotto'* (a type of essence made by heating the wine), plus brandy are added, after which the various wines are blended and then go into a type of *solera*, similar to that of sherry. The huge casks are referred to as 'pipes', each containing 423 litres. The wines are drawn off to make the various blends as and when required.

A huge range of different Marsalas is in fact produced: the finest, according to the tastes of most readers, will be the dry type, much favoured by our ancestors; it is a delectable drink when one comes in on a cold night and has the leisure to sit down and sip some with a piece of sponge cake or fruit cake. Anyone who has only associated Marsala with the cooking wine, used for many Italian dishes but specially for *zabaglione*, will be delighted by the quality of such a dry wine. The best dry Marsala will usually be labelled *'Vergine'* and have been matured for at least five years in wood. Marsala *all'uovo* is enriched with egg yolks and fairly sweet; there are other Marsalas flavoured with almonds, coffee, chocolate, strawberries, mandarins and even bananas, but one is unlikely to find them outside Sicily or places where the Italian or Sicilian population is high.

OTHER FORTIFIED WINES

Other wines higher in alcohol than table wines include Málaga and Tarragona, the latter having been at one time in the nineteenth century nicknamed 'poor man's port'. Both nowadays tend to be sweet, full and somewhat lacking in appeal for drinkers of our time, but the finer dry examples can achieve quality. The best Málaga does go through a type of *solera* system, but is not fortified with brandy. The type called Lágrima ('tear') is white and definitely sweetish. Old wine labels bearing the name 'Mountain' refer to Málaga, because the vineyards are on the hillsides.

Another category of wines that are likely to be encountered by travellers in France are the *vins doux naturels*. They are slightly above table wine strength, which is why it is difficult to sell them on export markets where they are penalized with paying higher duty because of this strength, but they can be very pleasant as apéritifs or between-times drinks.

The *vins doux naturels* get their additional strength either by means of *mistelle*, a type of concentrate of grape juice and spirit, or by the blending in of some spirit, according to the individual formulae of the different makers. Production is strictly controlled and, although these wines can be pleasant drinks, they are not likely to undergo significant changes in bottle and, if matured in wood, they will be blended and bottled as required. Some of the best known are those made from the Muscat grape, and along the Mediterranean coast of France and at the bottom of the Rhône Valley there are many local versions, especially Muscat de Frontignan, also, nearer the Spanish frontier, the Grands Roussillons, such as Banyuls, Rivesaltes, Maury and many others.

VERMOUTH

This wine – for it is a wine and therefore a bottle, once opened, will begin to deteriorate with exposure to the air – is curiously neglected by many writers, yet it is one of the most widely-made wines of the world and, certainly, the oldest form of wine. The aromatized wines of ancient Egypt and Greece, when herbs and flavourings were blended for individual consumption (often, one feels, merely to make a beverage drinkable or at least slightly more so), were not only used for social purposes, but formed an important part of the repertoire of the physician. From the earliest times almost to the present day various forms of vermouth were made in the stillrooms and dispensaries of the great noble houses and religious establishments, some as medicinal drinks, some as digestives or soporifics, some as preventatives against disease. Along the great trade routes travellers brought the herbs and spices – and recipes picked up from hospices and 'wise women'.

In the eighteenth century vermouth began to be made commercially in Turin, where the local wine and the proximity of the supplies of mountain herbs, as well as spices along the pilgrim and trade routes, were propitious to its production. At first customers each had their own mixtures made up for them in the bars, but the founders of what are now the mighty vermouth establishments achieved their own recipes that made them famous. In the nineteenth century, vermouth began to be made in and near Marseilles and also at Chambéry.

The name comes from the wormwood plant, *Artemisia absinthum*, known as *'wermut'* in German, which featured in most of the original recipes. (Vermouth does not, however, contain absinthe.)

Today vermouth is made in many wine-producing regions and, although it was originally intended to be drunk neat, its popularity in mixes, notably cocktails, makes it an essential bottle in any bar. Each of the great vermouth houses has its own style and, although the methods of production in Italy differ somewhat from those of France, it is usual for each establishment to put out a range of vermouths: it is erroneous to assume that 'French' is dry and 'Italian' sweet. These days white vermouth, or *'bianco'*, is an Italian speciality and this is on the sweet side. Pink or *rosé* vermouths are also made and, in Chambéry, some are flavoured with Alpine strawberries to make a strawberry vermouth. Elsewhere in the world vermouth is made either under licence with one of the great firms, or simply to fulfil a need locally; in Crete, for example, the vermouth is very good because, one is told, of the inclusion of the herb dittany, very much a speciality of the island and bought by major vermouth makers in huge quantities. The Cretans still use their vermouth in semi-medicinal ways, for cuts, stings, rashes and bruises.

Although until recently much regional wine that could not be made palatable for ordinary consumption was made into vermouth (or used for distillation), the improved methods of wine making have set quite a problem as regards supplies for the vermouth manufacturers, who could previously utilize wines from parts of Sicily and the south of France. Now these wines are able to be sold under their own regional names or used in branded blends and the vermouth makers have to seek other sources of supply.

Although generalizations about the exact methods of production of vermouth are risky, it remains true that it is still aromatized wine, the processes of infusion, maceration and distillation being involved, sometimes all three of them. No other wine is made in this way – indeed, if it were, it would be vermouth!

EIGHT

PRACTICALITIES

It is surprising that anybody should suppose that wine is in any way 'difficult' to enjoy – all that is necessary is to draw the cork and see whether or not you like the contents of the bottle. With so many articles and books written about wine the basics are easy to learn, wherever you are and whatever your resources may be. So this brief account of the few essentials involved should not be intimidating.

BUYING WINE

There is a wide range of suppliers and, even in remote parts of the world, it is possible to order from lists of merchants who will mail these to you. If possible, make use of this wide range of retailers, for not even the largest firms can stock every single type of wine, nor may one concern invariably offer the most competitive prices. The huge retailers can pass on the benefits as regards cost that they achieve by buying on a large scale; the smaller firms can feature wines that are simply not available in the quantities required by the mighty multiples for all their retail outlets. One merchant may specialize in the wines of a particular country or region, another may be able to offer advantageous services to buyers – free delivery, invitations to tastings, regular lists of 'bin ends' or remnants; some offer lower prices if wines are sold on a 'cash-and-carry' basis; others arrange to be open at weekends for people to sample and select at leisure. Many retailers provide lists that are full of detailed information about stocks. Some may run wine courses, arrange visits to vineyards, offer substantial discounts on purchases of two or three 'case lots' (a dozen bottles) or more, so that wine lovers can join together to buy in bulk. Ask or look at the terms of sale given in any list and you may find a variety of ways of saving when buying, even if the retailer merely provides a 24-hour telephone answering service to receive orders in the cheap period, or includes a stamped card for orders.

Anyone beginning to learn about wine should shop around as much as possible. Even moderate acquaintance with the wines of, say, a supermarket or licensed grocer can be rewarding in gaining experience. Don't expect inevitably to find anyone behind the counter of a modest shop who can provide detailed information about a wide variety of wines, although the wine trade do run many training courses for students these days; you may be certain, however, that there will be someone highly qualified who has been responsible for the buying behind the bottles – so any letter of inquiry should bring a rewarding reply.

Wine clubs, originally providing a means of buying in bulk without the additional costs of keeping a shop or lavish offices, also mail order offers, are still popular in the UK. But bear in mind that any firm running them is *in business* – to make a profit. What, apart from certain wines, can such sales outlets provide? Can you, for example, buy in mixed case lots, or only single dozens at a time? Can you easily get advice from someone qualified to give it – not merely a 'personality' whose name looks well on the list or letterhead? Are you easily able to take deliveries or to return wines you don't care for without much trouble? Is it possible for you to buy spirits in this way and, if so, then are they 'club lines' or 'own brands' – which may be perfectly good, but are they your own favourites? Do you get any 'extras', such as tastings or newsletters or, perhaps, the chance of buying certain wines before the ordinary public and at a lower price?

People often inquire about buying at auction, but this – unless you can join with a group of friends to buy several dozen at a time – is not always ideal for the ordinary consumer; sometimes the identical wine or wines may be in the local off-licence at a lower price! As regards the 'fine and rare' bottles, although sales of these usually attract much publicity, you ought – as with sales of any quality goods or works of art – to know more than a little as to what you are doing before you get carried away by the excitement of the bidding. If you do have a hankering for something special, a wine merchant can usually arrange to bid for you – and will have a calmer notion as to what a fair price may be.

Another frequent query is about wines that the buyer thinks may make a nice little profit if sold again in the future. The reason why any reputable wine merchant condemns this sort of thing is because there never is enough fine wine to go round; it is worth buying all the finer wines at opening prices – but for your own enjoyment when they are ready to drink, by which time they may be very expensive on the open market. And it infuriates the true lover of wine to hear anyone who has some fine bottles, either given, bequeathed or bought on advice when first on the market, announce that they 'can't afford' to drink such things! This, to me, is like telling people that you 'can't afford' to give them adequate food when inviting them. As the experience of sharing a memorable wine is wholly rewarding, I say that, if you consider cash more important than friendship, you are unlikely ever to be more than the sort of wine snob who 'drinks the label'.

People who merely speculate in wine also forget one thing – unlike works of art, wine is a perishable commodity and not only does it need careful keeping (which may cost money if you haven't a suitable cellar), but, after a certain stage, it will decline. Buy at opening prices when you can – but for yourself or, at worst, for your heirs, who will remember you with affection. A merchant can certainly arrange to lay down a 'cellar' for you and will, if you inherit one, value it, but informed advice is necessary if you are to benefit by this. The discovery of the odd old bottle somewhere won't make you a fortune. Wines for laying down should be in case lots, be properly kept and a report be available as to the rate at which they are maturing. (If you make a habit of buying and selling wine and do not possess a licence to do so, then you may be in trouble with the law, and if you do this kind of thing on a large scale, you may need the advice of your accountant to avoid certain tax liabilities.)

Finally – buying wine abroad, getting it home and bottling it yourself. This is something that may sound fun but cannot be much more. Anything really good nowadays will have been either bought by the locals or snapped up by visiting trade buyers. Do you want to cope with the paperwork and, possibly, the complications of the customs, can you put right anything that may go wrong with the wine, and do you really want several dozens of something that, at best, may only be a very 'everyday' beverage? It is significant that no one I know in the wine trade indulges in this method of buying – and they, after all, have both the know-how and the mechanics of the procedure easily available.

TASTING AND DRINKING

When you seriously 'taste' a wine you are appraising it in detail. When you drink, you are – it is to be hoped – enjoying doing so. It is not necessary to be solemn about tasting, but the distractions of social chat, people smoking and wearing scent (which, these days, may be men as well as women) do make it very difficult for anybody to concentrate on a range of wines that may be both interesting as such and, for the student of wine, of great value – some of the bottles may be rare, many may be expensive; for the member of the wine trade or someone whose job it is to write about wine, noise and conflicting smells make the task very hard.

But people who bore fellow guests at a dinner with gratuitous information about wine or try to turn a pleasant get-together into a study session are equally thoughtless and, probably, wine snobs. Tasting is one thing, drinking another.

Tasting

The basic procedure for tasting seriously is simple. Use a suitable glass – such as a 'Paris' goblet, or tulip-shaped glass or something similar, with a bowl slightly curved in at the rim, on a stem and of clear glass. This makes it easy to see the wine's colour, to swing the small amount of wine – equivalent to about a mouthful – that forms the tasting sample around in the glass to release the bouquet.

The heat of the hand need not affect the temperature of the wine if the glass is held by its stem or foot and the bowl-shape in which the wine is contained projects both the smell and the wine itself satisfactorily towards nose and mouth.

Look at the wine – tilt the glass away from you slightly, preferably over something white – to note the limpidity and any shades of colour tones. Swing the wine around and sniff at it. Then pull a small amount into your mouth, plus a little air (this emphasizes the taste), draw the wine around the mouth so as to 'feel' it as well as noting the flavour. Then, if possible, spit the wine out and 'huff' an outward breath, which will give an additional impression of both smell and taste in the cavities of the face.

Make a note of anything that strikes you at that moment, not simply 'nice' or 'nasty', but a word or phrase that will evoke the experience when you refer to your tasting sheet in the future. Do this *immediately* – tasting impressions are very hard to describe and, even half an hour later, may leave you with only a vague idea of what the wine said to you when it was actually in your mouth.

That's all essentially involved with tasting. But bear in mind that, done with serious intent, it is *hard work*, involving complete concentration; even people with many years of experience within and outside the wine trade find tasting both exhilarating – when the wines are good – and taxing. If you suppose a tasting is really a type of drinks party, you should try tackling a range of fifty or more cheap wines, many of which may be utterly dull, even defective, with the possible awareness that, on your 'say-so', thousands of pounds' worth of wine may be bought, affecting the economy of the region producing it and the profit or otherwise of the firm selling it! This is why a trade tasting is inevitably a serious exercise.

Sampling young wines, as in these circumstances, is something that many people find difficult to enjoy, because the wines are seldom pleasant drinks at this stage in their lives. A wine merchant's tasting, however, usually presents a range of wines that are ready to drink. This can indeed turn into a bit of a party.

People also find it fun to give 'tasting parties' of their own, possibly with advice from a friend in the trade: wine and cheese parties are another pleasant form of entertaining. There is one big difference between these and any serious tasting, however: 'We buy on apples, sell on cheese,' say the wine trade, because an apple freshens the palate and reveals any deficiencies in the wine, whereas cheese makes any wine taste better (on account of the acidity of the apple and the alkalinity of the cheese). The only food likely to be seen in any professional tasting will be dry bread and/or biscuits.

Drinking

Advice on serving and enjoying wine also often makes it sound more complicated than it is. It is wise to observe a few rules when you are beginning to love wine, however, simply because they have established what most people find agreeable. Once you know what these rules are and have gained some experience, you can do as you like.

Glasses, such as those described in the section on tasting, should show off wine – if a glass is coloured, the wine may look strange; if it is heavily cut or engraved, the wine's colour may be distorted and, ideally, a glass should be thin as well as plain, so that there is no distraction from the presence of a thick glass in one's mouth. I have sometimes said that to try to drink a fine wine from a thick glass is somewhat like it must be trying to make love to a female wearing thick underwear, with all the bumps and folds showing through her dress.

It is obvious that no glass should smell of anything except the wine in it, but it is astonishing how frequently a wine may be rejected as 'off' when what is really the matter is that the glass has not been thoroughly rinsed after being washed in detergent (which will also flatten the finest Champagne) or has been dried with a cloth impregnated with grease after being used for other purposes than simply polishing glasses. Sniff any glass you have not washed up yourself to make certain that it has no smell. For the same reason, glasses should be stored upright, or hanging upside down but open to the air; if turned upside down on a shelf, not only will they smell stale from the air held in the bowl but, in many instances, they may have acquired an additional odour from the shelf – plastic is revolting, a pine shelf may make you suppose you are drinking diluted turpentine. Don't spoil a wine that someone has taken care to make and buy by ignoring routine checks when you are going to serve it.

TEMPERATURE

White, pink and sparkling wines are more enjoyable when served cool, red wines at the temperature of the room in which they are to be drunk. But of course, this varies enormously – on a stuffy day, you may prefer to chill a wine more than on a bright, fine, cool one. Very sweet wines can be chilled more than delicate dry ones. The relevant adjective should be 'cool' – semi-frozen wine will have virtually no bouquet (and one of the reasons why you buy it is to enjoy the smell) and not much taste. It's affectation to take the temperature of a bottle or glass – what you require is a wine at the temperature that will make it most agreeable *to you* when it goes into *your mouth*. This is why it sometimes surprises people that even authoritative members of the wine trade don't make much fuss about cooling any wine – they will put their hand on the bottle to test its temperature against that of themselves and, very often, serve a wine merely at the temperature at which it might come from an ordinary cool cellar. This, incidentally, can polish up the delicious fruitiness of many small-scale red wines – which is why young Beaujolais and similar red wines are sometimes served in the ice bucket.

If you wish to cool a wine, remember that a bucket of ice and water (not ice alone) will cool a bottle to pleasant freshness within a quarter of an hour. In a refrigerator it may take an hour. Do not keep wine in the refrigerator indefinitely, because it acquires an odd, flat flavour which cannot be dispersed.

Red wines should certainly not be served tepid – as some people tend to insist in 'chi-chi' eating-places. It is always possible to warm a wine gently by cupping one's hand round the bowl of the glass or, even, cuddling bottle or decanter for a few minutes. If you really haven't allowed time for a wine to take on the temperature of the room in which it is to be served, then you can dip the bottle into warm (but never hot) water for a few seconds. But to subject any bottle to being put before the fire, over the stove, or suddenly heated in any way is to shock the wine and it cannot be at its best when it is drunk. Also, currents stir up any deposit.

Decanting is the subject of endless discussions. If, by the way, you pour wine through air, this in itself gently warms the wine. You decant to aerate the wine as well as to pour it off any deposit that may have formed in the bottom of the bottle. This means that, if you want to 'bring on' a wine that may be still far from its prime, decanting can help it and smooth out any roughness. Indeed, some people would agree with the saying that 'An old wine deserves decanting, a young wine needs it.' But decanting is very much a matter of personal preference, so it is wise to experiment with two bottles of the same wine; decant one and not the other and see which you enjoy most. You may, of course, draw the cork of a wine a couple of hours ahead of drinking time, just so as to disperse the stale air or 'bottle stink' that has been under the cork and to allow the wine a little 'breathing'; this slight airing is also useful when you serve fine white wines – ten or fifteen minutes with the cork drawn and lightly replaced or even left out will not harm any wine.

If you don't finish the contents of a bottle, the wine should be perfectly drinkable (sometimes even better) for the next twenty-four hours or, sometimes, even longer, if you cork up the bottle and keep it in a cool place. Indeed, some very cheap wines can improve enormously by being left overnight. Some great wines, notably vintage port, should, however, be consumed at a sitting and the delicate *fino* sherries can begin to lose their freshness after a day or two – one authority can even tell if a sherry has been opened in the morning when it is served in the evening!

Sweeter wines stand up to exposure to air – which causes deterioration – longer than the light dry ones, so a medium or sweet sherry will remain in condition for days, even for a couple of weeks after being opened. Vermouth, which is also a wine, is subject to the same risks; it won't last indefinitely. Vermouths that are sweet stand up far longer than the dry types, but two to three weeks is their limit. As all wines can be used up in the kitchen or in the vinegar crock, there need be no waste of dregs.

OPENING WINE

It's surprising how difficult many people find it to draw a cork – but perhaps not so when it is realized that many corkscrews are not helpful. A good corkscrew, of whatever type, should have a rounded spiral screw, ending in a curve, so that you can look up it like a spiral staircase. This spiral will go into the cork and hold it, whereas the sharp-edged, pointed-end types of screw merely pierce and may break the cork.

Wipe the capsule and remove it. If you cut off the top, be sure to do this neatly, below the rim of the bottle, because, if wine is poured over the jagged remnants of a metal or plastic capsule, it may take on the smell of this. Wipe the top of the cork. Never open any bottle without holding it in a napkin. Bottles do not often split these days, but it is better to be safe. Insert the corkscrew steadily, until the end just reaches the bottom of the cork – if it pierces this, a little cork may drop into the wine, although this does not make the wine 'corked' (see p. 233. Pull the cork out slowly and steadily, without jerking. If it is stuck very tight, put the bottle between your ankles and push down with your other hand while pulling up the corkscrew. When the cork comes out, wipe the inside of the neck of the bottle before pouring any wine.

Ideally, any wine bottle should have been standing up prior to serving, but, if you have to draw one from the bin or rack, where it lies on its side so that the cork is kept damp, do not tilt the recumbent bottle upright at once, as there may be some deposit in the bottom. Look against a light to see. If there is a lot of deposit you may have to decant from the bottle while this is lying in a basket or cradle but, if you do so, refrain from tilting the bottle up and down while pouring, because this will merely churn up the deposit and all the drinkers risk getting a mouthful of 'bits'. It won't harm them, but it spoils the impression of the wine. Decanting from the bin is, it should be stressed, the only use of the cradle or wine basket that is acceptable to the serious wine lover: its presence on the table is silly for, if there is no deposit, why not stand the bottle up? If there is a deposit, then the tilting up and down of the bottle while the wine is poured from the basket will merely distribute deposit in all the glasses. Gradually incline the bottle. Restaurateurs say that 'the public' require wine to be served in baskets. (Personally, I do not think that the basket has any more right on a civilized table than the chamberpot has underneath it.)

If you are going to decant a wine, follow the same procedure for opening it. Then, position the decanter or carafe (or a jug, or a clean bottle) plus a glass, near either a candle, torch or bicycle lamp – something that will shine through the shoulder and neck of the bottle. Pour the wine gently and steadily into the decanter, without splashing, holding the bottle so that the light behind it shows you when the deposit begins to move and comes up into the shoulder of the bottle. Before any of it can pass into the decanter, lift the bottle – without tilting it back – away from the decanter, and direct the wine into the glass, pouring gently until some deposit is about to flow into the glass. It is surprising how much more wine can often be 'persuaded' from the bottle in this way. Finally, decide whether you will add the wine in the glass to that in the decanter or whether you will merely use it for a preliminary sampling and use the rest in the kitchen. Stand the bottle up and, if more than a very little wine remains, pour this into a bottle for kitchen use. Decide whether to stopper the decanter or leave it open for additional 'breathing'.

Decanting is not difficult but, if you are nervous, ask a wine merchant to do the decanting for you and watch the process.

Opening sparkling wine needs care: every year, hospitals report instances of people losing an eye because of letting the cork of a sparkling wine fly. It is dangerous and wasteful of wine to let this happen.

Hold the bottle in a napkin and incline it at an angle of about 45°, making certain that it is not pointing at anyone or anything that a flying cork might damage. If a bottle has been standing up, or if you have shaken it in your shopping basket or the boot of the car, the wine will be extra 'lively', so be ready for the cork to rush out. Remove the top of the metal capsule and untwist the loop that secures the wire muzzle – lift this right off if possible. From this moment, never for an instant leave hold of the cork (or any plastic stopper). Hold it firmly. Then turn the bottle, not the cork – if you turn the cork, you are likely to break off the top of the 'mushroom'. The cork should gradually emerge with a discreet sound and jump into your hand – not fly. Have a glass ready to receive the immediate rush of wine.

If the cork sticks, so that not even a little upward pressure with your thumb below the mushroom will start it to move, you can always extract it by holding the neck of the bottle for a few seconds under the hot tap – the increased pressure inside will push out the cork, but never let go of it or you may waste a lot of wine. If the mushroom top does break off, you then have to pierce the cork that is left, so as to release some of the pressure, then insert a corkscrew and pull in the usual way. Do not try to use the corkscrew until some pressure behind the cork has been released.

If you use the type of cork extractor that pumps air or gas below the cork so as to push it out, remember that such extractors should *never* be used for sparkling or *pétillant* wines. Increased pressure can make a bottle split or explode.

Because in any wine – except those sealed with a small plastic stopper with the wine able to come right up to the base of this – there is a small amount of air between the level of the wine and the bottom of the cork, this air may have become stale. It is this that is termed 'bottle stink' and can be apparent when the cork is first drawn. Only a few moments will suffice to disperse it, but the initial impression may be that the wine is somehow 'off'. This is why, with any wine, red, white or *rosé*, it is always a prudent policy to draw the cork 5–15 minutes before pouring; even fine white wines should have this slight initial aeration, although the cork may be lightly reinserted during the period of waiting.

KEEPING WINE

Wine bottles should be stored on their sides, so that the cork is kept in contact with the wine and therefore swollen, so as to keep the bottle sealed. If you do find some 'weeping' from a bottle, it may be wise to use it fairly soon – though there need be nothing wrong with the wine.

Quiet, dark and a fairly constant temperature are what wines like. But even the house or flat lacking a true 'cellar' can usually find a place away from noise and vibration, away from direct light and not too dry. Even if you only tip a bottle carton on its side, this will do for short-term use. A damp cellar is ideal, although you may get labels rotting unless you wrap the bottles in tissue (not plastic, as this keeps them warm). A temperature of 10–12°C is perfect, but even up to 17–18°C is not too warm, providing that the place does not get appreciably hotter in summer and cooler in winter – this is why an attic is not always a good storage place, unless it is insulated. Central heating, unfortunately, is not good, except for short-term wine storage.

Wine bins can be ordered to fit quite small spaces and the simple types are perfectly serviceable, so don't waste money on the elaborate ones that, too often, are found in smart restaurants where wines may be stored over the hotplate, alongside the bar and, anyway, in brilliant light (which, remember, is also a source of warmth).

Always keep a record of what you have in your 'cellar' and, if possible, buy wines at least in pairs so that, if there is one defective bottle – this invariably happens on important occasions – you are not without something to drink. A record of what you have is also essential if any merchant cellars wine for you, when an annual charge may be made; however, the merchant is also usually able to report on the progress of the wines and, when you wish to draw any out, he will, if you wish, not merely advise on service, but decant vintage port, for example, which must be decanted. A list of what you own where, however, is really important, as there are still stocks of superb wines forgotten in many merchants' cellars, the owners having died and no record having been left for their heirs.

FAULTS IN WINE

Improved wine technology has fortunately made many previously common defects rather rare, but there are still a few – and there are still conditions suspected by the public that often cause bottles to be returned when there is really nothing amiss.

'Corked' and 'Corky' Wine

It is possible to differentiate between a wine that is 'corky' – that is, one that definitely smells of cork – and one that is 'corked', which, at least to me, doesn't evoke a smell of cork at all, but gives a flat, dull impression to the nose. This may sometimes also be a slightly oxidized wine, affected by the entrance of air into the bottle, whether because of a too-porous cork or the action of the cork weevil boring into it. But it is curious that, in my experience, the sensitivity of the British nose to corked wines appears to be more acute than in some famous wine regions: the word *'bouchonné'* (corked) is not often heard around a French table and, when a visitor sufficiently qualified and senior to venture the comment has done so, I have several times known the entire party, while agreeing, continue to drink the – albeit slightly – faulty bottle, whereas I doubt that any Anglo-Saxon host would have hesitated to change it immediately the condition was acknowledged. It should possibly be emphasized that a wine that is either corky or corked is not in any way harmful to drink – it is simply not very pleasant; the smell is alien to that of any sound wine and this inevitably detracts from the flavour. It's doubly unfortunate if somebody is not familiar with the defect and supposes that the wine *ought* to taste like that!

However, it is often rather difficult when the bottle is first opened to decide whether the wine really *is* corked. This, incidentally, is why the host tastes the wine first in a restaurant – it should be inspected prior to opening to check that it is definitely the bottle ordered, then appraised for temperature and condition and, if any minute bits of cork have gone into the first sample-sized pouring, this will only affect the host. Corkiness develops after quite a short while, however, so if you are in doubt, leave the wine for five or ten minutes – if it then stinks, the bottle should be sealed up and returned to the source of supply. People are naïve about this – no reputable restaurant or merchant will charge for a defective bottle and it will be replaced free of charge; but if you've consumed all but an inch of the wine in the bottle and then complain, the source of supply may wonder what you are complaining about!

A complete absence of smell is one thing to beware of, also, as far as I am concerned, the slightly chlorine 'swimming-bath' stink that indicates a corked bottle. Appreciate that this is not the fault of anybody.

One important caveat, however – if you order more than one bottle when in a restaurant, insist that you, the host, taste *each* bottle as it comes, in a clean glass, before it is served. Should the second bottle be defective and the wine waiter simply top up glasses around the table before you – who are paying for the wine – have approved it, then this defective second bottle will pollute all the remaining wine in all the glasses. This happens time and again, so be on the watch. No one will suffer from drinking a corked wine – but it isn't pleasant.

Deposit

Deposit in a wine, white as well as red, is by no means a fault. Indeed, fine red wines from certain regions ought to have this 'gunge' in the bottom. One important market, however, is so suspicious of 'bits in wine' and so lacking, one presumes, in adequate *sommeliers*, that all fine reds shipped to it have to be siphoned off any deposit before they are sent away. This, of course, shortens their lives and, as deposit varies, it deprives the serious wine-lover of finding something interesting in the different amount and type of deposit.

White wines can throw a slight sludge – again, it is easy with care to pour the wine off this. Our Victorian ancestors used tinted glasses for German wines, to avoid seeing the 'flyers' or bits that might appear floating in the wine, but modern filtration makes these rare today. They don't hurt the wine or the drinker, and their presence essentially means that the wine hasn't been subjected to excessive filtration to provide the 'star bright' wines that the public like – and which, alas, lose something, however infinitesimal, each time they go through the filter.

Crystals

One thing that causes some anxiety to customers is the presence of crystals in wine. These, which can appear in red wines but are more easily seen in whites, are in fact quite a sign of quality – again, the wine hasn't had the guts knocked out of it by treatment. (Returned bottles usually end up in the directors' luncheon room.) The crystals are tartrates, often produced because the wine has been subjected to some sudden change of temperature. In the bottom of the bottle they look like small pieces of grit, stuck into the cork they look like slivers of glass. They will not do you the slightest harm – indeed, they don't possess any flavour even if you eat them.

Otherwise, if you are in any doubt as to the 'goodness' or 'badness' of a wine, certainly return it if you can, with an explanation as to your objection. There are wines that may be out of condition; the odd bottle from impeccable suppliers may, for no detectable reason, be unsatisfactory. This may be because the wine has been badly kept, such as in the light or heat (many people suppose Cyprus wines to be inferior merely because, alas, they have been served from bottles that have been stacked outside in the Mediterranean heat for days or weeks), or because one bottle was dirty – it can happen, even with sterilized bottles being delivered in sealed pallets – or because the cork has dried and let in air. All such should be returned. These wines will not harm you but you won't enjoy them.

It is also fair to ask yourself, before you complain, whether the fault is in the wine or yourself. You may not like it – this doesn't mean that it is 'bad'. You may have been eating or drinking something that has changed your palate so that the wine does not taste as you expected. Remember to check that the glass does not smell or that you have not imparted some alien smell from yourself to the glass and, incidentally, to the wine. (This is why wine-minded people will use their left hands to squeeze any segment of lemon as this, on the right hand, makes the glass and the wine redolent of citrus.)

There are some dreary wines, some poor wines, even among widely advertised and popular brands. But there are far more good wines, those that are value for money – and those that, occasionally, make you realize 'what all the fuss is about'. Concentrate on what you like and what reliable people recommend – and leave those alone who make a business of promulgating adverse criticism and making a fuss about wine scandals.

NINE

WINES WITH FOOD

Many wines are specifically intended for consumption with meals – hence the term 'table wine'. There are large books and innumerable articles that purport to give advice on 'what to serve with what', but it is difficult to accept that there is only *one* wine for *one* particular dish – and is this one likely to be available both widely and indefinitely? Too much detail complicates the matter too much. So I propose only to give some general counsels. The wine lover will cater for his or her personal preferences, the individual way of life and what can be afforded, as well as what can be found locally.

Enemies to wine are foods that so change the palate that the wine doesn't taste as pleasant as it might. Very piquant or violently flavoured foods come into this category – books that recommend any specific wine for curry are being somewhat affected! Anything with a lot of pepper, strong pickles, a high proportion of malt vinegar, lots of sharp-flavoured ingredients, such as pickled herrings, pineapple, lemon, citrus in general, watercress (which is peppery), and, top of the palate stunners, chocolate, all make it difficult to appreciate wines of any delicacy, and they are not usually the ideal accompaniments even to wines in the cheap and cheerful robust category.

Some vegetables, too, tend to 'take over' the flavours of a dish: tomatoes can be somewhat acidic, carrots sweet, any vegetables dressed with an eggy sauce (see p. 242) or having some additional strong taste should be taken into account when planning the wines. Onions, shallots and, of course, garlic tend to make themselves evident and, much as I love them, it cannot be denied that, if

237

you propose to serve fine wines, these should all be used with moderation and discretion if at all. I have, on occasions, also had vegetable dishes so enthusiastically combined with various herbs – especially sage and rosemary – that one had difficulty in tasting anything else, the food as well as the wine; if anyone incorporates more than a very small quantity of caraway, coconut, curry powder into any dish, then this also tends to dominate and affect the palate, even slightly.

Salad is another item that is often denounced as inimical to wine, but I think it sensible to consider when and how it is served – and of what it is composed. It does not, conventionally, feature in a formal British menu, though this is a convention now often disregarded. When it is served, it is often eaten after the main course, by which time it may be supposed that most of the main wine is finished. If, however, something salady forms the first course of a meal or is part of the principal dish – sometimes being eaten at the same time as any cheese – then the ingredients are relevant: if they are sharp or piquant – peppers, onions with 'bite', celeriac, radishes, garlic-anointed *croûtons* – then they can certainly be too strong for a delicate wine. But the dressing would seem to be the thing most likely adversely to affect the drink. If this is any form of mayonnaise or salad cream, then the caveats about eggs (see p. 242) apply. But, to my mind, it is the use of vinegar that can do the most harm.

The British have always used a great deal of vinegar. It can, of course, be made from other things than wine and it is a preservative and disinfectant. But it is definitely an enemy to wine. In wine installations where vinegar is also made it must be kept far apart from the wine, as the vinegar bacteria 'turns' wine, especially while the latter is young and vulnerable. If you take a mouthful of wine while your palate is still drenched in vinegar, the wine will be 'turned' in your mouth – and taste acid and unpleasant. But the British fondness for vinegar, especially malt vinegar as opposed to wine vinegar, has resulted in a high proportion of this featuring in many 'salad dressings'; indeed, there are numerous cookery books in which 'French dressing' consists of one-third vinegar to two-thirds oil. This is definitely strong and piquant. Malt vinegar is coarse in flavour anyway; I don't go quite as far as the late Raymond Postgate, who said it was only useful for stripping varnish off furniture, but its culinary rôle seems to me to be in certain strong pickles and chutneys and for sprinkling on chips when you eat these out of a newspaper!

My own salads are dressed with six or seven parts of oil to one of vinegar – and the latter is wine vinegar I make myself, much milder than even commercial wine vinegar (see pp. 246–8). The oil is used – as it used to be in the early nineteenth century – as a primary coating for the salad vegetables, the vinegar being added by itself only just before serving, as a condiment. Not only will the salad not wilt quickly, but the small amount of vinegar will usually not affect the wine or wines being served, any more than a moderate amount of mustard or fruity sauce (apple, redcurrant, cranberry) might do. And, as several illustrious members of the wine trade and critical friends have eaten salads at my table, with some very fine wines at least in the offing, I can only say that no one has ever objected to this type of salad and its dressing.

So – if you like a two or three to one dressing, it may be prudent to serve a salad of this type after the wine is finished or at least with plenty of bread to counteract the piquancy. Otherwise, with a light touch as regards the dressing, also the ingredients, the problem is not too serious – and a salady first course with no accompanying wine can be a very good way of making the transition between the apéritifs and the wines with the food. It should be noted that a sparkling wine apéritif, which may be slightly higher in alcohol than a table wine anyway, is likely to make any delicate, light-bodied wine coming immediately on its heels taste somewhat indifferent.

It seems as if I have already pronounced too many warnings – but it does not take long for anyone to work out what they like, by doing a little experimenting. After all, as the host, it's reasonable for *you* to enjoy the meal; do not, therefore, be a slave to any advice in book, article or speech – use your own sense and discrimination.

The palate, washed by saliva, can recover quite quickly and return to a neutral and receptive condition (not, in my experience,

239

from chocolate, however, for at least a couple of hours), so menus need not be disrupted too much. What is fair to wine is to plan any meal so that, if possible, you are not putting the drink at a disadvantage throughout.

If spirit-based cocktails are lavishly served before a meal, then these, by reason of their strength and, possibly, their ingredients, do make it difficult to appreciate the subtleties of any fine wine. But you can serve plenty of the medium-range wines if you and your friends like spirits by way of apéritifs, or start the meal with a 'blotting-paper' course, such as *consommé*, or something with which wine isn't served anyway. You may in any case have chosen one of the inimical dishes – anything with a piquant or salady sauce or, perhaps, an egg recipe; eggs tend to stick on the palate and wine simply doesn't taste as well as it might unless it is a very assertive one.

Do programme any meal so as to include the before-dinner drinks as well as those taken with food. If, for example, you have been drinking a medium or sweetish apéritif, such as a medium sherry or one of the many proprietary branded apéritifs, then the finest dry wine in the world is bound to taste 'bitter' immediately afterwards. Either have no wine with the first course, or opt either to continue with the apéritif wine or else have something quite different – even something sweeter. People are not always so conservative that they will not try something new, even if they are devotees of gin and tonic in the ordinary way! Remember, too, that it is always acceptable to have a glass of wine instead of a cocktail or sherry should you wish and, naturally, for any kind of celebration, a glass of sparkling wine is delightful.

Otherwise, it is a reliable maxim to progress from dry to sweet and, usually, young to old. You can see the sense of this if you translate it into food terms – would you relish a dish of caviare or smoked salmon if you'd just eaten a slice of strawberry shortcake? Sweet things tend to cut the appetite. Also, if you have a weighty, important wine early in the meal, then any wine following it must be weightier and more important, or else, even if it is first-rate of its kind, it will seem weak and disappointing. In many instances, naturally, there will be only the one wine to accompany the food, but for special occasions two or even three can provide the opportunity for most interesting comparisons in company.

Generally, with fine wines, fine food – but this last can be very simple; indeed, if the wine is superb, then rather plain food is probably ideal, although the ingredients must be first-rate. Sometimes, I know, a wife may complain that one of her husband's 'wine dinners' doesn't give her much scope to show off her skill in cooking – but far from it! A perfect roast, prime vegetables, a combination of different colours and contrasting textures is something really hard to achieve, but discriminating guests will find it memorable. No amount of 'garnishing' and decorating and short-cut versions of elaborate recipes that are really for the chef rather than the cook to accomplish will compensate for second-rate materials and inexpert versions of something outside the scope of the household. Remember – people whose palates are tuned up to appreciate wine will also appreciate the details of food; fresh, perfect ingredients, beautifully cooked, are not only a treat even to the international diner-out, but the best possible context in which to enjoy fine wines.

Another sound piece of advice is that a wine should either complement or contrast with a dish. This means that, with very rich food, you might choose a crisp, dry wine – white or red – or else a rich, weighty wine. With roast duck, for example, which is quite fatty, you might have a brisk, young white wine, such as an Alsace Riesling, or a crisp red, such as a Cabernet Franc from the Loire or a young Beaujolais; or, for a richer wine, you could have a spicy Gewürztraminer or even a late-picked Chenin Blanc, or else a velvety Pinot Noir from the Côte de Nuits, or an impressive Italian Brunello or Barolo. In the Sauternes region, they even serve a glass of one of the great sweet wines with *foie gras*! But this is rather an exciting idea – such as serving a red wine with poached salmon (which I myself often do) – and you may prefer to play safe if you don't know whether or not your guests are feeling adventurous. There is, incidentally, no reason why you should not serve red wine with fish or crustacea or shellfish – it is often done in the wine regions – but some people do find that, when they are eating fish, a red wine in their mouth acquires an odd metallic flavour. But it is certainly not necessary to stick to the old 'white with white' adage – how 'white' is, for example, turkey with all the trimmings?

There are some problem dishes and recipes. Smoked salmon, for example, tends to be rich, slightly fatty and sometimes a bit salty; it can overwhelm many a fine wine, and perhaps salt fish and cured or salted meats should either be eaten without wine or else accompanied by an uncomplicated wine that will stand up to the food and that 'cuts' any richness. A Portuguese *vinho verde*, for example, or a Franconian *steinwein* or a robust *rosé* will be possible choices.

Dishes or foods with very eggy sauces also pose problems. Eggs tend to coat the mouth – again, a delicate wine tends to make scant impression in such a context. Opt for a dryish assertive wine – white, red or pink and, unless you dislike acidity, a wine fairly high in this, such as Muscadet, or a Loire Sauvignon or one of the minerally dry Sicilian wines from volcanic vineyards.

Ham is another food that seems to get a different wine recommended in every guide. It depends – as with other foods – on how it is cooked. If something is poached in wine, basted with wine, served with a wine-based sauce, then at least a similar style of wine is generally the one to drink. The same applies to foods – fish and meat – that have stuffings or garnishes or gravies incorporating wine. With stews and casseroles the wine involved is also the wine to drink.

Personally, I would always serve a red wine with roast or grilled meat and poultry. But the style of the food should accord with the style of the wine and, as roast beef is fuller-flavoured than roast chicken, a fuller, weightier wine is appropriate; lamb cutlets are more delicate than, say, a mixed grill or pork chop, a veal escalope is lighter in taste than a rump steak. There need be no affectation about selecting a suitable wine for any dish, because, for most people these days, the choice is wide, but it is sense to consider the partnership of the dish and the drink in detail – and, if you consult a merchant, don't expect his choice to be all-purpose and satisfactory if you have to alter the menu for some reason. A pair of wines selected for, say, a meal starting with smoked trout and going on to crown roast of lamb may not ideally accompany avocado vinaigrette and baked gammon!

Game, from the humble pigeon or rabbit to grouse, woodcock, venison, is usually partnered by a red wine, both because of the acceptable fruitiness of the wine and, in many recipes, because red wine goes into the sauce or gravy. These days, however, it has been discovered that some people have an odd reaction to red wine, feeling sick and developing a bad headache so, unless you are sure, it is considerate to offer guests an alternative of something white – which may be the first course wine anyway – if you have a dinner party. A white wine capable of partnering a roast or game, however, must have some assertiveness and this is one reason why it is at least fairly true to say that a white Burgundy or Chardonnay is possibly the best 'when in doubt' wine in the world, because a good example will combine the sleek elegance of a good Chardonnay with sufficient weight not to be swamped by the food. You might, however, also serve a white Rhône or a fairly big New World Rheinriesling in such circumstances.

'Pudding wines' have suffered a decline, mainly, I think, because people who have drunk before and during a meal do not always want another wine before the end. But a revival has begun for a single glass of one of the luscious sweet wines that are delectable with fruity or creamy puddings. Sweetish sparkling wines can be excellent at this stage of the meal, especially for a birthday or some form of celebration. If, however, the sweet course is something laced with liqueur – such as a traditional English trifle or a sweet *soufflé* – or unctuous with chocolate, then wine is virtually wasted. But the great sweet wines may also be served quite by themselves, either after a meal or sipped (before any coffee) if you offer hospitality to friends between times.

It is so easy to adopt some of the habits of our ancestors – a dry Marsala with a slice of sponge cake is excellently reviving to anyone 'home from the City' on a winter evening; a glass of a golden Muscat wine with a macaroon or slightly sweet biscuit is an elegant form of refreshment any time in the summer and, of course, a fruity sparkling wine is delicious with an ice. The full sweet sherries and the many ports are admirable postprandial drinks, up to the 'greats' of the fine old tawnies and vintage ports.

In general, fine food with fine wines, medium range wines with

243

more everyday dishes, is a reliable saying. If you serve a particular regional recipe, try to match it with either a wine from the region, or something similar. Remember, though – a good bottle, which may not by any means be an expensive one, can lift quite ordinary fare into the 'something to ask a man to' category, but the most elaborate culinary creation will not do anything to improve a dreary or inferior wine. If in doubt, put your money on the bottle! Wine is the supreme 'convenience food' and, even if you do not like a particular example, it is not discourteous to comment interestedly and even critically, whereas you would risk insulting any host or hostess by criticizing the food put before you.

WINE IN ACTION

If anyone needs some practical advice on buying wine for serving or selecting at a meal, I would suggest the following: if in doubt in a restaurant, opt for the cheapest wine on the list, unless you see one that you already know and like listed. If the wine is indifferent, you won't have wasted too much money. If it's good – you have a bargain and may be able to order the second bottle! 'By their cheapest shall ye know them' is a sound maxim – the cheapest wine of a shipper, merchant or restaurant should be the best value; it will be the wine the boss, the managing director and the *maître d'* drink frequently.

Then, when buying wine from a specialist, never be hesitant to specify what you can afford and, if it's for any special occasion, detail the menu (if you change this, change the wine). No one minds being told what price range you are shopping in, nor that you are serving tomato soup followed by cottage pie and apple crumble; or potted shrimps and crown roast of lamb, followed by *zabaglione*; or caviare before *consommé double* and then *goujons* of sole, roast partridge or ribs of beef, *charlotte russe* or baked alaska; or a mere dozen oysters or smoked salmon or platter of *fruits de mer*, plus grouse or a game pie, then a cheese *soufflé*, followed by a *sorbet d'ananas* or coffee *profiteroles* . . . The people behind the counter have the same problems as yourself – they have to cope with bills, shortage of time, guests who may be difficult and those who – such as in-laws and employers – need to be impressed. Tell them! State your problem, detail your menu – and, if you change it, be prepared to change the wines. Something that may be admirable with lamb cutlets may be less so with stuffed cabbage, should the income tax demand arrive in between the original order and menu and the event. Remember, always, that a fine wine to end the meal, or, even, be served immediately afterwards can be most effective. Any meal should always end on a high note.

Unfortunately you cannot always expect informed counsel from the wine waiter. The good *sommelier* – and these do exist – should, if he doesn't already know, ask what you are eating. If he doesn't, tell him. He should, ideally, recommend two sorts of wine – the cheap and the expensive. Don't hesitate to opt for the former – if it's good you may order another bottle and come back for the latter another time! If he – or she – simply says 'So-and-so is very nice', then you've either got to get some more definite opinion or simply back your fancy. Don't be too hard on the *sommelier*, however; in many establishments he may have had no instructions except to push the wines – which is why he may irritatingly overfill or keep topping up glasses – and have had no chance to taste them.

If you haven't time to take advice and are faced with a fairly important guest at short notice and have to pull a bottle from the 'bin' or case on its side that is your home 'cellar', select a dryish white wine for the apéritif, a fairly full, fruity red with the main course. Otherwise, either you should have thought in advance, consulted with somebody (even if not your wine merchant, at least a friend with more experience), and bear in mind that, even if the guest whom you are honouring by your invitation is an authority on wine, he or she will be more interested in something unusual, out of the ordinary, rather than the sort of fine wine that they may have in their cellar and drink regularly. A good supermarket 'discovery' or recently introduced wine is the sort of thing I have often pleased guests – many of them owners of great wine estates – by offering. Don't be hesitant to do the same. And don't always play safe – a widely advertised brand can be a sound standby in many

245

circumstances when a selection is limited, but a choice of something unfamiliar can be rewarding and a bargain.

WINE VINEGAR

Vinegar is made from a 'vinegar mother' or culture and, as this is a living organism, it cannot be easily obtained unless you already know someone who has one that is reproducing. It looks rather like a piece of liver.

Ideally, it should be kept in a vinegar crock, with a spigot from which the vinegar can be drawn off and a loose-fitting lid to allow the air to get in. However, a glass jar or pot will do, providing that whatever lid or stopper is used does not contain metal. Contact with anything metal will kill the culture. The type of jar used for preserves – such as a Kilner jar – or a plastic-topped glass jar in which instant coffee is supplied is a possible container for the vinegar. The culture should be kept just covered with wine. If you strain off any heavy deposit, remember to use a plastic funnel for this and, if you move a culture into another container, take off any rings you may be wearing and use a wooden, plastic or china spoon – nothing metal. Unless you are fortunate enough to obtain a sherry vinegar culture, which is a very strong one, do not use any fortified wine, vermouth, or any spirits for nourishing the culture, and opt for dry rather than sweet wines.

The culture will 'turn' the wine, sometimes within hours, definitely within days, and the vinegar may be poured or drawn off as required. The culture will also reproduce itself, another layer forming on top of the original one, first looking rather like a fine film, then thickening; at this stage pour on any additional wine with care, so as not to break the embryonic culture. At times the cultures cease to reproduce, but will continue to turn wine. Then they will go into action again, particularly as the result of the appearance of minute 'vinegar flies', and also if air is allowed to circulate within the crock or jar – it is wise to leave this loose at all times, unless the vinegar has to be carried around.

Red wine vinegar is easiest to make, but a red wine culture may be put in a jar and fed with dry or dryish white wine, when it will

246

eventually lighten in colour; the vinegar will be white or pale amber. It does, however, usually take some months or even years for a really good white wine vinegar to develop, whereas a good culture will make good red wine vinegar quite quickly; it is not necessary to use any particular wine to feed the culture, but really coarse wine is not desirable. A wine that is half-way to being vinegar, of course, which can be noticed if you sniff it, is ideal for the vinegar crock. Merchants sometimes have the odd dud bottle.

It is important for anyone engaged in making wine not to keep any vinegar in its vicinity, but as far as the domestic consumer is concerned the proximity of vinegar to bottled wine will not be harmful. If vinegar is decanted off into any bottles, however, it is wise to label it clearly in case anyone supposes it to be cooking wine. If you wish to put a culture into a bottle, this is not difficult if you can select a smallish one or portion of one and coil it round so that it will slip through the lip of the bottle or pass through via a plastic funnel.

Flavoured vinegars are easy to make. Simply put the requisite herbs or spices – garlic, tarragon, coriander, chilli, mustard seed and so on – into a bottle or pot and allow them to impart their flavour or flavours to the added vinegar. They will do this to plain vinegar or can be used in conjunction with a container holding a culture.

At all times keep the vinegar 'fed' with a little wine – red or white – so that it does not dry up. A certain amount of deposit, in the form of a light, sludge-like substance, will probably develop after some time and, if it is wished to get rid of this (it does no harm, however), then the crock or pot or jar should be emptied, the cultures retained in a plastic colander and the vinegar itself in a plastic or glass bowl, while the original container is cleaned with water. If a washing-up brush is used, make sure it does not have any metal on it.

It should be noted that the acid content of home-made vinegar is lower than that of the commercial product. It has been stated to me, by vinegar manufacturers, that it is not 'possible' to use home-made vinegar satisfactorily for making chutneys, pickles and general preserving because of this lower acid content, but I have had no failures in pickling eggs, onions and making a wide range of chutneys and pickles over many years. What will certainly be noticed, however, is that home-made wine vinegar made from a vigorous culture has a particularly delicate flavour; it is always far better with any salad, indeed, it is the vinegar that is the most important condiment in my view. It should be used very sparingly – although this is something the British find difficult to understand – and, ideally, the salad should first be turned in the oil and any seasonings, the vinegar only being added immediately before the salad is to be served. This will prevent the salad wilting and, with the proportion of the vinegar being (in my dressings) one to seven of oil, the presence of the vinegar in the mixture is unlikely to affect the flavour of any but the most delicate of wines – at least, none of my guests has ever found it to do so! The 'vinegar on last' method is a practice often followed by Alexandre Dumas, who noted that it originated with Napoleon I's Minister of Agriculture, Comte J.-A. Chaptal (who issued the decree permitting the process now known as 'chaptalization'); he, after studying salads in various northern countries, was definite that to add the vinegar last distributes the seasoning evenly and, if there should be any excess, the vinegar simply drops to the bottom of the salad bowl. Dumas comments that, as salt is not soluble in oil, it is certainly better to season the salad ingredients first, not attempt to mix the dressing and seasonings all together.

[TEN]

DIRECTORY OF THE WORLD'S WINES

It would obviously be impossible, in a book of this size, to give even an approximate description of the main wine-producing regions of the world. There are a number of pocket guides that purport to do this, but, when every statement in such a mini-manual is inevitably a generalization, this may not be very helpful. In the following, therefore, I am listing the main wine regions of the world, such as are likely to feature their wines on export lists; there will be, of course, many others in the numerous areas now being planted, even experimentally, with vines, but, if you visit such regions, there will probably be someone on the spot to provide additional information. Otherwise, for up to date background and statistical information as to production, regulations, and styles of wines from individual vineyard areas, it is wisest to consult a well-respected, detailed and up to date work of reference, of which there are some listed on p. 260–61. Or, of course, if you see a wine that is unfamiliar in a shop, the person to ask is whoever bought it in the first place. Remember, however, that regulations applying to labelling and other controls, also to nomenclature, are subject to frequent and sometimes sudden changes; do not, therefore, be suspicious if you see a description on a label or something referred to in a wine list that differs from anything that you have read in an otherwise reputable book – the quality of both the wine and the writer need not be doubted, only the circumstance of both not being able to coincide with whatever is up to date at the time each was produced.

VINTAGES

For similar reasons to the above, there are no vintage charts or appraisals of particular years given in this book. Obviously, even in an otherwise indifferent year, some good wine will be made, and it is possible that carelessness or lack of knowledge may cause indifferent wine to be produced even in an otherwise great vintage. But people who are slaves to vintage charts, like those who are equally bound by 'known names' in their buying, are likely to miss a great deal of enjoyment, for there are many occasions when the light year of a good property may produce wine suitable, say, for a luncheon, whereas a great wine of a fine vintage might be too overwhelming, not able to be prepared in time and perhaps of rather too specialized appeal. The way to find out about vintages is to keep in touch with the regular progress reports from the various vineyards from which you are likely to be making your choice, preferably by having the lists of reliable merchants or by reading the specialized publications which issue vintage reports of this sort. Many of the wines intended for immediate enjoyment will be non-vintage.

Note: Remember that, in export markets, wines may be sold under different names from those of their homeland, which may be difficult for foreigners to pronounce. Individual export buyers may also put their own brand or other names on many inexpensive wines. Their origin, however, must be stated on the label in the E.E.C. and often elsewhere.

Algeria: The vineyards of the Algerian coast have been established for many centuries, but the wines as they are known today were first made by French colonists in the early nineteenth century, in the provinces of Oran, Alger and Constantine. Mostly red wines are made, although some white is produced. Red Algerian wine, especially when properly made and matured, can give considerable pleasure, but the future of the vineyards in this now Islamic country is in some doubt, so wines may not often feature on export markets.

Argentina: This country is the fourth largest wine-producer in the world, making virtually all styles of wine, although the red and white still table wines are those likely to feature on export lists.

They can be good, even very good, and visitors to the country may find more of outstanding quality.

Australia: Wines of all styles are made in this vast country, those of the different regions possessing as much individuality as those of different European countries. Plantations of vines are being extended and although the produce of the enormous firms may dominate export lists, with their overall good quality but not particularly individual regional styles, other remarkable wines can be made, both by them and by the specific estates. One interesting circumstance is that there are huge areas where the *phylloxera* has never invaded the vineyards, so vines in these are not grafted. In addition to many classic grapes being used, some are featured that may be unfamiliar for making table wines. The best of Australian wines are as good as any in the world.

Brazil: A comprehensive range of wines is made in this country, many of them making use of classic grapes. As yet, they are seldom seen on export lists outside the United States, but it seems as if production will widen their availability in the future.

Bulgaria: A wide range of wines is made, the trade being controlled by a monopoly concern. Both local and classic grape varieties are used and although adequate quality in both red and white wines is usually achieved for export markets, there seems to be no attempt made to produce estate wines or any of outstanding individuality or very fine quality.

Canada: Vines have been grown here for wine since the early settlers arrived from Europe, but the progress of the wine trade would appear to have been possibly inhibited by the giant concerns producing spirits, and, certainly, by the licensing laws. The wineries now make table, fortified and sparkling wines, but export markets have not yet received them in any quantity.

Chile: A complete range of wines is made in this country, but it is the red and white table wines, notably the former, that tend to feature on export lists and these can be extremely good; the grapes used are mostly European classic varieties, and the significant thing is that the Chilean vineyards have never been attacked by *phylloxera*, hence none of the vines are grafted. Always worth sampling.

Cyprus: This island has been famous for wine since classical times.

The rehabilitation of the wine industry after the Second World War has resulted in huge exports of both the fortified sherry-style wines and table wines. Several native grapes are used but classic varieties are also being introduced. The business is in the hands of several large concerns, each of whom produces an individual range. The most famous historic wine of Cyprus is Commandaria, a dessert wine.

Czechoslovakia: Wine has been made in this country for several centuries, the best today usually being the white from the Slovakian region as far as export markets are concerned.

Egypt: Wine has been made in this country for thousands of years, but the modern wine business was only started in the twentieth century; although a variety of wines is produced, they are not usually available for export.

Elba: There are a number of wines made on this island, but some of the most interesting are not table wines, being slightly higher in strength. One called Aleatico di Portoferraio is luscious and rather sweet, made from one of the varieties of the Moscato.

England: Wine has been made since before 1066 but English wines today began when, in 1965, the English Vineyards Association was started. Today the EVA members make a variety of wines, most of the vineyards being in the south, although some are even as far north as Lincolnshire. Some classic grapes are used, also certain hybrids, the majority of the wines being white, although a few red and pink wines are now being produced. English wines are no longer a subject for mirth – when they are available in sufficient quality, commercial concerns have found that they are profitable. Some are even exported.

France: This country jostles Italy for maximum production. However, French wines have set the standard for many wines of the world and therefore the basic French styles are of great importance to anyone who wishes to learn about wine. The tradition of wine production is old and, although even the most devoted Francophile would not necessarily claim that all French wines are better than any others, nevertheless they have established traditions that must be respected. France produces the world's greatest sparkling wine – Champagne – together with many other sparkling wines including those of the Loire, and Blanquette de Limoux in the south-east,

252

certain wines which are higher in strength than ordinary table wines, *vins doux naturels*, made in the south-east, plus the great red and white table wines of Alsace, Bordeaux, Burgundy, the Loire, the Rhône Valley, Languedoc-Roussillon, and other areas which, thanks to modern improved methods of wine making, are now producing wines able to feature on many export lists. France is also the country in which many of the greatest classic wine grapes have shown what they can produce in the top quality ranges, therefore they have virtually issued a challenge to any newer vineyards, using these grapes, to do as well. In addition, there is an enormous amount of everyday wine made, most going into the big commercial blends that give ordinary pleasure to vast numbers of people. Anyone seriously studying wine must study some of the major French wines, simply because their influence has spread all over the wine world and the wines they have made, both in the past and present, influence by their style as well as their quality anything that is to be made in the future.

Germany: Although this country produces some red wine (mostly in the Ahr Valley) and a lot of sparkling wine, made by both the Champagne and the sealed vat processes, the reputation of German wines has been established because of their whites. The main regions are the Rhine, the Mosel, the Palatinate or Pfalz, Hessiche-Bergstrasse, Nahe, Franconia and Baden-Württemberg. The different styles of German wines range from the everyday to the very special and from dry, or at least dryish, to sweet, and, in the higher quality categories, according to when the grapes were picked: late, selected grapes, selected over-ripe grapes. The fact that some of the very finest German wines are suitable only for drinking apart from food has in recent years resulted in the creation of *trocken* (dry) or *halbtrocken* (half-dry) wines for accompanying food.

Greece: Wine features in the earliest writings of the Greek classics. Today, a wide range of table wines, some dessert wines and others are made in Greece, but these are mostly the product of large wineries, many of them intended for short-term consumption. Retsina is the famous resinated wine of this country, plus the sweet dark brown Mavrodaphne and Muscat of Samos, the last also being sweet.

Hungary: A wide range of wines is made in this country, including what are considered to be the best whites, dry, medium dry and sweet, of the whole of central and south-eastern Europe. Some native grapes are used, also classic varieties. The whites are perhaps slightly more widely featured on export lists than the reds. The most famous and widely known wine, however, is Tokay, which is best known for the different degrees of sweetness it can attain; it is made by a unique method, although there is a dry version also produced. Bull's Blood is the best-known red.

Israel: Although wine has been made in this country since very early times, it became a modern industry at the turn of the nineteenth and twentieth centuries. There is a tradition for the production of sweetish whites – well known for featuring in religious ceremonies – but red wine is also made.

Italy: In some years this is the top wine-producing country of the world. Virtually every province makes wine, some of them a complete range of table wines of every variety, plus sparkling and sweet wines. The production of vermouth, also extremely important, is influential in the economy of regions that cannot make ordinary wines for more than local consumption. There are special wines made in both Sardinia and Sicily, including the world-famous Marsala in the latter island, but, in general, the finest wines come from the northern regions of Italy, especially Tuscany, Lombardy, Piedmont and the Veneto. The Alto Adige wines are also of interest. But there are many others, and the detailed study of Italian wines requires reference to a large book.

Madeira: This Portuguese island is famous for one of the great fortified wines of the world, most of it being made by separate grape varieties, Sercial, Verdelho, Bual and Malmsey. The first two may be served as apéritifs or with first courses, the last two are definitely dessert wines. A little table wine is made but is usually only available for visitors to the island.

Mexico: Wine is made here, but tends to be consumed locally, although some reaches the United States.

Morocco: Wines have been made for many centuries in this country, but the French who took over control in 1912 began to produce wine on a commercial scale. At present, the religious traditions of Morocco make it difficult to foresee much future for wine production, but visitors can enjoy the Moroccan reds, some of which are exported, and there are other styles available.

New Zealand: The first vines were planted in 1819, but only since the Second World War have table wines and some others been made of a quality and on a scale that makes them acceptable on export markets. In addition to several large companies, many small wineries make wines of interesting quality and the future for the table wines on export markets is good.

Portugal: A wide range of wine is made in this country, the most famous of which is certainly the fortified wine from the port region in the upper Douro in the north of the country. Red, white and pink wines are made in many other regions, including the *pétillant* 'green wine' of the Minho in the north, which is red or white; the Dão area, Colares, Setúbal (whose wines are sometimes sweet) are other well-known regions which should provide great interest for visitors. The Portuguese have never tried to liken any of their wines to those made with classic grapes or according to established styles and have kept Portuguese names. Their wines can attain high quality and the use of many otherwise unknown local or locally named grapes does not seem to have been a handicap. Colares vines, in the sand-dunes, are not grafted.

Romania: A variety of wines are made here, one of the best known being the dessert wine, Cotnari, made from certain native grapes. Some classic grapes as well as the local varieties are used, but the ones listed for export do not usually seem to attain more than everyday quality.

South Africa: Vines were planted and wine has been made in the Cape region of South Africa from the latter part of the seventeenth century. There are therefore many traditions associated with wine production, and a number of picturesque and historic estates. Although until fairly recently the twentieth-century export markets were principally aware of South Africa as a producer of sherry-style wines, a huge range of table wines and some sparkling wine is also made, plus some port-style, and the installations are second to none in the world for technical knowledge and up-to-date equipment. A number of classic wine grapes are used, also Pinotage, evolved from a cross of the Pinot Noir and Cinsaut, the latter being known as Hermitage at the Cape. This is now grown in other wine regions of the southern hemisphere. The Steen or Stein grape, often mentioned on labels and at one time thought to be native to the country, has now been identified as the Chenin Blanc, though long residence in this country has modified its main characteristics somewhat. At one time there was the 'Imperial preference' system of duty (applying to all the then U K 'colonies'), whereby heavy wines from the Cape paid less duty when brought into the U K than similar wines from countries not previously associated with this British preference scheme; therefore the comparative cheapness of Cape wines resulted in some people supposing them to be inferior in quality. Nowadays they are both competitively priced and able to stand comparison in quality with any other wines of the world.

Spain: Wine is made in nearly all the provinces of this large country, although it is the wine of Jerez, sherry, that is perhaps the most famous. Montilla, coming from a region near that of Jerez, is not a fortified wine, although similar in style. Málaga and Tarragona are wines our ancestors enjoyed, sweetish for the most part and higher than table wines in strength, but today they have a rather limited appeal. Huge quantities of sparkling wine are made in the Penedés region in the hinterland of Barcelona, the better wines produced by the Champagne method, and vast quantities of others. The Penedés region also makes first-rate table wines of many styles, making use of classic wine grapes as well as some of those principally used only in Spain. The Rioja region in the northwest is possibly the best known table wine region, red and white wines being made, some of them according to very traditional methods, giving great individuality; among other regions whose wines are now beginning to be featured on export lists are those of Navarre, Valdepeñas, Alicante, La Mancha, Priorato and Alella. For many years after the Second World War inexpensive Spanish wines were often labelled with classic wine names such as 'Spanish Chablis', 'Spanish Burgundy', 'Spanish Claret' and 'Spanish Sauternes', which caused many discriminating drinkers to regard them as inferior imitations – today the firms sell them either as branded wines under the name of the installation or as quality wines in their own right.

Switzerland: A great deal of wine is made in this country, mainly around the Lake of Geneva and in the valley of the Rhône. Most of the wines are white, some of them slightly *pétillant*, but a few reds are also produced. They tend to be at a disadvantage on export markets because their limited production means that their prices are inevitably high.

United States of America: Wild vines were found in this country by the very first settlers over a thousand years ago, but these and other types of vine which are not *Vitis vinifera* tend to make wines with a curious taste, not appealing to those accustomed to the classics. Since the seventeenth century attempts have been made to plant *vinifera* vines in various areas, but for many reasons these were not successful until comparatively recently, except in California, where cuttings from Mexico were introduced in the late eighteenth century. Both the ravages of *phylloxera* and various problems, including prohibition, have handicapped contemporary development of vine-growing until almost the present day, except in California, which is by far the most important for quality of wines at the time of writing. It is considered, however, that Washington, Oregon, and a number of other states which may as yet not be known to drinkers in export markets may well produce the quality wines of the future. New York State is second in production to California, best known outside the US for its sparkling wines. In California the technical developments are very advanced, the individual estates and makers are famous and the production of bulk or 'jug' wines is enormous and increasing.

USSR: This vast country usually comes about fifth in world wine production. A huge range is made, notably in Georgia, but for various reasons few of the wines are seen outside Russia, the script with which they are labelled making names difficult for people to interpret. The bulk of production comes from large installations; hybrid as well as classic vines are used and vast quantities of sparkling wines are made. Reports and experience indicate that in general the Russian taste is for sweet or at least slightly sweet wines of all types, of predominantly everyday quality.

Yugoslavia: Wine is produced in several regions of this country, the most important being Serbia and Croatia, some also coming from Bosnia-Herzogovina. The production seems to be controlled mostly by co-operatives and state concerns, but peasant owners still have possession of vineyards. Classic grapes are used both for the red and white wines, but some local grapes are also influential in production, especially for certain sweetish red wines which are locally popular.

FOR FURTHER READING

It is obviously impossible in a book of this modest size to provide a comprehensive bibliography. Even if all the reference works were listed, many of them would be inaccessible to the general reader, out of print, in another language than English, or simply so out of date as to be unreliable except for someone aware of the possible pitfalls of this. Anyone able to use a good library will find many books listed there, the universities usually have a fair number of books on wine and related matters in their reference sections and, in London, the Guildhall Library is particularly fortunate in possessing a collection that includes the library of the Institute of Masters of Wine, which has frequently been enriched by gifts and bequests from writers and members of the wine trade.

The books listed here are a basic collection such as I should recommend to anyone wanting to study wine in further detail than in this book. Some, of course, overlap others, some are expensive, others low in price, but anyone owning them – they were all in print at the time of writing – will have a useful set of works to consult; bear in mind that authors do not always agree, so in some instances I have included more than one book on a single subject. It is, I think, a great mistake to concentrate too much on the wine classics of the past – it is very interesting to read what André Simon said in the 1930s, or what George Saintsbury wrote before 1914, but does this help the beginner of today, who wants to buy a bottle in a supermarket? Unlikely. Indeed, the advice of past pundits can be very misleading and inadequate.

There are two other caveats. Members of the wine trade naturally speak from their specialized experience – they may have certain prejudices that the beginner in wine may not notice. Someone meriting great respect may be very good on a particular aspect of wine – they should not be assumed to be God. With some wine writers who may write extremely well, the technical background can be deficient and, because wine is such a subjective topic, they may recommend as 'good' something which is merely a wine that they themselves like and enjoy; it is *extremely* difficult to be objective but I think the experienced should try not to confound 'I like' with 'This is invariably excellent' and keep their personal preferences quite definitely separate from their general recommendations.

Then – what does a writer do about his or her own books? One cannot leave them out – it is false modesty to do so. Yet some will probably be more appropriate than others for particular purposes. I have included some of mine that I think are good and, in several instances, provide information not easily to be found elsewhere.

For General Reference

Encyclopaedia of Wines and Spirits – Alexis Lichine (Cassell). Regularly revised and massive in scope, this is the 'one' book if you have to make do with a single tome.

The Wine Book – Jancis Robinson (Fontana). Sensible, practical, often original, by an outsider who is now an established young wine writer.

A World Atlas of Wine – Hugh Johnson (Mitchell Beazley). Superb maps and helpful diagrams.

Dictionary of Wines and Spirits – Pamela Vandyke Price (Northwood). In directory format, this includes notes on the practicalities of wines and spirits, also some of the past writers and odd trade terms.

Understanding Wines and Spirits – Pamela Vandyke Price (Corgi). A paperback for the beginner buyer.

Wine Tasting – Michael Broadbent, MW (Cassell). The professional's approach by the head of Christie's wine department.

Enjoying Wine – Pamela Vandyke Price (Heinemann). How the outsider can tackle tasting.

Specialized Studies

The Faber series of wine books is always a valuable addition to any wine library. Some are perhaps rather hard going for the beginner, but the following should be tackled by the serious: *Sherry* – Julian Jeffs; *The Wines of Spain* and *The Wines of Portugal* – both by Jan Read; *Burgundy* – Anthony Hanson, MW; *Bordeaux* – David Peppercorn, MW; *Italian Wines* – Philip Dallas; *German Wines* – S. F. Hallgarten; *Wines of the Rhône* – John Livingstone-Learmonth and Melvyn Master.

Rich, Rare and Red – Ben Howkins (Heinemann). Port and port-style wines from all over the world.
Guide to the Wines of the Rhône – Peter Hallgarten (Century).
Guide to the Wines of Burgundy – Graham Chidgey (Century).
Guide to the Wines of Champagne – Pamela Vandyke Price (Century).
Guide to the Wines of Bordeaux – Pamela Vandyke Price (Century).
The Wines of Bordeaux – Edmund Penning-Rowsell (Allen Lane).
Burgundy – John Arlott and Christopher Fielden (Quartet Books).
Champagne, the Wine, the Land and the People – Patrick Forbes (Gollancz). Perhaps the most important and detailed book on the subject in existence, although now a little dated as to production methods.
The German Wine Atlas and Vineyard Register (Davis Poynter).
A Tradition of English Wine – Hugh Barty-King (Oxford Illustrated Press).

Wine lovers in the United States, South Africa, Australia, New Zealand and South America will be able to get up-to-date publications specializing in the wines of their countries – or simply consult the general reference works as a start. Periodicals dealing with wine are also fairly widely available, and the government bureaux of the main wine-producing countries often have informative brochures and booklets.

GLOSSARY

The following lists some of the most commonly used terms that may be heard in any wine talk; many of them – such as those referring to 'light' or 'heavy' wines – bear a special significance in this context. Although every wine-producing country naturally has its own terminology for describing wines in detail and for the names of various devices in use in the vineyard or in making wine, French is the most recurrent language, and it is probably fair to say that most members of the wine trade will be familiar with the meanings of many French words and expressions, even if they cannot speak the language.

It is unwise to rely on any dictionary or phrase-book definition of a particular word because, in relation to wine, it may mean something highly specialized. It should also be remembered that, as labelling regulations vary considerably between country and country, the use of a term on a label may be quite in order in, for example, the US, whereas it would be illegal in the UK. Labels of EEC wines are subject to different regulations from those of 'other countries' outside the EEC, and French wines have a different system of regulations governing their labels even within the EEC basic requirements. Wines from other parts of the world that are to be offered for sale in certain export markets must also comply with the regulations controlling the labelling within those markets as well as those that apply in the country of origin. This, as will be appreciated, makes the interpretation of many terms, especially those appearing on labels, somewhat complex; it may irritate the potential wine buyer to be told repeatedly that the best consumer protection is a good source of supply, preferably one with a reputation to maintain, but from the above it will be seen that, until there is an organization that internationally dictates and supervises the labelling of wines from every part of the world, no simple solution exists to the problems of what may and what may not go on the label of a bottle.

Acid: There are various acids in wine, which would be flabby and short-lived if it did not contain any. The acidity should be part of the tripartite

262

components – alcohol and fruit being the others – in any balanced wine. Tartaric acid in particular gives a wine freshness and zip. Some very young wines may appear unpleasantly high in acidity, but this can change as they mature; even the most luscious wine must have some acidity to provide a resilient tautness of style. Certain acids, however, are undesirable, notably the *acetobacter*, which turns wine into vinegar. If a wine seems harsh and sharp, unlike its typical smell and taste, then this may be due to volatile acidity, indicating that the wine is on the way to becoming vinegar. Among examples of mature but youngish wines that naturally possess pronounced acidity, extremely agreeable to those who like the wines, are the *vinhos verdes* from the Minho in north Portugal and the red wines made from the Cabernet Franc grape along the River Loire in France. The term 'acetic' as applied to wine usually means a fault.

Aftertaste: The 'echo' of the wine as it comes into the mouth and passes through the nose when it has either been swallowed or spat out. Sometimes, especially with a wine that appears very reserved or 'closed up', the aftertaste can indicate what may be its future development.

Alcohol: There are different sorts of alcohol but it is only ethyl alcohol that concerns the wine drinker. The alcoholic content of a wine is important if it is to be adequately healthy and resist the hazards of keeping and travel, but it is impossible to make an exact estimate of the alcoholic strength in any wine merely by tasting – this is a job for the laboratory. What is sometimes possible is to detect that a table wine may be fairly high in alcohol but, if it contains more than $14°–14.5°$ in terms of percentage of alcohol by volume (Gay Lussac) it is categorized as a 'heavy wine' and pays correspondingly higher duty. Sometimes, in regions where wines are made by peasant proprietors, a wine highish in alcohol may be praised as 'better' than one lower in strength, but this is because those concerned require the 'lift' given by the alcohol; to the civilized wine drinker, a table wine too high in alcohol can be unbalanced and not particularly enjoyable to drink. (See also *Strength.*)

Aldehydes: These are one of the important components of wine, formed by the oxidation of alcohol and, according to Alexis Lichine, 'a half-way step between alcohols and acids'.

Ampelography: The study of grapes.

Aroma: 'The smell of the taste'.

Aspect: In relation to a vineyard, this word means the outlook, not what the vineyard looks like.

Balance: A good wine should have the various elements – smell, flavour, aftertaste – harmoniously proportioned in relation to each other. Sometimes, while a wine is maturing, its balance may be somewhat out of true, but this can right itself in time.

Balling: Method of measuring the sugar content of grapes, which is done by means of a saccharometer. 1° Balling equals 1% total extract – sugar, acid and other non-sugar extracts. The term is widely used, but especially in South Africa. (See *Brix, Oechsle, Baumé.*)

Baumé: Measurement of sugar in wine. 1° Baumé is approximately equal to 0.6 oz (18 g) of sugar to each 1.76 pint (a litre) of wine. A luscious wine may have a Baumé of 3.5°, a fairly dry wine about 1°. But there can be few generalizations except in relation to the controls that govern wine production in the different areas, because one maker's 'dry' may be his neighbour's 'medium'. (See also *Brix, Balling, Oechsle.*)

Beerenauslese: Usually only applied to certain German wines, this term means 'selected berries', the grapes having been picked individually.

Bianco: Italian term meaning 'white', applied to both wines and vermouths. But dryness is not inevitably implied – in fact most *bianco* vermouths are sweeter than the ordinary dry type.

Bin: Series of racks, where bottles are kept lying on their sides – so that the cork remains in contact with the wine and therefore stays wet and swollen, preventing air from entering the bottle.

Blanc de blancs: Literally 'white from white (grapes)'. Originally the term tended to be used mainly for Champagnes made solely from the permitted varieties of white grapes, but is now frequently used for other wines – idiotically, in fact, because a wine made solely from the Sauvignon Blanc could not be anything but a 'white from white'.

Blanc de noirs: A white wine made from black grapes, no skin contact being involved.

Blanc fumé: The name used locally for the Sauvignon in the Upper Loire region. Supposedly adroit labelling has made California wines labelled 'Fumé blanc' successful, but I have never been able to understand why. *Blanc fumé* is in no way supposed to describe the wines as having a 'smoky' taste as some people imagine.

Blend: The term 'a blended wine' is endowed with pejorative significance by some people, but in fact, unless a wine could be made simply from a single vinestock, it is obvious that all wine is and must be a blend – of plots within the overall vineyard, of differently aged vines, sometimes of different grape varieties, often of different years. The art of the blender in composing a successful blend is considerable.

Bodega: Used generally in Spain to designate where a wine is made and stored, but particularly in reference to sherry.

Botrytis cinerea (noble rot, *pourriture noble, muffa nobile, Edelfäule*): This is the particular fungus or mould which, in certain conditions, attacks certain grapes so that they shrivel, the skin becoming fuzzy and crinkled, the juice inside concentrated to a particular type of sweetness. Picking requires skill, because a whole bunch of grapes will not be attacked at once, so individual grapes have to be picked one by one when just at the required stage of over-ripeness and rot. This is one reason for the high price of most wines on which the action of noble rot has been allowed to develop.

Bottles: There is no 'standard' bottle, but generally bottles have evolved in shape from various regions according to the type of wine they are to contain – thus, a wine likely to throw a heavy deposit will usually be put into a bottle with a shoulder, which will hold back this deposit when the wine is poured. It is difficult to establish an exact size for wine bottles, because space is obviously taken up by the cork or stopper and this can vary in length; the ullage, or amount of space of air between the level of the wine and the cork, can also vary. Certain types of bottle are traditional in certain regions but, at least in the fine wine areas of Europe, their shape and colour (wines for long-term maturation are usually put into bottles dark in tone) are controlled. It is usually considered that, with the finer wines, the larger bottles will mature them best, because of the smaller ratio of air to wine in the container, but it should be remembered that the wine in a large container will age more slowly than that in a smaller one.

Some basic bottle sizes:	*Approximate capacity in centilitres*
Bordeaux	74/75
Burgundy	75/78
Champagne	80/81 (remember the bottle has to be thicker)
Alsace	72/73
Rhine	70/72
Chianti flask	50 cl or 1 litre
Tokay	50 cl

Large bottles:

Champagne sizes:	
	Magnum (2 bottles)
	Jeroboam (4)
	Rehoboam (6)
	Methusaleh (8)
	Salmanazar (12)
	Balthazar (16)
	Nebuchadnezzar (20)

A Bordeaux jeroboam was 6 bottles until 1978; it is now 6 litres.

A Bordeaux impériale is 8 bottles.

A Marie Jeanne of the Coteaux du Layon is 1.50 litres.

A Chiantigianna is 1.75 litres.

(Many wines today are in 70 cl bottles also.)

Bottle age: The time a wine spends in bottle, when it undergoes certain changes and can develop to advantage. With some wines, even non-vintage cheap ones, a little additional bottle age can improve them enormously – such as with non-vintage Champagne.

Bottle stink: The stale, flat smell of the minute amount of air that is in the bottle in addition to the wine. It can, when the cork is first drawn, give an unfavourable impression of mustiness, but is soon dissipated with a little contact with the fresh air.

Bouquet: The collection of smells given off by the wine, to be appraised only by the nose. The term implies quality. Every wine in a healthy state has a smell, some wines in poor condition have a stink, only quite good wines have a bouquet.

Breaking-up: Term used to describe a wine that is distintegrating, either because of great age or not having been well made.

Breed, breeding: Term used to describe wines that may be produced in a great tradition, when, even as young wines, they demonstrate this quality.

Bright: Wines are today obliged to be 'star bright', or without any trace of 'bits' or 'flyers' in them. If made so that they can naturally 'fall bright', they will possess a beautiful limpidity, but the stress on brightness has resulted in many wines being put through the filter so that, while the 'bits' are removed, so is at least something of the quality and individuality. No 'bits' in wine ever harmed any drinker, although our ancestors did use tinted glasses for German wines so that their eyes were not affronted.

Brix: System of calculating the sugar content of must (q.v.) so as to anticipate the ultimate alcoholic strength and sugar in a finished wine. 1° Brix equals 1° alcohol, 1.8° Brix equals 1° Baumé (q.v.).

Brut: Although this term, meaning 'dry', is usually applied to Champagne, it can be used in relation to other wines. With Champagne, there is a vogue for *'Brut zéro'* wines, meaning that no *dosage* of any kind has been added – but it takes a very fine wine in an exceptional year to make a satisfactory drink in this vineyard in this way.

Capsule: The cap, of metal foil or plastic, that goes over the cork. This should always be cut down below the lip of the bottle, so that wine cannot be poured over it, as any contact may impart a metallic or plastic taste. If it is difficult to cut off the capsule neatly, then it can be completely removed.

Carafe: This container for open wine must now, in the UK, have its contents stated: 25 cl, 50 cl, 75 cl, 1 litre, in catering establishments.

Carbon dioxide: This gas is given off during the process of fermentation (q.v.) but in certain sparkling wines, such as Champagne, production enables it to be retained and incorporated with the wine – hence the sparkle. A wine can be made sparkling simply by pumping in carbon dioxide gas, but although this seldom results in more than a pleasant, casual drink, the slight shot of CO_2 added to some cheap wines nowadays does prevent them maderizing (q.v.) and retains a fresh, crisp style, without their necessarily being obviously *pétillant* (q.v.).

Chai: French word often translated as 'wine store'. But it has special significance in the Bordeaux region, because, as the water table is high in most areas, cellars as such cannot be excavated and the wine is therefore kept, often, in wood in an above-ground *'chai'*.

Chaptalization: Napoleon I's Minister of Agriculture, Chaptal, gave his name to the process whereby it is permitted to add sugar to musts (q.v.) in certain vineyards where the climatic conditions are such that the process of fermentation has to be assisted. In the northern hemisphere beet sugar is used, in the south, cane sugar. The process is usually subject to controls – badly chaptalized Burgundy, for example, is a treacly, soupy, vulgar wine – but the maker should anyway take care never to unbalance the ultimate wine by the addition of sugar, which, it must be stressed, does not make the wine sweet or sweeter.

Claret: This word started in the Middle Ages as *'clairette'*, meaning a light-toned wine from the Bordeaux area, as distinct from the dark-coloured wines of the hinterland. Today, *'clairet'* is a pinkish wine from the Gironde region, subject to controls, but not to be confused with 'claret'. The latter term was the subject of much argument in the EEC, but the British, from long-established usage (we owned the Bordeaux region for 299 years, after all) are now allowed to use the word, although most of the rest of the world says 'Red Bordeaux'.

Classed, classified: These terms are generally in use for certain of the wines of Bordeaux, but although all the main producing areas have now been 'classified' except for Pomerol, it should not be inevitably assumed that the term implies more than fine quality – any of the 'first growths' or *'grand crus'* are usually very fine wines, but the original classifications were based on the sort of prices the wines might fetch and for the guidance of buyers. Therefore, a second or third 'classed growth' is not necessarily to be rated as 'better' than one that is fourth or fifth; with changes in ownership and individual estate practice, no definite classification of quality can be made that will stand up to the test of time – or the varying fashions and preferences in certain markets for certain wines.

Climat: A specific plot within a vineyard, a term used in Burgundy and of great importance with the finer wines, as regards quality and price.

Clone: Vine term, meaning a specific strain deriving from one particular vine. Of increasing importance in vineyard layout.

Commune: The French word means 'parish' and is used for wines typical of the particular area. Some may be famous estates, others humbler, non-vintage wines. Sometimes the English version will be 'generics', but this is used rather more widely, as in 'the Médocs', 'the Graves', 'the St Émilionnais', when speaking of the Bordeaux region.

Consumo: Portuguese word, used for red or white table wine for everyday drinking – the type that is made at, for example, a port estate for domestic consumption. Nowadays more of these wines are made available to the public on export markets.

Corked, corky: There are two theories about a wine that is, to use the French word, *'bouchonné'*: one is that the defective cork makes the wine actually smell – or stink – of cork. This may indeed be said to be a 'corky wine'. A 'corked' wine, however, may be the result either of the cork weevil or of other deficiencies. If a wine stinks of cork, it is, of course, 'corky'. If there is a somewhat obvious absence of smell or a faint odour of chlorine – what I term 'the swimming bath smell' – then this is a corked wine. The smell, in either case, tends to get stronger with exposure to the air. It is disagreeable, but there is nothing harmful if the wine has, for social reasons, to be drunk. No one who is able to replace a wine with this defect should, in theory, hesitate to do so – however, many may either be unaware of the smell (even if they've made the wine!) or not bother. Sometimes it is quite difficult to detect a wine that is corked, but the British are fortunate in that, on occasions, there will usually be someone around a hospitable table who can make the decision that the wine isn't as it should be – and, in a restaurant, it should be replaced without charge. In someone's home, it rather depends on whether there is another bottle! It should be stressed that there is no reflection on any wine maker whose wine is corked on some occasion – it's a condition that appears to be capricious in making itself evident.

Corks, types: There are various types of cork, ranging from the expensive 'full long' used for vintage port and sometimes the finest red wines – this is 5 cm in length and made of top quality cork (from the bark of the cork oak). Other corks are either 4.75 cm or 'short long', 4.5 cm. A stopper cork is one where a metal or plastic top is attached on to a fairly short tapered cork – as often used for port or sherry. A crown cork is the type that has a layer of cork within a metal cap – as used for many fizzy mineral water bottles. (See also *Stoppers*.) Branded corks are important with the finest wines, and, according to the local regulations of the region of production, may bear the name and vintage of the wine. A Champagne second cork is usually branded on its base. Sometimes a cork will have been waxed before being inserted, and then the stain imparted by the wine tends to take longer to permeate the cork. For certain export markets, the wine may have to be decanted off its deposit (q.v.) so that the final cork may be only slightly stained.

Cosecha: Spanish for 'harvest'; the word implies a vintage.

Côte/Coteaux: French words, the first meaning 'slope', the second 'hillsides', often prefacing regional names. The implication is that wines from a vineyard on some sort of slope will be superior in quality to those made from vines grown on the flat.

Crémant: French for 'creaming', or 'foaming', used to denote a wine in Champagne that is not fully sparkling – that is, having about 4 atmospheres of pressure behind the cork, whereas a fully sparkling *mousseux* wine will have about 5.5 atmospheres. There are several *crémant* wines made in various regions of France today. The difference in 'fizz' is usually not perceptible unless it is possible to put a glass of a *crémant* alongside a fully *mousseux* wine. The notable exceptions are the Crémants d'Alsace, which are fully sparkling (*mousseux*).

Cru: French word meaning 'growth', often seen on labels as *'Grand cru'* or *'Cru bourgeois'* and so on.

Crust: Type of deposit (q.v.) associated often with vintage port, but any wine may throw a crust.

Crystals: Found in both red and white wines, these appear in the form of glass-like splinters in the cork and/or small solids in the bottom of the bottle. They are tartrates, precipitated for various reasons – such as when the wine is subjected to sudden changes of temperature – and their presence is usually a sign of a quality wine, one that has not had the guts knocked out of it by excessive filtration. The public get very suspicious about crystals, but you can eat them without the slightest harm – they do not taste of anything.

Cultivar: Term used in South Africa to denote a specific variety of vine.

Cut: Term now somewhat archaic, but signifying to blend in – certain wines used to be offered for sale 'cut' with some others. (See *Hermitagé*.)

Cuve/Cuverie/Cuvier/Cuvée: *'Une cuve'* is French for 'a vat', so *la cuvée* is both the contents of a vatting and also, in certain contexts (such as Champagne), the making up of the final blend of wines, one vatting possibly being different from another. The *cuverie* or *cuvier* are terms used to signify the vathouse or presshouse – if the fermentation vats and, possibly, the storage vats are kept in the same building as the presses. The term *tête de cuvée* is sometimes seen on labels, meaning that the wine has been selected as being the best from a particular lot. The term *'cuve close'* is, literally, 'sealed vat', used for the process involved with making sparkling wines by the Charmat method instead of the Champagne process. It may sometimes confuse visitors to a winery to find that a circular or rectangular tank, white-enamelled outside, stainless steel or vitreous enamel within, is still referred to as *'une cuve'*, like the huge wooden vats that are still in use in many places. It is perhaps worth stressing that a *cuve de fermentation*, a vat in which the process of fermentation (q.v.) takes place, is different from a *cuve de conservation*, a vat in which the wine may be kept after the fermentation.

Dégorgement/disgorging: The process whereby the first cork of a sparkling wine made by the Champagne process is replaced by the second cork.

Deposit: Many wines, both white and red, can throw a deposit, especially those that are capable of a long life and gradual maturation in bottle. According to the wine itself, the deposit varies, some deposits being light and dust-like, others much more solid, some, notably that of vintage port, being crusty in consistency. It is possible to make a wine so that it does not throw any deposit, it is also possible to handle it after making so that it will be 'star bright' in the bottle. It is one of the curious things about wine that deposit can vary so much, some wines from certain estates tending to throw a deposit, others, from nearby, even when made by the same wine maker, not doing so. In general, the presence of a deposit implies quality and informed handling of the bottle and, if necessary, decanting will ensure that the deposit does not get into the glass of the drinker.

Dessert wine: This term implies a wine that is to be drunk at the end of a meal, either with fruit and nuts – the word 'dessert' means the food served after the cloth has been removed – or with certain sweet dishes. In the UK and many English-speaking countries the word 'dessert' does not mean 'the sweet course', because obviously vintage port, dessert sherry, Madeira, are not wines to accompany puddings, ices, gâteaux, pastries. The great sweet wines, however, can be excellent with certain fruity dishes, such as fruit tarts and pies, compôtes of fruit and even creamy trifles and syllabubs.

Depth: Term often used in tasting to describe a wine that lures the drinker to explore the complexities of fragrance and flavour.

Esters: Alexis Lichine describes this as 'the reaction of the acids and alcohol in a wine, resulting in the ultimate smell' or, with luck, bouquet.

Eiswein: A phenomenon among German wines: usually made in a year when the conditions have not been particularly propitious and when at least some fully or even overripe grapes have been left on the vines long after the usual vintage. If a severe night frost occurs the grapes can then be picked and rushed to the press – they must go in still frozen. Their juice is naturally concentrated. *Eiswein* are curious and always highly priced – to me they are ghost wines of what the vintage might have been, but they deserve appraisal, if possible from a truly reputable grower; the price they can fetch has recently made their production somewhat 'commercial'.

Enzyme: A chemical substance secreted by yeast, responsible for fermentation (q.v.).

Extract: The elements that get into the grapes from the subsoil, via the roots of the vine. According to the way the vine is pruned, these elements are distributed among the ultimate fruit. Technically, extract is what would remain if a wine could be boiled down to dryness – the acids, glycerine, residual sugar (q.v.), various trace elements and other compounds, which can be noted in the analysis.

Fermentation: The process whereby certain juices containing particular yeasts – in this context grape juice – are converted into an alcoholic beverage. Specific yeast strains, known to achieve satisfactory results, excrete enzymes, which act on the natural sugar in the unfermented grape juice. It is the bloom on the grapes that holds the yeasts, either wild yeasts or suitable wine yeasts, in the atmosphere of the vineyard and the winery (see pp. 122–5).

Filtration: The process whereby any deposit and particles remaining in wine are removed prior to bottling, to satisfy the current insistence by consumers for 'star bright' wines. (See also *Crystals, Deposit.*) Not to be confused with fining (q.v.).

Fining: A process (the French verb is *'coller'*) whereby particles in suspension in a wine, likely to cause problems by their action if allowed to remain, are clarified and removed. Various substances are used, including egg whites, gelatine, blood, fish finings. The various fining agents are subject to controls; in certain regions, the use of some chemicals is prohibited. (See p. 141.)

Finish: The final impression a wine makes on both nose and palate.

Flyer: Term for a particle floating in wine – not a piece of cork that may simply have dropped in. Not necessarily in any way harmful. (See *Crystals, Deposit.*)

Fortified wine: This term is used in the UK to signify wines 'made stronger' by the addition at some stage in their production of brandy. In the EEC the term is *'vin de liqueur'* but Britain opposed this, because of obvious possible confusion with 'liqueurs', based on spirits. The French, if they are being particular, may use the term *'vin muté'* – that is, 'changed wine'. In the US the term cannot be used on labels, but, as some US state regulations require alcoholic strength to be stated, the difficulty of a general name is still under discussion. (See *Heavy wines*.)

Fouloir-égrappoir: French terms to signify the 'crusher-destalker' in the process of making wine. The *'fouloir'* crushes the grapes, the *'égrappoir'* strips them of any skins and stems, and in the production of many wines the two processes are combined, although in some instances the grapes may only be submitted to the crusher. Not identical with pressing (see p. 82).

Frizzante: Italian term implying that a wine is slightly sparkling or definitely *pétillant* (q.v.). Not the same as *'spumante'*, which is fully sparkling.

Grip: The tasting term used to describe the way a wine holds on to the mouth – ideally firmly and definitely.

Green: The fresh, almost sharp smell and taste characteristic of many young wines. It can also be partly due to the presence of young vines in the blend. It can be very agreeable and is not a pejorative term.

Gran spumante: Italian white fully sparkling wine, made by the Champagne method. It is produced in several regions and may be dry to sweetish.

Heavy wines: Those that, being above the strength of light or table wines (14–14.5° Gay Lussac), pay additional duty in the UK.

Hectare: One hectare (abbreviated to 'ha.') equals 2.471 acres. 10,000 square metres.

Hectolitre: One hectolitre (abbreviated to 'hl.') is 21.9976 gallons (UK). In speech the term is usually shortened to 'hecto'.

Hermitage/Ermitage/Hermitagé: Term derived from the great Hermitage vineyard in the Rhône Valley, but also in former times somewhat loosely used to imply a robust red wine style. In the nineteenth century many wines were deliberately made to appeal to the British and certain other export markets by being 'Ermitagé', in some instances this meaning that they were blended with the direct, somewhat powerful Rhône reds. particularly popular in Britain at this time. (George Saintsbury's opinion of Hermitage of a particular vintage that it was 'the manliest wine I ever drank' is a typical reaction, and the name occurs in several novels of the period, including at least one by George Meredith.) Some lists show that certain clarets were offered 'cut' (blended) or 'uncut', and those that were 'Ermitagé' – that is, having had a judicious admixture of a wine at least vaguely similar in style to a big Rhône red (such as some of the great red Riojas and, even, certain Catalan wines) – could be more expensive than the 'natural' wines. Today, the Hermitage vineyard is one of the finest of the Rhône Valley, making both white and red wines of great character – by no means the 'blackstrap' assertiveness that many people suppose.

Hollow (French *'creux'*): Term used to describe wines that have a beginning and an end, but somehow no 'middle'. The Australians refer to them as 'donut wines' – their 'donut' is circular with a hole in the middle, not like the UK doughnut.

Hybrids: Vines that yield grapes for wine, but are not in the *Vitis vinifera* category. Many are used for experimental purposes and, in some countries, including the UK, their grapes are permitted for wine making, but as yet it seems impossible for any hybrid to achieve top quality in wine grapes, although some pleasant wines from hybrids are increasingly being made.

Irrigation: At one time it was considered that wines from irrigated vineyards could never be more than adequate. However, improved and subtle methods of irrigation have achieved wines of great quality in the New World. (See p. 77–8.)

Labels: Most wine labels are subject to controls but unfortunately, as these vary not only from country to country (and within and without the EEC), but also from region to region, what they say is subject to no world-wide overall controlling set of regulations. In very general terms, the finer the wine, the stricter the labelling laws and, usually, the more information that should be given. But different controls are continually being imposed and, in order to interpret a wine's label (or labels) it is necessary to know the prevailing regulations both within the producing country and within the export market where it is offered for sale.

Lagar: Portuguese for 'treading tank' – used especially in the port region, where the grapes are crushed by the action of the human foot, in many instances even to this day.

Lees: The deposit left in a cask or vat of wine after the wine has been drawn or pumped off into another container. A wine bottled directly off the lees (*'sur lie'*), such as certain Muscadets, may continue to evince a certain slight liveliness and impression of 'working' or undergoing some minor fermentation.

Legs/tears/larmes/Gothic windows: English, French and German terms for the trails that flow down the side of a glass when the wine has been swirled around, indicating its viscosity – usually a sign of quality and not restricted only to sweet wines.

Light wines: This is the term that, in a context of wine, implies one of table wine strength. (See *Heavy wines.*)

Lively: Term implying that a wine has some vivacity – that is, it has a touch of *pétillance* (q.v.) or 'prickle' of fizz, implying that it is still 'working' (q.v), i.e., undergoing some process during that overall stage of fermentation (q.v.).

Maceration: The softening of some element by steeping it in a liquid, such as is involved with the production of vermouth. (See p. 220.)

Macération carbonique: Process which, nowadays, renders many wines or some part of the blend contributing to them fruity, easy to drink and agreeable (see p. 165–7). Many of the previously considered 'little, local' wines are now pleasant, widely enjoyed drinks as a result of using this process.

Maderization: This term, associated with 'Madeira', means that the wine has been altered by some exposure to air. In white wines the colour will darken. It does not necessarily mean that the wine is unpleasant to drink.

Malo-lactic fermentation: see p. 134–6).

Meniscus: The edge of the liquid – in this context wine – where it makes contact with the glass. Its colour, tone and texture can be significantly indicative as to the wine.

Micro-climate: The prevailing climatic conditions within a particular area – which may be quite small.

Mis en bouteille: The term means 'put into bottle' in French. Used generally for the bottling process.

Moelleux: French word used to describe wines with a soft, concentrated style – most usually of sweet wines. (The term in fact means 'like bone marrow'.)

Mousseux: French word used to describe a fully sparkling wine.

Must: Grape juice before it is transformed into an alcoholic beverage by the actions of the yeasts during fermentation (q.v.).

Mycoderma vini: Latin term for what, in the sherry region, is termed *'flor'*, in the Jura *'le voile'* (the veil), signifying the fungus that forms on the surface of certain wines, resulting in a particular flavour and style.

Nose, nosing: A wine's 'nose' is, essentially, its smell, and the action of smelling it is 'nosing'.

Oechsle: German term, relating to the measurement of sugar in the must. One degree Oechsle equals the number of grams (0.04 oz) by which 1.75 pints (1 litre) of must is heavier than 1.75 pints (1 litre) of water. The sugar content is about 25% of this calibration. In relation to the finer sweet German wines and those of similar style, the higher the degree of Oechsle the better, but fine wines in the category of 'dry' can also be made with comparatively low Oechsle degrees.

Oenology: The study or knowledge of wine. A firm's oenologist is usually the person responsible for making and keeping the wine.

Oïdium Tuckerii: Powdery mildew, one of the great vine diseases, discovered just prior to the *phylloxera* plague in the nineteenth century and named for the Mr Tucker in whose garden it was first found in Britain. It is thought by the authority George Ordish that it was through the importing of American vines in various attempts to research and counteract the downy mildew (*peronospora*) that *phylloxera* (q.v.) was first brought to Europe. The many traces of vines grown over porches and on the walls of Victorian houses show how much the plant was formerly cultivated, and it was the mildew that killed so many at this period.

Organoleptic: The appraisal of drink – or food – by means of the senses. A word somewhat in vogue at present, especially by those who attempt to enshroud wine in pompous terminology. The word 'tasting' is simpler and adequate.

Oxidation: The effect of air on wine – when this lasts too long the wine will break up and become dreary, though not harmful to drink until or if it becomes unpleasant and, possibly, vinegary. Some aeration is most helpful to wines prior to their being served.

pH factor: (See p. 78.)

Pricked: A sharp smell, tending to make a taster wrinkle the nose, usually indicating the presence of volatile acidity (q.v.).

Proportioned/equilibré/balanced: A good wine of any sort should display a harmony of appearance, smell, taste.

Pasteurization: Named for the great scientist, Louis Pasteur, this is a means of sterilizing by heat, so that potentially or actually harmful bacteria are killed. Carried to excess in relation to wine, it can result in 'mummified' wines, but certain methods can be helpful to some robust wines, assisting them to resist the hazards of travel.

Perlant: See *Sparkling wines.*

Perlwein: German term for wines that are *pétillant* (q.v.).

Phylloxera vastatrix: Aphis that attacks vine roots and, because of its life cycle, cannot be removed from the soil once it has got there, unless the vineyard is flooded. Brought to Europe in the latter part of the nineteenth century. After inflicting terrible damage on most vineyard regions, it was found that grafting national vinestocks on to the resistant roots of American vinestocks enabled replanting to take place. Although most European and US vineyards are planted with grafted stock, there are also various *phylloxera* – free regions in the New World where ungrafted vines flourish and, even, disease-resistant strains that can yield well in areas where the aphis is in the soil.

Pipette/velenche: Device for drawing wine from cask or vat for sampling.

Pétillant: French word meaning slightly sparkling or 'fizzy'. Less fizzy than any fully sparkling wine and, usually, than any wine described as *'crémant'*. The Portuguese *vinhos verdes* are typical of *pétillant* wines.

Punt: The hollow at the base of many wine bottles. It serves as a gutter to retain the deposit.

Quinta: Portuguese word for a farm or estate, particularly used in relation to the various single port estates of the Douro Valley.

Rack: Procedure of transferring the contents of a cask or vat to another, leaving any lees (q.v.) or deposit (q.v.) behind. According to the type of wine, this may be done several times.

Residual sugar: Even with a fully fermented wine, there will be a minute trace of sugar remaining naturally. If the residual sugars are subtracted by the laboratory from the total extract (q.v.), the remaining sugar-free extract is a measure of the 'body' of the wine.

Rich: Term that implies intensity and concentration in a wine, not necessarily sweetness.

Saccharometer: Instrument used to measure the weights of musts (q.v.).

Sick: Wines can pass through certain phases when they taste less well than they should and, although they need not be harmful or even unpleasant to drink, this sort of malady should be noted and, if possible, the bottle returned to the supplier. A wine can be 'bottle sick' for some time after it has just gone into bottle, but it may throw this off quite soon.

Schaumwein: German for sparkling wines (q.v.).

Sec: French word meaning dry – but this, also the Italian term *'secco'* and others, are relative: one firm's 'dry' may be another's 'medium sweet' unless the wines are subject to exact controls on the amount of sweetness.

Sekt: German term for sparkling wine (q.v.).

Solera: Spanish word, used to signify the place and, sometimes, the method whereby sherry is made – the *solera* system takes place in the *solera* – in the finest qualities, also in the production of Montilla, Marsala and Madeira, and wines made according to the sherry method throughout the world.

Souche: French for the root or stock of a vine. To buy *'sur souche'* is to buy on spec, before the vintage has taken place, counting on a vineyard's reputation and one's own knowledge and, of course, so as to achieve some form of bargain price before the wine is generally offered on the market.

Sparkling wines: The French term for a fully sparkling wine is *'vin mousseux'*, whether or not it is made according to the Champagne method. The Spanish word is *'espumoso'*, Italian *'spumante'*. Wines that are slightly less than fully sparkling may be referred to as *'crémant'* (foaming), or, with even less sparkle, *'pétillant'* (q.v.).

Spritzig: German for the slight natural liveliness or mini-sparkle present in certain fine young wines, which can often last for some years. It is a thoroughly good thing and should not be confused with a wine that is in any way 'working' or undergoing some stage of fermentation, or one that has been given a shot of carbon dioxide (CO_2) to prevent maderization (q.v.) and maintain freshness.

Strength: It should be emphasized that alcoholic strength cannot be exactly determined by tasting – sometimes people assume that a wine that seems 'heady' (by which they mean possessing a marked bouquet) or else 'heavy' (by which they usually mean a complex, interesting wine, making demands on the intelligence because of its quality) is 'strong' – i.e., high in alcohol. This is not necessarily so at all. A pale-toned carafe wine, in some of the bars or cafés patronized mainly by manual workers or peasants, may well be 'stronger' than, say, a fine red Burgundy; such *'vins traîtres'* only make the drinker realize their comparatively high strength after they've been consumed! What is possible, on occasions, is to feel an additional warmth and assertiveness behind the wine, which may be the alcohol: it sometimes has the effect of making the cheeks feel glowing (whether they are or not). A wine that is too high in alcohol for the fruit and acidity is unbalanced and, therefore, not usually pleasant to the discriminating, but there are drinkers who like to 'feel' the effect of even a table wine – particularly those who do not habitually resort to spirits when they require a quick 'lift' or reviver.

In general, the following shows the approximate alcoholic strength of wines, expressed in terms of percentage of alcohol by volume – a system evolved by Joseph Gay Lussac (1778–1850), whose name is associated with it.

Table wines – white, rosé, sparkling and still	7–14.5 Gay Lussac
Fortified wines – sherry, port, Madeira	18–21 Gay Lussac
Vermouths and many wine-based apéritifs and a few very delicate examples of fortified wines that for various reasons have not had their strength increased to 18	16–20 Gay Lussac

In any discussion of strength, reference should also be made to the terms Balling, Baumé, Brix, Oechsle (q.v.), which refer to the measurement of sugar in the must and/or finished wine. A wine that is naturally high in its sugars (as in various hot vineyards) will tend to be higher in alcohol when the process of fermentation has been completed, because the yeasts will have benefited by the sugars, on which they feed, and can therefore go on working without hindrance or problems. It is not compulsory to put the alcoholic content of a wine on its label in the UK, although many firms who do their own bottling may do so.

Sulphur: Sulphur dioxide (SO_2) is possibly the most important disinfectant involved in wine making, as its informed use enables harmful bacteria to be killed and equipment kept ready for wine making.

Süssreserve: German process, whereby certain wines that might lack fruit and appeal receive an addition of special must (q.v.) to improve them. This is forbidden with all the finer wines. In New Zealand the process of 'back blending' is similar. The subject is complicated, with many controls.

Table wine/Tafelwein/vin de table/vino da tavola: English, German, French and Italian terms for wines intended for casual drinking or consumption with food but, in various different ways, subject to controls – e.g. the French *vins de tables* are in a special category below that of '*vins de pays*'.

Tannin: The product of the stalks, pips and stems of the grapes, this is the element that gives long life to many great wines, notably the 'big reds'. In young wines it makes itself evident by a certain astringency and tendency to pucker the mouth.

Tartrates: See *Crystals.*

Tastevin: Shallow irregularly indented cup used for tasting in Burgundy, where wine must often be first appraised in badly-lit cellars by a candle flame. In former times such tasting cups were carried by many dealing in wine. The Bordeaux '*tas de vin*' is not indented, merely a shallow cup with a bulge in the centre. The white '*tomboladero*' of the port trade fulfils the same purpose.

Tonneau: French word, signifying 'cask', meaning a liquid measure of 900 litres in which the production of many Bordeaux estates is stated – although there is no such thing as a *tonneau* in existence or use today.

Transfer method: Process involved with making various sparkling wines, some of them of good quality, that may be more suited to this method than the '*cuve close*' or Charmat method.

Ullage: Space between the level of wine in a bottle or any form of container, such as a cask, and the closure – it is therefore occupied by air. In bottles of very old wines the ullage may be considerable. (See also *Bottle stink.*)

Trocken: German for 'dry'. Today some of their wines are made *trocken* or '*halb* (half) *trocken*' in an attempt to gain appeal for drinking with food.

Trockenbeerenauslese: Categorization of grapes picked when they have dried on the vine and been attacked by *botrytis cinerea* (q.v.). Mostly used in Germany.

Venencia: Device whereby samples of sherry can be drawn through the bunghole of a cask and penetrate any *'flor'* on the surface.

Vin de table/vin de pays: Two categories of French wines of a modest regional type, the latter slightly superior. A *'vin de marque'* is a branded wine, a *'vin de tête'* usually means made from the first pressings or even mostly free-run juice, whereas a *'vin de presse'* implies that the final squeezings of the grapes have gone into the wine.

Working: Term used to indicate that a wine is still 'making itself', i.e. undergoing some part of the process of fermentation (q.v.).

Yeast: Aptly termed 'the workhorses of wine', but yeasts do not themselves cause fermentation (q.v.) – it is the enzymes that cause it to take place. There are many different types of yeasts and the action of this curious thing is complex (see pp. 122 ff.).

Note: For details as to the controls implied by the French AOC, VDQS, *vin de pays, vin de table* systems, the German Wine Law, the Italian DOC, the Portuguese and Spanish regulations and those of other wine-producing countries and regions, reference must be made to the specialist books and current decrees concerning these particulars.

LIST OF PLATES

Plates

1. A traditional estate: the Marienberg, Würzburg, Germany. (*Photo: Deutsche Wein Information.*)
2. The 'space age winery' at Te Kauwhata, near Auckland, New Zealand. (*Photo: Cook's New Zealand Wine Company.*)
3. A typical landscape of the Douro region, looking across the river to Quinta da Roeda. (*Photo: Teófilo Rego.*)
4. The Stellenbosch vineyards of South Africa. (*Photo: South African Wine Farmers' Association.*)
5. California vineyards. (*Photo: J. Allan Cash.*)
6. A Champagne vineyard. (*Photo: Champagne Bureau.*)
7. The vineyard at Mitchelton, Victoria, Australia. (*Photo: Patrick Eagar.*)
8. Smudge pots in a Champagne vineyard. (*Photo: Champagne Bureau.*)
9. Grapes being unloaded from a lorry. (*Photo: J. Allan Cash.*)
10. A mechanical harvester in a Bordeaux vineyard. (*Photo: Denis Hughes-Gilbey.*)
11. Spraying by helicopter above Épernay, in Champagne. (*Photo: J. Allan Cash.*)
12. Spraying by tractor in Champagne. (*Photo: CIVC.*)
13. Grapes going into the press. (*Photo: Denis Hughes-Gilbey.*)
14. The must being pumped into an open cask. (*Photo: Denis Hughes-Gilbey.*)
15. A modern press at Rully in southern Burgundy. (*Photo: Patrick Eagar.*)
16. The white wine cellars at the KWT in Paarl, South Africa. (*Photo: Chris Jansen.*)
17. The 'Cathedral of Wine' at Paarl. (*Photo: Cape Wine Centre.*)
18. Champagne frames, automatic remuage. (*Photo: Matthew Clarke & Sons.*)
19. Casks of sweet sherry at Limassol, Cyprus. (*Photo: J. Allan Cash.*)
20. A winery in the Barossa Valley, South Australia. (*Photo: J. Allan Cash.*)

INDEX

MORE ABOUT PENGUINS, PELICANS
AND PUFFINS

For further information about books available from Penguins please write to Dept EP, Penguin Books Ltd, Harmondsworth, Middlesex UB7 0DA.

In the U.S.A.: For a complete list of books available from Penguins in the United States write to Dept DG, Penguin Books, 299 Murray Hill Parkway, East Rutherford, New Jersey 07073.

In Canada: For a complete list of books available from Penguins in Canada write to Penguin Books Canada Ltd, 2801 John Street, Markham, Ontario L3R 1B4.

In Australia: For a complete list of books available from Penguins in Australia write to the Marketing Department, Penguin Books Australia Ltd, P.O. Box 257, Ringwood, Victoria 3134.

In New Zealand: For a complete list of books available from Penguins in New Zealand write to the Marketing Department, Penguin Books (N.Z.) Ltd, P.O. Box 4019, Auckland 10.

In India: For a complete list of books available from Penguins in India write to Penguin Overseas Ltd, 706 Eros Apartments, 56 Nehru Place, New Delhi 110019.

Wine in Penguin Handbooks

THE WINES OF BORDEAUX
New Edition
Edmund Penning-Rowsell

Admired throughout Europe as the unsurpassed authority on the world's largest fine wine region, The Wines of Bordeaux is compulsively readable as well as comprehensive and discriminating.

The landscape, architecture and anecdotes of the Gironde and some 500 châteaux all play their part in Edmund Penning-Rowsell's absorbing descriptions of the region's character, the making of the wines, the grapes used and the diseases that have afflicted them. He records the rise of Bordeaux through the centuries, the growth of the great estates and the influence of world trade, and minutely details the character of each district – from the celebrated Médoc to the Graves. And, for connoisseur and amateur alike, his chapter assessing the Bordeaux vintages from the late eighteenth century to the present day is an indispensable guide.

The Wines of Bordeaux has been meticulously revised and updated for this fifth edition.

'A most accurate, encyclopaedic and immensely valuable work' – *The Times Literary Supplement*

'The comprehensiveness and intellectual integrity of *The Wines of Bordeaux* will ensure it an honoured place on the shelves of every wine lover' – *Daily Telegraph*

ITALIAN WINE

Victor Hazan

Victor Hazan's excellent and comprehensive guide to *Italian Wine* is a real source of inspiration to all those interested in finding out more about Italian wines.

By grouping the wines according to their taste and grape variety, rather than their geographic origin, the author gives all the essential information; organizing his selections by category – The Big Red Wines, The Medium-Range Wines, The Light Red Wines, Light and Crisp White Wines, Full and Fruity White Wines, and Italy's Sweet Wines.

In addition he provides
   * a brief essay on how to taste wine
   * a lucid explanation of the D.O.C. law
   * a glossary of terms and an illustrated guide to reading an Italian wine label
   * the most up-to-date maps of the wine producing regions, and
   * a guide to the selection of wine to drink with food

Clearly a classic in its own right, the ever growing number of wine drinkers will discover with Victor Hazan the special qualities of animation and ripeness which distinguish all Italian wines.

'You will find this remarkable book on the wines of Italy an absolute treasure' – Craig Claiborne

CHARCUTERIE AND FRENCH PORK COOKERY

Jane Grigson

'A remarkable research job on the pig, from head to tail' – *Evening Standard*

'Fully comprehensive ... a detailed and enlightening insight into the preparation and cooking of pork. Altogether a unique book' – *Wine and Food*

ENGLISH FOOD

Jane Grigson

'Jane Grigson is perhaps the most serious and discriminating of the younger generation of cookery writers, and *English Food* is an anthology all who follow her recipes will want to buy for themselves as well as for friends who may wish to know about *real* English food' – Pamela Vandyke Price in the *Spectator*.

COOKING FOR SPECIAL DIETS

Bee Nilson

This revised edition, from the author of the bestselling *Penguin Cookery Book*, gives short explanations of such illnesses as diabetes, anaemia, ulcers, heart diseases and obesity, with reasons for prescribing fat-free, low protein, liquid or other restricted diets, and descriptions of the diets themselves. A general meal pattern, suggestions for eating out, ideas for packed lunches and a set of fourteen menus for main and snack meals round off the discussion of each variety of disease and diet.

THE VEGETARIAN EPICURE

Anna Thomas

The answer to all those who consider vegetarian food boring and fit only for rabbits. In Anna Thomas's imaginative and skilful hands vegetarian cookery becomes a rich, exciting and varied way of eating that should appeal not only to the confirmed vegetarian but to the confirmed meat-eater as well.

QUICK COOK
Beryl Downing

This is a cookery book for victims of the twentieth century ... That is, for all those people who love eating but don't have much time to devote to actual cooking. Imagination, planning and economy are the thirty-minute cook's chief weapons – and as the recipes here confirm, that's a combination which will ensure exciting and varied meals for years to come.

THE CHOCOLATE BOOK
Helge Rubinstein

Enter the world of chocolate – the most luxurious, sumptuous (and sinful) of all foods. Here is a tantalizing selection of recipes – chocolate cakes, ice-creams, pies, truffles, drinks and savoury dishes galore. Both cookery book and expertly written social history, this is an anthology to treasure.

PICNIC
The Complete guide to outdoor food
Claudia Roden

'Wonderfully evocative and useful ... *Picnic* covers every sort of outdoor feast, from backyard to grouse moor, from Japan to the Middle East, from Ancient Greece to John Betjeman's "sand in the sandwiches" ' – *Sunday Times*

SIMPLE FRENCH FOOD
Richard Olney

'The most marvellous French food to appear in print since Elizabeth David's *French Provincial Cooking*' – *The New York Times*

'There is no other book about food that is anything like it ... essential and exciting reading' – *Observer*

Cookery in Penguin Handbooks

A BOOK OF MIDDLE EASTERN FOOD
Claudia Roden

This fascinating cook's tour of the Middle East contains more than 500 recipes from a number of countries – Greece and the Yemen to Algeria and Morocco.

'Absolutely gripping . . . the way a cookery book should be' – Caroline Conran in the *Sunday Times*

CHINESE FOOD
Kenneth Lo

To help you go *à la carte* in a Chinese restaurant, as well as to 'cook Chinese' at home, this excellent handbook outlines the philosophy and practice of the various Chinese meals; provides a guide to the food found in restaurants outside China and devotes a section to the four quarters of China and the four seasons of the year in an intriguing and authoritative introduction to the classic fare of the country.

JAPANESE COOKING
Peter and Joan Martin

A simple, working introduction to the indigenous Japanese cooking of homes and small eating houses, with some 250 recipes covering soups, rice and noodle dishes, fish meat, vegetables and salads, eggs and pickles.

AN INVITATION TO INDIAN COOKING
Madhur Jaffrey

A loving and practical guide to Indian cooking, which pays special attention to the dishes of Delhi and includes a comprehensive list of the spices and herbs used in India alongside a wide range of recipes and some suggested menus.

PENGUIN COOKERY BOOKS

☐ *Mediterranean Cookbook* **Arabella Boxer** £2.50

A gastronomic grand tour of the region: 'The best book on Mediterranean cookery I have read since Elizabeth David' – *Sunday Express*

☐ *Josceline Dimbleby's Book of Puddings, Desserts and Savouries* £1.75

By the *Sunday Telegraph*'s popular cookery columnist, a book 'full of the most delicious and novel ideas for every type of pudding, from the tasty, filling family variety to exotic pastry concoctions' – *Lady*

☐ *Penguin Cordon Bleu Cookery* £2.50

Find the highest quality of European cooking with a French accent in this classic Penguin cookery book, prepared by Rosemary Hume and Muriel Downes, co-principals of the English Cordon Bleu School.

☐ *A Concise Encyclopedia of Gastronomy* **André Simon** £6.95

Expertly edited, with wit and wisdom, this is the most comprehensive survey ever published, and a treasure-house of good food.

☐ *Barbecues* **James F. Marks** £1.95

From choosing your barbecue to smoke-cooking, and from tandoori chicken to pizza and bananas Diana – the new, updated edition of this bestselling handbook is indispensable to everyone wanting to dine out deliciously in their own back garden.

☐ *The Chocolate Book* **Helge Rubinstein** £2.95

Part cookery book, part social history, this sumptuous book offers an unbeatable selection of recipes – chocolate cakes, ice-creams, pies, truffles, drinks and savoury dishes galore.

PENGUIN COOKERY BOOKS

☐ *Scottish Regional Recipes* **Catherine Brown**   £2.95

Bridal Cake from Orkney, Chicken Stovies from the Highlands, Morayshire Apples from the North-East, Cock-a-Leekie from Edinburgh – this book of rich and satisfying recipes proves the cuisine of Scotland to be as varied as her scenery.

☐ *Jane Grigson's Fruit Book*   £3.95

An alphabetical guide to fruit, packed with information and recipes. 'Not only my book of the year, but one that will have a permanent place on my shelves' – Paul Levy

☐ *Jane Grigson's Vegetable Book*   £3.95

From the cabbage to the Chinese leaf, a modern kitchen guide to the cooking of vegetables by 'the most engaging food writer to emerge during the last few years' – *The Times*

☐ *Food Facts* **David Briggs and Mark Wahlqvist**   £4.95

Whether you are young or old, fat or slim, fit or unwell, pregnant, or vegetarian, this lively handbook contains a comprehensive round-up of nutritional facts to help you create a satisfying diet, and live healthily.

☐ *Simple French Food* **Richard Olney**   £2.95

A cookery cult, and now a classic, this book contains 'the most marvellous French food to appear in print since Elizabeth David's *French Provincial Cooking*' – *The New York Times*

☐ *Geraldene Holt's Cake Stall*   £1.95

'Mouthwatering fare . . . There are scones and tea-breads, sponge and fruit cakes, family cakes, tray-baked cakes, special occasion cakes . . . Reading about them makes me feel hungry . . .' – Philippa Davenport

IN COOKERY BOOKS

Kenneth Lo   £1.75

ophy, practice, menus and delicious recipes of
his well-known, step-by-step introduction.

ookbook **Evelyn and Judi Rose**   £1.95

Equipment, stores, soups, sauces, egg dishes, meat, pastry, puddings, party food and more are covered in this excellent and easy-to-
follow introduction for the novice cook.

☐ *An Invitation to Indian Cooking* **Madhur Jaffrey**   £2.95

A witty, practical and irresistible handbook on Indian cooking by the
presenter of the highly successful BBC television series.

These books should be available at all good bookshops or news-
agents, but if you live in the UK or the Republic of Ireland and have
difficulty in getting to a bookshop, they can be ordered by post.
Please indicate the titles required and fill in the form below.

NAME _____ BLOCK CAPITALS

ADDRESS _____

_____

_____

Enclose a cheque or postal order payable to The Penguin Bookshop
to cover the total price of books ordered, plus 50p for postage.
Readers in the Republic of Ireland should send £IR equivalent to the
sterling prices, plus 67p for postage. Send to: The Penguin Bookshop, 54/56 Bridlesmith Gate, Nottingham, NG1 2GP.

You can also order by phoning (0602) 599295, and quoting your
Barclaycard or Access number.

Every effort is made to ensure the accuracy of the price and availability of
books at the time of going to press, but it is sometimes necessary to increase
prices and in these circumstances retail prices may be shown on the covers of
books which may differ from the prices shown in this list or elsewhere. This list
is not an offer to supply any book.

**This order service is only available to residents in the UK and the Republic of
Ireland.**

PENGUIN COOKERY BOOKS

☐ *Scottish Regional Recipes* **Catherine Brown**   £2.95

Bridal Cake from Orkney, Chicken Stovies from the Highlands, Morayshire Apples from the North-East, Cock-a-Leekie from Edinburgh – this book of rich and satisfying recipes proves the cuisine of Scotland to be as varied as her scenery.

☐ *Jane Grigson's Fruit Book*   £3.95

An alphabetical guide to fruit, packed with information and recipes. 'Not only my book of the year, but one that will have a permanent place on my shelves' – Paul Levy

☐ *Jane Grigson's Vegetable Book*   £3.95

From the cabbage to the Chinese leaf, a modern kitchen guide to the cooking of vegetables by 'the most engaging food writer to emerge during the last few years' – *The Times*

☐ *Food Facts* **David Briggs and Mark Wahlqvist**   £4.95

Whether you are young or old, fat or slim, fit or unwell, pregnant, or vegetarian, this lively handbook contains a comprehensive round-up of nutritional facts to help you create a satisfying diet, and live healthily.

☐ *Simple French Food* **Richard Olney**   £2.95

A cookery cult, and now a classic, this book contains 'the most marvellous French food to appear in print since Elizabeth David's *French Provincial Cooking*' – *The New York Times*

☐ *Geraldene Holt's Cake Stall*   £1.95

'Mouthwatering fare . . . There are scones and tea-breads, sponge and fruit cakes, family cakes, tray-baked cakes, special occasion cakes . . . Reading about them makes me feel hungry . . .' – Philippa Davenport

PENGUIN COOKERY BOOKS

☐ *Chinese Food* **Kenneth Lo** £1.75

Discover the philosophy, practice, menus and delicious recipes of Chinese food with this well-known, step-by-step introduction.

☐ *First-Time Cookbook* **Evelyn and Judi Rose** £1.95

Equipment, stores, soups, sauces, egg dishes, meat, pastry, puddings, party food and more are covered in this excellent and easy-to-follow introduction for the novice cook.

☐ *An Invitation to Indian Cooking* **Madhur Jaffrey** £2.95

A witty, practical and irresistible handbook on Indian cooking by the presenter of the highly successful BBC television series.